MW01278182

POLITICAL IDEOLOGY IN PARTIES, POLICY, AND CIVIL SOCIETY

POLITICAL IDEOLOGY IN PARTIES, POLICY, AND CIVIL SOCIETY
Interdisciplinary Insights

Edited by David Laycock

UBCPress · Vancouver · Toronto

© UBC Press 2019

All rights reserved. No part of this publication may be reproduced, stored in a retrieval system, or transmitted, in any form or by any means, without prior written permission of the publisher, or, in Canada, in the case of photocopying or other reprographic copying, a licence from Access Copyright, www.accesscopyright.ca.

28 27 26 25 24 23 22 21 20 19   5 4 3 2 1

Printed in Canada on FSC-certified ancient-forest-free paper (100% post-consumer recycled) that is processed chlorine- and acid-free.

Library and Archives Canada Cataloguing in Publication

Title: Political ideology in parties, policy, and civil society : interdisciplinary insights / edited by David Laycock.
Names: Laycock, David H., 1954– editor.
Description: Includes bibliographical references and index.
Identifiers: Canadiana (print) 20190092955 | Canadiana (ebook) 2019009303X | ISBN 9780774861311 (hardcover) | ISBN 9780774861328 (paperback) | ISBN 9780774861335 (PDF) | ISBN 9780774861342 (EPUB) | ISBN 9780774861359 (Kindle)
Subjects: LCSH: Ideology—Political aspects—Canada. | LCSH: Political science—Canada.
Classification: LCC JA84.C3 P65 2019 | DDC 320.50973—dc23

Canadä

UBC Press gratefully acknowledges the financial support for our publishing program of the Government of Canada (through the Canada Book Fund), the Canada Council for the Arts, and the British Columbia Arts Council.

Printed and bound in Canada by Friesens
Set in Futura and Warnock by Apex CoVantage, LLC
Copy editor: Frank Chow
Proofreader: Caitlin Gordon-Walker
Indexer: Noeline Bridge
Cover designer: David Drummond

UBC Press
The University of British Columbia
2029 West Mall
Vancouver, BC V6T 1Z2
ubcpress.ca

Contents

Acknowledgments / vii

Introduction / 3
David Laycock

Part 1: Ideology in Partisan, Policy, and Academic Contexts

1 Consent, Representation, and Liberty:
America as the Last Medieval Society – or a
Footnote to Louis Hartz / 21
Ivan Jankovic

2 Canadian Development Assistance and
Mediated Geopolitics / 41
Katherine Reilly

3 Right-Wing Populism, Conservative Governance,
and Multiculturalism in Canada / 61
David Laycock and Steven Weldon

4 Not Merely Playing: Game Theory's Subversive
Proclivities / 91
Laurent Dobuzinskis

Part 2: Ideology in the Politics of Civil Society

5 The Contribution of Rhetorical Analysis and Discourse
Theory to the Study of Political Ideologies: The Cases of
Multiculturalism and Environmentalism / 115
Ian Angus

6 Mobilizing Political Strategy: The Global Practices of
Taxpayer Groups / 132
Kyle Willmott

7 Telling Their Stories: Ideology and the Subject of Prairie
Agriculture / 149
Katherine Strand and Darin Barney

8 Laborlore and the Ideology of the British Columbia
Labour Bureaucracy, 1900–2015 / 169
Mark Leier

9 A Reconnaissance of Everyday Working Class Ideology in
British Columbia / 187
Dennis Pilon

Conclusion / 205
David Laycock

Contributors / 215
Index / 218

Acknowledgments

Several generous contributions made this volume possible. The collaborative project was partly funded by a Social Sciences and Humanities Research Council of Canada Connections Grant, which included a publication subvention. At Simon Fraser University, the Faculty of Arts and Social Sciences, the Vice-President's University Publication Fund, and the Departments of Political Science and History all made important financial contributions, as did the Centre for the Study of Political Ideology at the University of Nottingham.

I would also like to thank participants at the "Ideologies and Conceptual Travel" workshop whose presentations are being published elsewhere: Richard Bates, Mathew Humphrey, and Maiken Umbach (University of Nottingham); Howard Brick (University of Michigan), Avigail Eisenberg (University of Victoria), Jim Farney (University of Regina), Michael Freeden (Oxford University), Margaret Kohn (University of Toronto), Eryk Martin and Aaron Windel (Simon Fraser University), Cayley Sorochan (McGill University), Mark Warren (University of British Columbia), and Yang Yang (Shanghai Jiao Tong University).

A special thanks to Mark Leier, Miriam Polman, and Lynn Kool, for their help with the workshop, to a particularly helpful anonymous reviewer, and to Darin Barney, for his valuable feedback on a draft of the Introduction. Finally, my gratitude to Randy Schmidt and Michelle van der Merwe at UBC Press, whose fine editorial support and assistance have been crucial to the volume that follows.

POLITICAL IDEOLOGY IN PARTIES, POLICY, AND CIVIL SOCIETY

Introduction

DAVID LAYCOCK

This volume investigates how political ideologies innovate through conceptual adaptation in a variety of social, cultural, historical, and political settings, crossing borders of time, space, and theory. Contributors share the view that ideology is a ubiquitous, continuously innovating, and ineliminable dimension of human experience that cannot be definitively understood using only one set of academic disciplinary tools. Our shared purpose is to reveal key aspects of the conceptual structure, social meaning, adaptability, and power of ideologies as they are practised in changing settings. We wish to spur development of interdisciplinary theoretical approaches to the study of political ideology that are attentive to the impact that host institutions, cultures, organizations, and social, economic, and political events have on ideological concepts and themes.

In their diverse analyses of the impacts of ideology on political life and social analysis, contributors reach across the methodological differences that separate our academic disciplines, ranging from philosophy to history, communications and sociology to political science (political theory and political behaviour), and anthropology to economic history. Methodological "cross-pollination" from various disciplines is evident in the chapters, which benefit from a range of theoretical traditions. Our hope is that this and related publications (e.g., Humphrey, Laycock, and Umbach 2019) will stimulate interdisciplinary creativity in the applied study of political ideology, adding to earlier cross-disciplinary theorization of ideology (Freeden, Sargeant, and Stears 2013).

The essays in this volume address a wide range of political ideologies, all involving some type of border crossing by concepts, the building blocks of all ideological structures. The most obvious such travel is across national boundaries, and the questions that most readily arise in such situations have to do with transformation of concepts, given specific shape by institutional and cultural contextual factors, political or other crises, political innovations, or major changes in the political competition. A variation on such cross-border travel occurs across regional and national political cultures, and across generations, sometimes skipping decades or even centuries. In North America, for example, the concept of direct democracy emerged in the United States to have a profound impact on populist movements in the 1880s and 1890s, experienced a rebirth in both the United States and Canada during the 1910–25 period, went into political hibernation across most of the continent until the mid-1970s, and roared back on both sides of the US/Canada border for the next forty years. More recently, it has appeared in the demands of populist parties and movements of the left and right in Europe.

Conceptual travel also occurs within and between the analytically distinct spheres of social, economic, cultural, and political life, as illustrated in two examples. Between spheres, the originally economic concept of "deficit" has recently been adapted to the notion of "democratic deficit" to help explain deficiencies in political representation and electoral accountability. Broadly within the political sphere, the concept of a "social contract" originated in the seventeenth century to address the problem of rational political obligation, and, with several reconceptualizations along the way, emerged again in the twentieth century in influential attempts to address the problem of social justice and the state's role in redistributing resources and opportunities to advance that justice. This re-emergence has occurred at the level of "high theory," with John Rawls and his commentators, and also at the level of political discourse among various political actors, policy professionals, and advocates. (See below for discussion of these "macro" and "meso" levels of ideological action and analysis.)

In each of these first two types of conceptual travel, one inevitably finds adaptation to specific features of the new environments as well as retention of some key features of the original conceptualization. This raises a semantic point: it is conceptualizations of enduring concepts that change by travelling, not the actual concepts themselves. This distinction flows from the approach to ideological analysis developed by Michael Freeden, which draws on the idea of "essential contestability" of all key ideological concepts to understand both conceptual variability across ideologies and the mutual influences of all major concepts within a given ideological field (Freeden 1996, 2013a).

An overview of Freeden's promising theoretical meeting point for interdisciplinary research on ideologies is presented in this introduction, followed by summaries of the chapters in this volume as a whole. It should be emphasized that while I have adopted Freeden's broad approach to the study of ideologies in Chapter 3 and other recent research (Laycock 2014, 2019; Humphrey, Laycock, and Umbach 2019), this approach was only occasionally engaged by contributors to this volume. The concluding chapter will discuss key themes in the volume as an invitation to future research and creative theorization.

* * *

The ideological structuring of cultural and organizational experience has long been acknowledged by anthropologists and sociologists in Europe and North America. Anglo-American historians and political scientists have either tended to resist structural understandings of ideology by treating it simply as a package of attitudes, orientations, and values that accompanies and somewhat shapes political and social experience, or by adopting Marxist perspectives on ideology that give social class and relations of production primary causal force in the creation of ideological perspectives in distinctive socio-political settings. Acknowledging that the more loosely structuring, often subtle power of ideology can be appreciated using analytical tools developed for the study of political philosophy, psychology, and social theory has taken a variety of methodological paths. Analytically removing the stain of either false consciousness or extremism from the idea of ideology has been especially important to these developments, but more systematic theoretical advances have also been crucial (Freeden, Sargeant, and Stears 2013; Maynard 2013). One particularly valuable and methodologically pluralistic systematic approach to ideology has been provided by English political theorist Michael Freeden.

Over the past three decades, Freeden's work has drawn on a rich variety of philosophical traditions and methodological approaches to provide an influential analytical framework for the study of ideology. Among its advantages for the student of ideologies is the set of theoretically open bridges that Freeden's theory builds to other social and human sciences. Like other conceptually focused approaches, Freeden argues that the ideologies underlying and informing social and political action are systematically structured and closely interrelated assemblages of concepts. What sets his approach apart from other conceptual approaches is his account of ideological morphology, which is a philosophically synthetic, creative, and systematic extension of Gallie's theorization of "essentially contested concepts" (Freeden 1996). For a variety of logical, epistemological, and cultural reasons, key political concepts related to a vision of a desirable socio-political order are always open to dispute, and reasonably so; there is no definitively correct understanding of the meaning and implications of "freedom" independent of one's cultural environment and basic philosophical commitments (Gallie 1956).

Freeden explains that the meaning of an ideological concept arises from its (historically and culturally) specific relationship to other concepts in a given time and place. A concept is thus not autonomous but relational, produced and reproduced in relation to other concepts in particular, variable, and dynamic structures. The morphological, relational character of concepts allows a given concept to mean one thing in one context and another (even opposite) thing in a different context, and ensures that its meaning is "contestable" (Freeden 1996).

Citizens who share an ideology accept roughly the same specific versions of most key concepts, or what Freeden calls "decontestations" of these concepts, but they may share few precise ideological decontestations with other citizens who adhere to another ideology within the same broader ideological family. Liberalism, to take the most obvious example, is a very broad ideological family. Some liberal variants decontest key concepts like equality of opportunity and social justice in ways that border on social democratic decontestations. Other liberalisms are hard to distinguish from forms of contemporary conservatism, by virtue of how they decontest freedom, equality, and the human need for order.

Freeden's methodology emphasizes the analyst's role in carefully weighing the significance and ideology-structuring impact of different concepts. To facilitate this, he develops an analytical toolkit that allows us to identify overlapping logics that weave together prominent policy concerns, specific kinds of public appeals, understandings of social change, and underlying normative conceptual foundations within political discourse. Freeden proposes mapping the morphology of any ideology with core, adjacent, and peripheral concepts. Core concepts are typically basic normative commitments to a specific version of key ideas like equality, liberty, or solidarity that anchor an ideology over time. In some cases, an ideology's core concepts can be meta-commitments to political action or understanding, such as the conservative orientation to resist or manage social change (Freeden 1996, 333–34).

Adjacent concepts are also basic to an ideology, but less heavily weighted than its core concepts. They are often second-order normative concepts (such as conceptions of human rights) or general institutional orientations to political practice (such as participatory democracy or group representation) that are instrumental to the achievement of core normative objectives. Peripheral concepts are typically policy positions or heavily symbolic features of, or past events in, the political system (such as those concerning immigration, trade, climate change, or constitutional rights, or a country's war experience). They may be at the centre of political debate at any given time, but ought not to distract us from the job of discovering their roots in more structurally basic core and adjacent concepts.

On Freeden's account, what makes any ideology distinctive is its system of mutual influences and relations among ideologically distinctive concepts – within the core, and across core, adjacent, and perimeter concepts. For Freeden, the dynamic character of any ideology results from the essential contestability of almost all ideological concepts. Through the combined efforts of those who produce its texts, performances, and mediated transmissions, every ideology "decontests" each of its key concepts, especially when these are actively debated outside the ideology, and always in relation to other key concepts.

In party political competition, for example, the meaning of equality is given a party-specific meaning via its connection to the party's decontested concepts of freedom, human rights, democracy, the market, and gender, all influenced by and influencing the party's (evolving) understanding of equality. Competing ideologies' proponents and carriers directly and indirectly contest the "real" meaning and policy implications of key concepts such as equality, liberty, or democracy. These remain a matter of fundamental dispute within party systems and across civil society, but a party or movement loyalist accepts the party or movement's efforts to decontest key concepts in political life. In effect, partisans and loyal political audiences share not just an enthusiasm for and attitudes towards particular policy proposals, but also an ideological vocabulary structured by a set of distinctively decontested concepts. This view of the linguistic structure of ideologies is similar to Roland Barthes's concept of an "idiolect," which merges understandings of the concepts of "ideology" and "dialect" (Barthes 1972).

Why does Freeden's analytical framework lend itself to bridge building across various disciplines? First, it can do this because it is constructed from a variety of political and social theoretical perspectives, drawing on everything from twentieth-century hermeneutics to Antonio Gramsci's understanding of "hegemony" to Louis Althusser's idea of "interpellation," from the post-structuralism of Foucault and Derrida to the linguistic analysis of Gallie, Austin, and Wittgenstein, and from the "Cambridge School's" conceptual histories to the comparative historical analysis of the *Begriffsgeschichte* school (Freeden 1996, 2013a). Second and more important, applying Freeden's approach to analysis of ideologies' conceptual morphologies requires serious and systematic attention to empirical details of political and social discourses and to the cultural, historical, and institutional environments in which they are deployed. In turn, these empirical details require careful and creative interpretation to generate comprehensive and nuanced understandings of ideological phenomena.

There is no clear reason why Freeden's conceptual morphology method cannot play complementary roles with other ideology-analyzing methods that focus on conceptual structure and meanings (Skinner 2002; Ball, Farr, and Hanson 1989; Howarth, Norval, and Stavrakakis 2000; Laclau 1993, 1994; Thagard 2014) in the analysis of the overall character and impacts of particular ideologies in specific settings (Humphrey 2005). And although his own studies have eschewed strong normative positions (Freeden 2013a), some of Freeden's analytical tools can readily be combined with various forms of social critique, as is acknowledged in Chapters 5 and 8 in this volume.

If these approaches can combine to good analytical effect, why not Freeden's approach combined with Freudian and Žižekian perspectives on social movement activity (Stavrakakis 1997), or with Laclau's critical discourse theory (Finlayson 2012), or with contemporary theorization of representation (Laycock 2019)? Other theoretical blends involving diverse conceptual, discursive, and even quantitative methods are well worth considering (Maynard 2013, Farney 2019).

The point of discussing Freeden's approach in some detail above is to broadly orient readers to the varied case studies that follow in a way that opens up theoretical space for a plurality of analytical/interpretive approaches within and across disciplines. His approach offers a theoretical orienting toolkit for this kind of multidisciplinary project, which requires openness to and compatibility with other approaches for particular case studies. Freeden's approach was not presented to this volume's contributors as a prescribed approach to the study of ideology. There is an important difference between such "prescription" and the provision of "orienting tools" that can share the stage with, or even yield, theoretically, to other analytical methods, as subject matter, explanatory purpose, or authorial intent require. As this volume demonstrates, such prescription would be counterproductive to building the multidisciplinary study of ideologies.

Of the many theoretical and methodological traditions in the study of ideology and ideologies, a good number appear in the contributions to this volume. Some aim primarily to explain the variety of *functions* that ideologies perform in social and political life (Althusser 1971; Converse 1964; Easton 1965; Geertz 1964; Gramsci 1971; Howarth, Norval, and Stavrakakis 2000; Laclau 1994; Weber 1958; and Žižek 1994, to name a few "functionalist" theories). Others focus their explanations on the *psychological dispositions and orientations* and/or *cognitive foundations* of different ideologies' adherents (Jost, Federico, and Napier 2013; Lakoff 1996; Haidt 2012). Still others aim to explain the connection between *attitudes, values, and policy preferences, voting, or other political behaviour,* often portrayed as unstructured by a coherent or consistent ideology (Ellis and Stimson 2012; Zaller 1992; Achen and Bartels 2016; Gidengil et al. 2012; Cochrane 2015).

Contributors to this volume all adopt, at least to some degree, a "morphological sensibility" towards ideology. That is, they all treat ideological expressions, discourses, actions, and convictions not as autonomous concepts with fixed meanings but as dynamic elements whose meaning arises from their structural relationships to other experiences, ideas, and concepts. All of them show that the study of ideology requires analytical work that is simultaneously empirical and interpretive.

Disagreements and tensions concerning the relationship between political/ideological analysis and truth have been inherent to, and often politicized in, the study of ideologies since the eighteenth century. The theoretical choices are often presented as binary: we must either argue that our critical approach to ideology leads to a return to "truth," or contend that ideology is simply what ideologists do. There is no way of knowing whether some ideologies are "true." Like other constructivist approaches to social and political analysis, and most post-1970s philosophy of social science, Freeden's theory of ideologies rejects the Marxist (or perhaps just Marxist-Leninist) and positivist binary of science/ideology. Like other constructivists, Freeden also accepts that the ultimate truth value of whole ideological perspectives and their normative underpinnings is beyond "proof" by the standards of the natural sciences.

Unlike postmodern theory, however, Freeden (1996, ch. 2) also insists that there is something beyond ideology with which we can evaluate the empirical and causal claims of ideologies. He argues that it is possible to show that some ideologies, and certainly specific ideological claims, are logically inconsistent, are dependent on objectively falsifiable claims about empirical reality, and have considerably less explanatory and "rational" political value than other ideologies – even if they come to shape many citizens' views of political life. Donald Trump's ideological success is by no means original in this sense. By providing us with a convincing way out of this analytically unproductive binary choice, Freeden has done analysts of ideology a considerable service.

Another important distinction to help readers navigate the chapters that follow is between the macro/canonical, meso, and micro levels of ideological expression, practice and experience. Thus we have: (1) the canonically articulated and defined, or macro level; (2) the intermediate or meso level of competitive political appeals, politically relevant public discourse, policy advocacy, and cultural criticism; and (3) the everyday or micro level of conceptual use by people making their way through ordinary life (Humphrey, Laycock, and Umbach 2019; see Freeden 2013b for a similar division between "elite, professional, and vernacular political thinking"). Briefly, these can be characterized as follows.

The macro level of ideological action is dominated by broadly influential canonical works, pitched at the level of "high theory." It is best to think here of "canonical" works in inclusive terms: not just the writings of major philosophers but also those of influential political writers or social theorists should count as canonical, encompassing everyone from Marx or Rawls, and from Gramsci or Friedrich Hayek to Ernesto Laclau or Sigmund Freud. Their philosophical depth and/or comprehensive accounts of "the political" lend them to analysis using Freeden's morphological approach or some other concept-centric analytical framework, such as critical discourse theory (Howarth, Norval, and Stavrakakis 2000; Van Dijk 2013), *Begriffsgeschichte* conceptual history (Koselleck 1985; Koselleck and Richter 2011), or that of Quentin Skinner and his "Cambridge School" (Skinner 2002; Ball, Farr, and Hanson 1989).

We can also identify a broadly encompassing meso or intermediate level of ideological activity, which involves highly varied "professional" efforts to shape and attach both policy and ideological specificity to political agendas, whether by governing or opposition parties, social movement organizations, or any number of other civil society actors. Such efforts are professional in the sense that they are conducted by individuals trained in persuasive presentation of policy ideas, shaping of public attitudes towards contentious policy questions, and analysis of the feedback provided to these efforts by target audiences. Freeden's approach can be applied at this meso level, as many articles in his *Journal of Political Ideologies* attest, but so can a variety of other approaches to textual/conceptual analysis, analysis of social movement motivations, activities, and policy processes, and efforts to place policy developments in a broader communicative and opinion-structuring context.

Finally, at the micro level of ideological action, individuals establish their own normatively oriented conceptual anchors in and perceptions of "the political," very broadly understood to incorporate their stance towards all relations of power that they perceive to affect them. Humphrey, Umbach, and Clolow (2019) demonstrate that Freeden's morphological approach can also be useful here. And Dennis Pilon demonstrates in Chapter 9 that auto-ethnographic analysis inspired by a Marxist perspective on working class experience can achieve valuable insights at the micro level.

Such differentiation among levels of ideological action and influence helps us to identify and appreciate the virtues of a variety of conceptual, discursive, and functionalist approaches taken to analysis of ideology within and beyond this volume. Making sense of ideological action across macro, meso, and micro levels is especially complicated when the main focus is the meso level inhabited by many different types of professional writers and political speakers, performing competitively and strategically with and to many other speakers and audiences. Such actors draw primarily on non-canonical sources in direct and hence traceable ways. They also draw indirectly on ideas formulated in consciously systematic and conceptually complex written canonical products, which percolate down to the meso level in both readily identifiable and highly mediated, often anonymized and "popularized" forms. At the meso level, materials from both the macro and micro levels will directly and indirectly impinge on actors' efforts to convey salient features of "the political" and to otherwise shape, sometimes unintentionally, citizens' micro level perceptions of and preferences about politics.

The chapters in this volume primarily analyze ideological dimensions of politics conducted at the meso level, examining the ideological production, dissemination, and conceptual contestation activities of social movement, trade union, organized interest, and political party leaders, activists, and public intellectuals. The actors whose discourses they analyze range from intellectuals inclined to tap directly into the macro level of canonical articulations, to well-known political figures quite removed from explicit connection to macro-level ideological "work," to figures prominent only within local and specific organizational borders. These actors are even less directly connected to canonical thinkers at the macro level, and their articulation of ideological concepts occurs primarily or exclusively at the vernacular level.

* * *

This volume is organized on a broad thematic basis to highlight the diverse and complementary perspectives brought to the study of ideology at macro, meso, and micro levels of social experience. Our contributors typically move between macro and meso levels of conceptual/discursive and functional analysis to illuminate the ideological complexity of strikingly diverse cases. These cases involve governing or opposition parties, social movement organizations, business associations, and other civil society actors. These actors' efforts are intended to recruit explicit citizen support for specific agendas or implicit, perhaps even subconscious, acquiescence, whether across a whole electorate or in a targeted, sometimes class- or group-specific constituency.

The broad thematic division among the chapters in this collection is between (1) ideology expressed via policy, partisan, or academic contests, and (2) ideology expressed through civil society organizational mobilization regarding broad domains of social change. A few words on how each chapter fits into these categories will round out this introduction.

In Chapter 1, Ivan Jankovic uses a combination of historical, conceptual, and discourse analytical methods to explore British eighteenth-century "country party" ideology and its influence on the United States in the aftermath of the American Revolution. Federalists and anti-federalists then approximated political parties attempting to shape the new regime. Jankovic engages a long-standing debate on the ideological origins of pre- and immediately post-revolutionary America. He argues that this British country party ideology, already on the wane on its home turf, fuelled a libertarian resistance movement against the modern state across the Atlantic in anti-federalist and Jeffersonian doctrines in America. He contends that this movement's leaders embraced an ideology with a marked medieval touch that was skeptical not of progress and modernity as such but of the centralized and mercantilist state created by the Walpolean regime in England and emulated by Hamiltonian nationalists in the United States.

From eighteenth-century America, we move to twenty-first-century Canada and two accounts of the ideological complexion and agenda of the 2006–15 Conservative federal government. In Chapter 2, Katherine Reilly examines efforts by the Conservatives to reorient Canada's approach to development assistance through mobilization of new imagery about Canada's role in the world. This involved reorganization of the relationship between the Canadian state and the development assistance policy community, and efforts to shift citizens' attitudes about what development assistance can and should aim to achieve. Reilly argues that this ideologically distinctive development policy agenda can best be understood as an example of mediated geopolitics, which involves a struggle to influence historical potential in and through the international arena. This analytical perspective is deployed primarily for functional explanatory purposes, though there is some cross-over into conceptual/substantive explanation as well.

In Chapter 3, David Laycock and Steven Weldon examine how populist conservatism in Canada attempted to redefine Canadian multiculturalism without relying on the nativism found in much European and American populism today. They argue that the Conservative Party and government attempted to normatively and politically detach multiculturalism from the liberal egalitarian foundations of the Canadian welfare state, while accepting the ethnic diversity of Canadian society. The Conservatives did so by selectively drawing on ideological themes from the Reform Party of Canada. The Reform Party had drawn heavily on ideological directions of the American new right, which has been successfully combining populist appeals and conservative ideology since the mid-1970s. The bulk of Chapter 3 uses conceptual and discursive analytical methods, though the question of how attitudes towards multiculturalism and the welfare state shape one another is explored quantitatively for functional explanatory purposes.

Only one contributor offers an account of how a particular theoretical approach used in academic analysis has incorporated a combination of theoretical and ideological assumptions. This singularity is unusual following a century in which the sociology of knowledge played a central role in studies of ideology (Berry and Kenny 2013). Laurent Dobuzinskis (Chapter 4) gives a detailed conceptual account of how game theory evolved, developed new methods and fields of analysis, travelled across many cultural, epistemological, and ideological divides, and gained academic reach and policy influence over the past century. However, he also defends game theory against critics who see it as a poorly disguised methodological generator of neoliberal economic nostrums and scepticism about non-altruistic behaviour or state intervention in markets.

To begin the second section, Ian Angus (Chapter 5) addresses the contribution that discourse theory and rhetorical analysis can make to the study of political ideologies. One of his case studies uses the notion of a "field of discourse" to analyze the framing of early debates concerning multiculturalism in Canada. The other case study utilizes the concept of rhetorical equivalence to understand how contemporary convergence between the concepts of "ecology" and "Mother Earth" has helped to mobilize social movement constituencies. Chapter 5 is also notable for its explicit theoretical statement concerning the difference between political philosophy, political theory, and political ideology, and the importance of these differences for the study of ideology, and for its clear endorsement of the inseparability of analysis of ideologies from political critique/engagement.

In Chapter 6, Kyle Willmott analyzes taxpayer advocacy groups as agents of political mobilization and ideological production. He argues that these distinct civil society organizations share a strategic imperative to provide what Foucault called "permanent political criticism" of any exercise of governing, in an attempt to encourage "taxpayer reason." Drawing upon the broadly functionalist "governmentality studies" and policy mobility literatures, Willmott positions taxpayer groups as circulatory networks that render complex ideological principles of liberalism into a practical, critical everyday political reason, and translate the work of governments into forms of knowledge tailored for "taxpayers." He uses ethnographic textual data to show how the ideas, strategies, and tactics of taxpayer groups circulate to globally advance "taxpayer reason" among everyday citizens.

In Chapter 7, Katherine Strand and Darin Barney offer an exploration of "agricultural subjectivity" as a key axis of ideological formation and contestation in the Canadian Prairie provinces. Taking their analytical cues initially from Althusser's functional account of ideologies as instruments for the reproduction of relations of production, Strand and Barney use critical discourse theory to compare two examples of extra-partisan cultural production that have attempted to "hail" distinct political subjects in different periods of Prairie political history. The first is a 1977 play, *Paper Wheat*, about the establishment of the Prairie wheat pools and cooperative movement; the second is *License to Farm*, a 2016 industry organization documentary that aims to promote genetically modified crops and chemical farming. The authors compare these two cultural products in Prairie experience as distinctive ideological formations intended to circulate ideological claims and mediate political subjects within a specific social class.

In Chapter 8, Mark Leier considers the importance of informal expression in labour movement ideology by examining jokes, songs, stories, and culture in British Columbia's labour movement. Leier draws on a diverse literature on working class history generally compatible with Freeden's injunction to analyze political concepts "through locating them within the patterns in which they actually appear." He argues that this "laborlore" has both supported and contested the movement's official ideologies as well as supporting and undermining its solidarities. The chapter focuses on the functions performed by informal ideologies associated with class, race, and gender in shaping the province's labour and left movements, arguing that they were as important as any manifesto or platform.

In Chapter 9, Dennis Pilon utilizes auto-ethnographic techniques and Eagleton's Marxist analysis of ideology to explore everyday ideology among working class people in British Columbia. Through a critical self-examination of his own "residual working class identity" and that of his parents and grandparents, Pilon sheds light on a broad area of practical, everyday ideological thinking that often fails to register with academics who tend to recognize ideology only as the product of political theorists or militant political actors. His objective in telling such stories – about himself and his union organizer and lifelong socialist grandparents – is to link such "ways of seeing" with the contexts that helped inform and sustain them. Though his broad view of this experience fits within a functionalist Marxist theoretical perspective, his fine-grained micro analysis also draws on conceptual and discursive analytical approaches.

The chapters in this volume provide new insights into historical and contemporary expressions of political ideology in North American political parties, public policy, and civil society actors' experiences. Taken together, they also make a case for studying ideology through a diverse range of disciplinary perspectives and methods.

References

Achen, Christopher, and Larry Bartels. 2016. *Democracy for Realists*. Princeton, NJ: Princeton University Press.

Althusser, Louis. 1971. "Ideology and Ideological State Apparatuses." In *Lenin and Philosophy and Other Essays*, ed. Louis Althusser, 121–76. New York: Monthly Review Press.

Ball, Terence, James Farr, and Russell Hanson, eds. 1989. *Political Innovation and Conceptual Change*. New York: Cambridge University Press.

Barthes, Roland. 1972. *Mythologies*. New York: Hill and Wang.

Berry, Craig, and Michael Kenny. 2013. "Ideology and the Intellectuals." In *The Oxford Handbook of Political Ideologies*, ed. M. Freeden, L.T. Sargeant, and M. Stears, 251–70. New York: Oxford University Press.

Cochrane, Christopher. 2015. *Left and Right: The Small World of Political Ideas*. Montreal and Kingston: McGill-Queen's University Press.

Converse, Philip E. 1964. "The Nature of Belief Systems in Mass Publics." In *Ideology and Discontent*, ed. David Apter, 206–61. New York: Free Press of Glencoe.

Easton, David. 1965. *A Systems Analysis of Political Life*. New York: John Wiley.

Ellis, Christopher, and James Stimson. 2012. *Ideology in America*. New York: Cambridge University Press.

Farney, Jim. 2019. "Cross-border influences or parallel developments? A process-tracing approach to the development of social conservatism in Canada and the USA." *Journal of Political Ideologies* 24: 2, 139–57.

Finlayson, Alan. 2012. "Rhetoric and the Political Theory of Ideologies." *Political Studies* 60: 751–67.

Freeden, Michael. 1996. *Ideologies and Political Theory*. New York: Oxford University Press.

–. 2013a. "The Morphological Analysis of Ideology." In *The Oxford Handbook of Political Ideologies*, ed. M. Freeden, L.T. Sargeant, and M. Stears, 115–37. New York: Oxford University Press.

–. 2013b. *The Political Theory of Political Thinking*. New York: Oxford University Press.

Freeden, Michael, L.T. Sargeant, and Mark Stears, eds. 2013. *The Oxford Handbook of Political Ideologies*. New York: Oxford University Press.

Gallie, W.B. 1956. "Essentially Contested Concepts." *Proceedings of the Aristotelian Society* (New Series) 56: 167–98.

Geertz, Clifford. 1964. "Ideology as a Cultural System." In *Ideology and Discontent*, ed. David Apter, 47–76. New York: Free Press.

Gidengil, Elisabeth, Neil Nevitte, André Blais, Joanna Everitt, and Patrick Fournier. 2012. *Dominance and Decline: Making Sense of Recent Canadian Elections*. Toronto: University of Toronto Press.

Gramsci, Antonio. 1971. *Selections from the Prison Notebooks of Antonio Gramsci*, ed. Quintin Hoare and Geoffrey Nowell-Smith. London: Lawrence and Wishart.

Haidt, Jonathan. 2012. *The Righteous Mind: Why Good People Are Divided by Politics and Religion*. New York: Pantheon Books.

Howarth, David, Aletta J. Norval, and Yannis Stavrakakis, eds. 2000. *Discourse Theory and Political Analysis: Identities, Hegemonies and Social Change*. Manchester: University of Manchester Press.

Humphrey, Mathew. 2005. "(De)contesting Ideology: The Struggle over the Meaning of the Struggle over Meaning." *Critical Review of International Social and Political Philosophy* 8 (2): 225–46.

Humphrey, Mathew, David Laycock and Maiken Umbach. 2019. "Introduction: Mediating between Macro and Micro Morphologies: Adaptation and Application in Political Ideology." *Journal of Political Ideologies* 24 (2): 113–20.

Humphrey, Mathew, Maiken Umbach, and Zeynep Clolow. 2019. "The Personal is Political: An Analysis of Crowd-Sourced Political Ideas from a Massive Open Online Course." *Journal of Political Ideologies* 24 (2): 121–38.

Jost, John, Christopher Federico, and Jaime Napier. 2013. "Political Ideologies and Their Social Psychological Functions." In *The Oxford Handbook of Political Ideologies*, ed. M. Freeden, L.T. Sargeant, and M. Stears, 232–50. New York: Oxford University Press.

Koselleck, Reinhart. 1985. *Futures Past: On the Semantics of Historical Time*. Cambridge, MA: MIT Press.

Koselleck, Reinhart, and Michaela Richter. 2011. "Introduction and Prefaces to the 'Geschichtliche Grundbegriffe.'" *Contributions to the History of Concepts* 6 (1): 1–5, 7–25, 27–37.

Laclau, Ernesto. 1993. "Discourse." In *A Companion to Contemporary Political Philosophy*, ed. R.E. Goodin and P. Pettit, 431–37. Oxford: Blackwell.

–. 1994. *The Making of Political Identities*. London: Verso.

Lakoff, George. 1996. *Moral Politics*. Chicago: University of Chicago Press.

Laycock, David. 2014. "Conceptual Foundations of Continuity and Change in NDP Ideology." In *Reviving Social Democracy: The Near Death and Surprising Rise of the Federal NDP*, ed. D. Laycock and L. Erickson, 109–39. Vancouver: UBC Press.

–. 2019. "Tax Revolts, Direct Democracy and Populist Politics in the USA and Canada." *Journal of Political Ideologies* 24 (2): 158–81.

Maynard, Jonathan. 2013. "A Map of the Field of Ideological Analysis." *Journal of Political Ideologies* 18 (3): 299–327.

Skinner, Quentin. 2002. *Visions of Politics, Volume 1: Regarding Method.* Cambridge: Cambridge University Press.

Stavrakakis, Yannis. 1997. "Green Ideology: A Discursive Reading." *Journal of Political Ideologies* 2 (3): 259–79.

Thagard, Paul. 2014. "Mapping Minds across Cultures." In *Grounding Social Sciences in Cognitive Sciences*, ed. Ron Sun, 157–83. Cambridge, MA: MIT Press.

Van Dijk, Teun A. 2013. "Ideology and Discourse." In *The Oxford Handbook of Political Ideologies*, ed. M. Freeden, L.T. Sargeant, and M. Stears, 175–96. New York: Oxford University Press.

Weber, Max. 1958. *The Protestant Ethic and the Spirit of Capitalism*, trans. and ed. Talcott Parsons. New York: Charles Scribner and Sons.

Zaller, John. 1992. *The Nature and Origins of Mass Opinion*. New York: Cambridge University Press.

Žižek, Slavoj. 1994. "The Spectre of Ideology." In *Mapping Ideology*, ed. S. Žižek, 1–33. London: Verso.

PART 1

IDEOLOGY IN PARTISAN, POLICY, AND ACADEMIC CONTEXTS

Consent, Representation, and Liberty
America as the Last Medieval Society – or a Footnote to Louis Hartz

IVAN JANKOVIC

This chapter re-evaluates the two basic pillars of Louis Hartz's interpretation of the ideological origins of American political culture: its Lockean liberal provenance, and its establishment and imposition in the United States through a seamless transplantation of the "liberal fragment of European history" (Hartz 1955). As one of the staunchest "Hartzians" of this age, Michael Zuckert had memorably said that "America was the Lockean country and Locke was the American philosopher," because in America Lockean liberalism was liberated from the challenge of pre-existing medieval and feudal institutions of Europe, and could thrive by creating *ab ovo* a new political, economic, and even constitutional structure. From Alexis de Tocqueville's *Democracy in America* to the variety of the most important *contemporary* thinkers of the American founding[1] this basic assumption of America's ideological Lockean purity and novelty is steadfastly maintained and reinforced.

I scrutinize this stubborn interpretive paradigm by going back to the historical "facts on the ground." Much of the evidence for Lockean liberal dominance of early American ideological discourse is derived from reading the contemporary official political and constitutional documents and assessing the relative significance of Locke in American culture of that age. Yet, even in this narrow focus, Bernard Bailyn's seminal work on the revolutionary pamphlet literature had shown convincingly that Lockean philosophy has been but a small part of American revolutionary conversation. Of far greater importance, in Bailyn's account, was a peculiar approach of outcast liberal old-Whigs. These included Trenchard and Gordon in their widely read (in America) *Cato's Letters,* and their English Tory ally Viscount Bolingbroke, with their passionate denunciations of cabinet government and a corrupting government-economy nexus, which were not conveyed with Lockean philosophical reasoning. As Bailyn's student Gordon Wood (1982) said much later, the revolutionary ideological upheaval was actually the first episode of "paranoid-style politics" in America, juxtaposing the usurpation of "power" with "traditional liberty" rather than being a self-assertion of the primordial American liberal Lockeanism against European monarchism, as the tradition exemplified by Hartz and Hartzians (Zuckert 1996; Dworetz 1990) would have it.

It has been already observed that, ironically, Bailyn was channelling Hartz when he argued that British "libertarian" old-Whig ideology was the true creative agent in American revolutionary thought; the "fragment" analysis was still in control, but the identification of the relevant transplanted fragment shifted from Lockean liberalism to Trenchard's and Gordon's "Catonian" republicanism/libertarianism. I attempt to revise the Bailyn-Wood account by picking up on one element of their analysis that was left completely unintegrated with the main narrative – a reactionary, medieval element of American political culture, especially crucial to an understanding of the institutions and political practices.

The "territorial" dimension of American democratic-liberal political thought and practice, localism, decentralization, and bottom-up federalism were all the remnants of the older, medieval political universe, opposed to the modernizing forces of state and nation building. By combining the Bailyn-Wood approach with Tocqueville's analysis of American and European history and the findings of the constitutionalist school of American founding, I will show that ironically, contrary to Hartz, the fragment of European history that was transplanted into America and that gave its "revolutionary" tradition its strongest flavour was a *medieval* fragment, which Hartz thought had been amputated from American history. In the time when Europe moved strongly from those localist principles and practices of the pre-modern period, America reasserted them in its revolutionary thought and practice. In this sense, the America of the late eighteenth century was the "last medieval society" in the West, and the American Revolution was the last European peasants' rebellion.

The result of this interpretive refocusing should be to offer us a new way of looking at how Americans in the early period of their history were decontesting liberty, to borrow the phrase from Michael Freeden (2003).

Our journey through American ideological origins will lead into a strange landscape where the modern coexists with the medieval, and individualism of the Lockean type coexists with the most ancient "communitariansm," in a seamless fabric of "territorial liberalism" that looks awkward and counterintuitive to the modern observer. This chapter will explore and document the degree to which a form of "decontestation" of liberty that both Hartz and Bailyn, with some variation, assume as given has to be supplemented by the forgotten medieval-territorial dimension.

American Localism

For historians of early America, claims about the reactionary nature of American political culture and institutions are not very radical or controversial. Localism as a pre-modern territorial framework of liberal order represented an antecedent condition of the revolutionary upheaval, an inherited feature of the customary baggage of colonial life that made the intellectual acceptance of radical Whig concepts easier and quicker. Most of the North American colonists in the seventeenth century came from Great Britain, a country that preserved its medieval forms of local self-government much more than the continental European lands such as France, Spain, or the Germanic states. During the seventeenth and early eighteenth centuries, these colonists were mostly on the sidelines of the gradual development of a modern state in Great Britain. Hence, the old-Whig sharp critiques of administrative centralization, taxation without consent, regulation of commerce, and other forms of consolidation struck a chord with the colonists, since these critiques were congenial to the notions of governance colonists derived from their own practical experience. The revolutionary experience grew from a happy conjunction of ideological influences from widely read literature and political and economic conditions of colonial life: "What the Whig radicals were saying about the English government and society had so long been a part of the American mind, had so often been reinforced by their first-hand observation of London life, and had possessed such an affinity to their own provincial interests and experience that it always seemed to the colonists to be what they had been trying to say all along" (Wood 1969, 17).

However, it was not only the ideology of the radical country party that was English in origin; the anachronistic institutional set-up that had been imported and fossilized in its previous forms gradually dissolved in England itself, under the assault of the advancing administrative centralization of the late seventeenth century. The ancient, medieval freedom of English parishes and boroughs is one of the strongest sources of this idiosyncratic American localism. Closely connected to it are the time-honoured American traditions of short electoral terms and local control of the politicians by the constituencies, which are the remnants and reflections of the medieval practice of attorneyship.[2] The practice was derived from the thirteenth-century institution of *plena potestas*, a revived Roman principle of representation in court, according to which local communities could send their representatives in the central political bodies to discuss taxes and other issues with a king or other nobles. This arrangement meant a delegation of power under a very precisely specified set of circumstances; it gave to a representative (attorney) a right to negotiate and conclude agreements with other parties, but at the same time retained his fiduciary duty towards the principal, or *dominus* (local community), similar to the way proxy representation functions in modern corporate firms (Post 1943; Edwards 1942). What is particularly important is that in medieval times this institution did not distinguish between "private" and "public" relationships among the contracting parties. An attorney representing a defendant in court, a political representative in the parliament, or an ambassador in foreign kingdoms all had exactly the same power of *plena potestas:* a power to act in the principal's interest as if he was physically present (Post 1943).

This paradox is similar to that identified by Otto Brunner in his analysis of the late Medieval feuds:[3] the fact that the medieval sources do not make any difference between the "private" and "'public," between the "state" and "civil society." Just as a quarrel of the two petty local nobles in Bavaria was regulated by the same laws of just war as a "real war" between the two powerful kings, a local parish representative in Southern England had essentially the same legal status as an English ambassador to France. John Edwards (1942) demonstrates that *plena potestas* was introduced in England in the late thirteenth century as a means of providing a stable tax revenue for the king: in order to have the local boroughs and communities assent to the tax levies, a medieval king had to ask and get a binding agreement and consent of every single local community.[4] He had no direct and autonomous power to tax: "As to the opinion that the king was under no legal necessity of obtaining the consent of shires and boroughs to taxation ... no convincing evidence has yet been adduced in support of it, and a great deal of evidence tells directly against it ... it seems clear that men in the thirteenth century inclined to the belief that consent to taxation should be personal, individual consent" (Edwards 1958, 147–48).

Hence the need for mandatory *plena potestas* as a means of circumventing the problem of consent to taxation: it allowed the local ambassadors ("knights of shire") to negotiate and to grant to the king a tax levy for a specific period of time on behalf of a given community. But even that did not mean that the king could enforce the obligation by force; it meant only that he had law on his side, and that justice required local communities to pay. As one historian notes, summarizing the fourteenth-century document about the English Parliament: "The king reigns, without him there can be no Parliament, but he is no more than the servant of the Commonwealth. His subjects could withdraw themselves from Parliament if they maintain, with particular instances that he has not ruled as he ought and he has no redress against their recalcitrance" (Clarke 1964, 9).

The concept of the monopoly of coercion and the power to tax as a prerogative of the "government" are inapplicable to the High Middle Ages in general, and specifically to medieval England.[5] In its historical origins, the formula made famous by the revolutionary Americans of the eighteenth century, "no taxation without representation," was just a reflection of a more fundamental medieval formula of a voluntary consent to taxation by the *local* territorial communities (boroughs and parishes). The formula was *quod omnes tangit, ab omnibus approbetur* ("what touches all must be approved by all"). This meant that any concrete grant of financial aid to the king needed to be approved by all estates and all individual local communities.

The historical record from the eleventh to the fourteenth century is full of examples of individual noblemen, clergymen, or commoners refusing to pay the subsidy to the king,[6] invoking the *quod omnes tangit* rationale because they did not freely consent to the subsidy. Originating in Catholic ecclesiastical thought, influenced by Roman law, the *quod omnes tangit* principle quickly found widespread acclaim among the secular magnates and commoner knights in Parliament. For example, the bishop of Winchester in 1217 refused to pay the tax to the king by arguing that he did not personally consent, and the Exchequer was forced to accept his explanation (no forcible collection of taxes in this "dark age"!). In 1270, the bishops granted to the king just one-twentieth of the requested sum, with the explanation that only those prelates and magnates present in Parliament were bound to pay. And the king had to accept this (Clarke 1964, 257).

This surprising method of parliamentary "representation" had one crucial aspect: localism. In the English Middle Ages, people sitting in Parliament did not represent the estates or social groups, even less the "nation," but only their local masters, who very tightly controlled them:

In its original medieval form elective representation to parliament had been a device by which "local men, locally minded, whose business began and ended with the interest of their constituency," were enabled, as attorneys for their electors to seek the redress from the royal court of Parliament, in return for which they were expected to commit their constituencies to grants and financial aid ... local communities bound their representatives to local interests in every way possible: by requiring local residency or the ownership of local property as a qualification for election, by closely controlling the payment of wages for official services performed, by instructing representatives minutely as to their powers and limits of permissible concessions, and by making them strictly accountable for all the actions taken in the name of the constituents. As a result, representatives of the commons in the medieval Parliament did not speak for that estate in general or for any other body or group larger than the specific one that had elected them. (Bailyn 1967, 162–63)

Seventeenth-century English immigrants to North America brought this ancient tradition of localist liberty and decentralized politics, this strange "territorial democracy" inimical to the claims of consolidated national power. And although these communal liberties of the Middle Ages began to fade away by the early seventeenth century in England,[7] conditions in North America forced the settlers to preserve them and even radicalize their use in the new circumstances. As Bernard Bailyn (1967, 164) suggests, utilizing seventeenth-century assumptions, Americans "out of necessity drifted backwards ... towards the medieval forms of attorneyship in representation. The colonial towns and counties, like their medieval counterparts, were largely autonomous, and they stood to lose more than they were likely to gain from loose acquiescence in the action of central government." Instead of moving from the medieval decentralized conditions towards political consolidation, as had been the case with England in the centuries before the American Revolution, the North American colonists went back to the original conception of the House of Commons as a confederation of localities. Seemingly hypermodern Americans reached back deeply into the Middle Ages to shape their political and social institutions in the New World.

The feebleness of colonial governments in America encouraged and in some sense even forced the colonials to rely on those older traditions and instruments. Since the power of colonial government was largely formal and ineffective, and colonial legislatures were formed and maintained on the basis of local representation, residential requirements, annual elections, and binding instructions to the legislators,[8] the resulting system was one of extreme decentralization of decision making, closely tracking that of medieval England or the Germanic states. The main governing units in the colonial period were the townships in New England and counties in the South and mid-Atlantic colonies (Jensen 1968; Wood 2011). They were the true sources from which the almost perennial American localism and particularism initially sprang up.

In colonial times, the governments of every individual colony were ruled by an appointed bureaucratic oligarchy and a rubber stamp upper house of the legislature, whereas the most local influence was felt in self-governing townships in the North and counties in the South.[9] There, the inhabitants could freely choose their representatives (or rule by direct democracy), and from the earliest period of colonization they had a significant and wide autonomy (Jensen 1968). Moreover, the lower houses of the colonial legislatures were not elected in colony-wide elections but rather selected and appointed by the said local governments as their ambassadors. Colonial legislatures were, in a way, confederations of local political communities (ibid.). While almost the entire European continent went in the direction of growing centralization and administrative consolidation, Americans went back to the essentially medieval system of local representation and self-rule.

Alexis de Tocqueville, paradoxically, was among the first to discover this. This is surprising insofar as Tocqueville, in his *Democracy in America,* saw America as a hypermodern society of enlightened republican egalitarianism, showing to Europe its inevitable democratic future. He saw New England township democracy as a radical novelty, a product of Enlightenment thinking and republican rejection of European conservative mores and hierarchical political ethos. According to *Democracy in America,* "the foundation of New England was something new in the world, all the attendant circumstances being both peculiar and original" (Tocqueville 1969, 35).

In his *Old Regime and the Revolution,* however, Tocqueville concedes that he was wrong in this regard, that the New England township democracy was everything but "something new in the world"; it was, in fact, a form of the very old medieval localist democracy. In analyzing the gradual disappearance of the communal institutions of self-government in modern French and German cities and villages, he pointed to a curious phenomenon, namely, that those cities appeared to have been much more autonomous and self-governing in the thirteenth and fourteenth centuries than in his own time: "In the organization of this small community, despite its poverty and servile state, I discovered some of the features which had struck me so much in the

rural townships of North America; the features that I had then – wrongly –
thought peculiar to the New World" (Tocqueville 1998, 48).

It suddenly dawned on Tocqueville that local American freedoms were
actually a direct descendant of European medieval freedoms. The New
England township was a medieval parish, surviving its transatlantic journey
on the ships carrying the English settlers, just removed from the feudal context of the old world: "They resembled each other [English parish and the
New England township] ... as much as the living could resemble the dead.
These two beings with such different fates had had, in reality, the same birth.
Suddenly transported far from feudalism and made absolute mistress of
itself, the medieval rural parish *became the New England township* [empha-
sis added]" (Tocqueville 1998, 48).[10]

The two most remarkable institutions, both medieval in their origin, were blooming in late colonial and revolutionary America, and were
front and centre of many constitutional debates during the revolutionary
period: annual elections and binding instructions to legislators. The practice of electing annual and sometimes shorter parliaments was prevalent in
England from the Middle Ages. In the thirteenth century, parliaments were
often called after much shorter periods than a year; for example, between
1272 and 1280, the parliament met fifteen times and only once granted tax
revenue to the king (Madicott 1981, 62). The strictly annual elections for
Parliament were legally introduced after 1330 and this practice persisted for
centuries. For the most part, the annual election meant that no single parliament could do business for much longer than several weeks.

All this started to change radically in the seventeenth and especially early
eighteenth centuries: first, the parliaments were prolonged to four years
and then, according to the Septennial Act of 1716, to seven years. Save for
a handful of radical Whigs and their allies among the gentry reactionar-
ies, annual elections were considered a relic of primitive medieval politics:
modern Parliament needed to participate in governance on a daily basis by
actually cooperating with the executive (Wood 1969, 26).[11]

In contrast to this, in America, this same fossil of British tradition was
very much alive and thriving. Annual elections were considered a cornerstone of democracy, especially after the experience with earlier colonial
legislatures, which, sitting for five or seven years, were often manipulated
and bribed by the governors and English bureaucrats. Americans relapsed
happily into the medieval-Gothic orthodoxy of annual elections as the sur-
est bulwark against "corruption" of colonial rule: "When annual elections
end Tyranny begins," proclaimed one South Carolinian in 1776. During the

revolutionary war, Massachusetts Arundel County militia members proposed annual elections because "they are most friendly to liberty, and the oftener power reverts to the people, the greater will be the security for a faithful discharge of it" (Jensen 1967, 336). After 1776, all new state constitutions except South Carolina's provided for annual elections and greatly increased the number of legislators (Wood 1969). A New York pamphlet published in 1778 echoed the widespread adherence to annual elections by attributing the transgressions of the British Parliament against the colonists to the abandonment of short electoral terms by the British themselves: "Long duration of the parliament is allowed by all to be principal Cause of its present corrupt State" because "the Ministry knowing that they [members of the parliament] are to continue for seven years, think it worth their while to attempt and seduce them with a high Bribe" (Publicola 1776).

In addition, to better effectuate the old notion of local, communal representation, annual elections were reinforced by a renaissance of binding instructions, also a very old English medieval institution. It came from the times when the local parishes were represented by plenipotentiaries – attorneys of local communities – when Parliament had very little real power, and when the very concepts of "body politic" and "political sovereignty" were unknown.[12] In those times, the plenipotentiary attorneys were the agents of local communities, and were denied a right of independent judgment that could go contrary to the will of the communities that sent them to Parliament.[13]

From the beginning of American colonial settlement, the practice of binding instructions was strongly entrenched:

> In the colonies, the practice of voting instructions commenced with the very beginning of New England. In 1641, the Massachusetts General Court asked the town to instruct their representatives on two issues, one of which was the method of elections. Plymouth had a statute providing that town meetings should hear from their representatives what had been done in the legislature and vote "instructions for any other business they should have donne." Dover, New Hampshire, instructed its representatives every year since 1658, and Boston did this almost annually since 1721. (Reid 1989, 98)

Americans of the late eighteenth century reinforced those old institutions and gave them constitutional status: in Pennsylvania, Vermont, and North Carolina, binding instructions to the legislatures were obligatory (Wood 1969). In many other states, although not constitutionalized, they were nevertheless common and widely accepted as a cornerstone of political liberty.

New England in particular had a long and uninterrupted history of local democracy coupled with the system of strict medieval attorneyship, including the instructions. Even after the American Revolution, representatives of New England townships often understood themselves as the new incarnation of the medieval "knights of shire," attorneys with the power to negotiate with other private parties.[14] As late as the 1830s, Alexis de Tocqueville (1969, 253–54) wrote that "the majority [in America] ... regards public functionaries as its passive agents and is glad to leave them the trouble of carrying out its plans ... It treats them as a master might treat his servants if, always seeing them act under his eyes, he could direct and correct them at any moment."

The popularity of binding instructions was immense, and was defended as a hallmark of American freedom. Metaphors of masters and servants were widely used to describe the relationship between the people and representatives. One of the leading critics of the planted aristocracy in South Carolina wrote that if binding instructions were to be relaxed, "it will at one stroke transform us into legal SLAVES to our lordly SERVANTS." Another writer argued explicitly for the republic of parishes that would create a state as a derived, composite community of local units, finding their least common denominator: "If after the election the members are free to act on their own accord, instead of abiding by the direction of their constituents ... it would be a matter of indifference from what part of the Republic the Legislative body was taken ... What nation in their senses ever sent ambassadors to another without limiting them by instructions" (Wood 1969, 190).

In his letter of instructions to Boston representatives in the colonial legislature of Massachusetts, Samuel Adams wrote that voters "delegated to you the power of acting in their publick Concerns in general as your own prudence shall direct you ... always reserving to themselves the[?] Constitutional Right of expressing their mind and giving you such Instruction upon particular matters as they at any Time shall Judge proper" (Reid 1989, 99). As one contemporary observer put it, "a representative who should act against the explicit recommendation of his constituency would most deservedly forfeit their regard and all pretension to their future confidence."[15] One Pennsylvanian writer in 1728 wrote in a tongue-in-cheek philosophical manner that there was "no transessentiating or transubstantiating of being from people to representative, no more than there is an absolute transferring of a title in a letter to an attorney" (Bailyn 1968, 85).

With this background, we should not be surprised that American colonists were not greatly enamoured of the concept of "virtual representation," well established in England and used by Parliament in the 1760s and 1770s to justify the British colonial policy of taxing Americans. This doctrine was considered by colonials to be appalling or, as one said, "the most monstrous, the most slavish doctrine that was ever heard." Echoing the English radical Whigs and their criticisms of ministerial and cabinet corruption, they offered a trenchant defence of binding instructions to legislators as a safeguard of American liberties that was, according to Arthur Lee, denied by the British government

> "since the system of corruption which is now arrived to so dangerous a height began first to predominate in our constitution. Then it was that arbitrary ministers and their prostitute dependents began to maintain this doctrine dangerous to our liberty, that the representatives are independent of the people. This was necessary to serve their tyrannical and selfish purposes ... [they are] trustees for their constituents to transact for them the business of government ... and for this service they, like all other agents, are paid by their constituents till they found it more advantageous to sell their voices in Parliament, and then ... wished to become independent of the people." (Bailyn 1967, 171)

Here again we have a full-throated defence of the same medieval form of representation via *plena potestas*, the same depiction of legislators as attorneys or proxy negotiators who do the "business of government" in the same way attorneys or real estate agents do other kinds of business for their principals and clients. And the concept of virtual representation that separates the rulers from the ruled, for a typical American pamphleteer of the 1760s and 1770s, was just a fraud concocted by the "arbitrary ministers and their prostitute dependents" to advance their own selfish interests.

The inhabitants of western New Hampshire articulated the idea in a more stringent and philosophical sense. In their view, the relationship between the towns and state legislatures was analogous to the relationship between the state legislatures and the British Parliament, and there were as many bodies politic in New Hampshire as there had been local communities: "To unite half a dozen or more towns together, equally privileged, in order to make them equal to some one other town, is a new practice in politics. We may as well take the souls of a number of different persons and say they make but one, while yet they remain separate and different" (Boutton 1877, 231). If a local representation was questioned, there was no difference in the mind of American colonials between the provincial and imperial governments:

"We are contending against the same enemy within which is also without," said a typical resolution written by the rebels of the Connecticut River valley, who were soon to secede from New York and create the republic of Vermont, "pursuing the same general cause ... that there cannot be taxation without representation." In 1769, the Reverend John Joachim Zubly ([1769] 1972, 17) attacked the British theory of virtual representation, invoking the medieval localist idea of representation: "Every representative in Parliament is not a representative for the whole nation, but only for the particular place for which he hath been elected; if not elected, he cannot represent them, and of course not consent to any thing in their behalf."

Just as the Continental Congress was an assembly of state ambassadors, in many ways the colonial and early revolutionary provincial/state legislatures were just collections of independent ambassadors of local communities. The basic unit of political representation, the living "soul" of the body politic, remained the local community, a town or a parish, whereas states represented just the derived composite forms, without any constitutional significance.

However, all this was not a new invention prompted by the revolutionary upheaval. On the contrary, this constitutional localism was well established from the very beginning of colonization. The colony of Connecticut was created in 1639 when three independent cities, Hartford, Windsor, and Whethersfield, came together and drew up an instrument of incorporation, creating thereby a central government for specific purposes. New Haven was created in 1643 when six cities joined together in a confederation to establish the separate colony of New Haven, and then in the 1660s joined Connecticut. Gordon Wood (2011, 713) points out that colonial Rhode Island was also a loose confederation of cities: "Although ostensibly a colony, seventeenth century Rhode Island was in reality four more or less independent towns: Providence, founded by Roger Williams; Portsmouth, founded by Anne Hutchinson, in flight from the Puritans in Boston; Newport, founded by William Coddington; and Warwick (or Shawomut, as it was called then) founded by a real radical, Samuel Gorton." Cities and localities were pre-existing political societies coalescing voluntarily to create a kind of federative structure in the colonial framework. A kind of federative duality between the state and national governments that we see in the period after 1787 existed also between the local and colonial or provincial governments in the seventeenth and early eighteenth centuries.

Many colonial political structures were created by a similar bottom-up process of federalization, in which the local communities would confederate and establish overarching political structures. But those provincial or colonial legislative structures remained entities of limited and delegated powers; localities such as the cities and towns in New England and parishes and counties in the Chesapeake area remained the basic constitutional units. This is best seen in the fact that throughout the colonial period there were independent cities that did not belong to any colony, and also in the fact that the same process of spontaneous bottom-up federalism with secessions and consolidations of independent cities and counties into new political units was repeated in the revolutionary period. The republic of Vermont was created by the secession of some counties of New York to establish an independent state. Northern regions of Massachusetts seceded from it to form the state of Maine; Kentucky seceded from Virginia and Tennessee from North Carolina. Not only in terms of institutional heritage and mental attitudes but also in terms of its kaleidoscopic, fragmented political geography, colonial and early revolutionary America was a true heir of the European High Middle Ages.

It is clear from this that Hartz's Lockean model ignores the highly contested nature not just of the idea of liberty but also of representation. Our corrective to him (stressing internal conceptual contestation within the liberal family) shows the diversity of late-eighteenth-century American liberalisms in a way that Hartz's rather determinist fragment theory, written from the point of view of the eventual victors, not the actual contestants, could not. The liberal individualism that triumphed in the late nineteenth century (capitalism of the Gilded Age, under whose long shadow Hartz wrote) was very different from the liberal individualism that triumphed, or rather settled for a draw, in 1787, and yet even more different from the liberalism that animated the events of 1773–76.

A form of "Lockean" philosophical continuity could be followed through all of these meanderings in American political history, but it cannot account for the diversity of views and the changes themselves. Most importantly for Hartz's thesis, the "original sin" of American liberalism – individualism and egalitarianism of the *Declaration of Independence* – were decisively influenced by an older, "medieval," anti-statist liberalism or libertarianism. Ironically, the "founding" liberal fragment of American history was reactionary, not modern; America did not transplant Old World Lockean individualism free of medieval remnants, as Hartz believed, but rather medieval remnants free of modern statist innovations. Therefore, not only did Hartz see much more continuity in American liberalism than there is but he seriously misidentified the starting point of its development.

Fiscal Military State and Liberalism

At this point, a note of caution is in order. The complicating factor we are facing in fleshing out the contours of American early liberalism is the fact that American political culture was in the process of fermentation and change in the late eighteenth century; the medieval, archaic, reactionary politics based on decentralization and localism was under attack from within, not only from without, by the growing intellectual, political, and commercial forces striving to forge "national unity" through a centralized nation-state. As Max Edling (2003) emphasized in *Revolution in the Name of Government*, the push to enact the US Constitution in 1787–88 was not a continuation of the American Revolution's anti-statist and anti-imperialist revolution in the name of local liberties, but a completely new revolution in the mould of European state building by absolutist monarchies to create a centralized "fiscal military state."

This state, formed in Europe under the aegis of absolute monarchy, and in America pushed by the nationalist politicians, included the central states' taxing power, regulation of commerce, right to erect trade tariffs and other barriers, central banking, and military organized in the form of standing armies. It united the powers of military sovereignty and the apparatus of fiscal coercion and trade regulation. A fiscal military state performs the two main functions of the government inspired by the imperialist and mercantilist philosophies of the early eighteenth century: waging war abroad efficiently and accumulating trade surpluses at home through subsidies, tariffs, and cheap central bank credit (Brewer 1989; Ertman 1994; Tilly 1975). In the American case, this spirit of fiscal military state is obvious in Article I, Section VIII of the Constitution, which establishes essentially the entire apparatus of government: "regulate commerce," "raise army and navy," "raise duties and imposts," "other taxes," "regulate commerce among the several states and with the foreign nations," and so on – the list mimics very closely the prerogatives of central government in absolute monarchies (Edling 2003; Jankovic 2019).

American traditional, reactionary localism and spirit or "anarchical" individualism were the obstacles to this process of creation of the fiscal military state. It is then not surprising that much before the revolution was completed (or even started), proponents of the new model – political sophisticates of the late eighteenth century – were already very wary of the unenlightened and reactionary localist tradition of politics in America. William Smith (1782, 243) of New York complained as early as 1750 that the provincial assembly consisted of "plain, illiterate husbandmen, whose views seldom extended farther than to the regulation of highways, the destruction of wolves, wild cats and foxes, and the advancement of their little interests of the particular counties, which they were chosen to represent." Tory politician Samuel Peters (1875) of Connecticut similarly complained that those same assemblies were composed of "contending factions whose different interests and pursuits it is generally found necessary mutually to consult, in order to produce a sufficient coalition to proceed on the business of the state."

So we have here developed the same argument against the "inefficiency" of American government that has come to be used pretty much until now: the government is too slow, too timid, too incapable of doing great things quickly. Moreover, the unenlightened, narrow-minded peasants see "the common interest only through the eyes of their deputies," who in return care only to provide "private or particular advantages to their own towns or persons, to the prejudice of other towns and the rest of their fellow subjects" (Wood 1969, 29). One of the modern, nationalist politicians in Massachusetts dismissed this widespread trend of "erecting small democracies" with local "ambassadors" within the new states of the union: "They [have to withdraw all their representatives from the legislature] for it is highly unreasonable that they should sit there as spies. The towns should send them as ambassadors, or commissioners plenipotentiary, and in that character they ought to be received, if received at all, not as representatives" (ibid.).

A similar sentiment against the medieval habits and ways of peasants was shared by later, post-revolutionary American nationalists. One of the principal advocates of political centralization and consolidation in the 1780s, James Madison, was equally dissatisfied with American petty localism. Commenting on Thomas Jefferson's proposal that the Virginia state senators should be appointed by the districts, he argued:

> The appointment of Senators by districts seems to be objectionable. A spirit of locality is inseparable from that mode. The evil is fully displayed in the County representations; the members of which are everywhere observed to lose sight of the aggregate interests of the Community, and even to sacrifice them to the interests or prejudices of their respective constituents ... so far from being the representatives of the people, they are only an assembly of private men, securing their own interests to the ruin of the Commonwealth. (Madison 1865, 186)

The same proud spirit of localism that Tocqueville and Jefferson extolled as a cornerstone of American liberty Madison disparages as an obstacle to efficient government.

Alexander Hamilton, James Madison, and John Jay's *Federalist Papers* is a typical and eloquent manifesto of the new nation-building creed intended to undercut the old political culture of "libertarian" decentralism and localism that Bailyn and Wood so praised. Federalist No. 9, 10, and 51 – the most important essays in the collection – all elaborate different aspects of the virtues of a centralized "military-fiscal state" vis-à-vis fragmented kaleidoscope of localities and states. All of this shows that the decentralist tradition analyzed in this chapter was not the only ideological paradigm of revolutionary America, and that it was challenged by internal opponents smuggling the European innovations of the modern state under the banner of "perfecting American republicanism," which made the conflict so much more difficult to perceive and properly evaluate.

One final theoretical question has to be asked at this point: if individualistic liberalism of the Lockean kind was indeed not in sync with proto-democratic local representation, inherited from the Middle Ages, how was it then possible that liberalism in America evolved from a localist to a centralizing mode, and that the spirit of liberty animating 1776 gave way to the spirit of state building of 1787?

In a certain sense, this is not surprising: the debate in the late eighteenth and early nineteenth centuries was not about different interpretations of Locke but rather about the European "fiscal military state" gradually suppressing all pre-existing political and constitutional structures and conditions, especially those based on localism and self-government. Locke's philosophy was to a degree "institutionally elastic" or compatible with different territorial frameworks of government and different degrees of consolidation. He advocated rotation in power and short electoral terms, the hallmarks of the older decentralist order, while espousing the centralist tenets of national democratic majoritarianism, enshrining Parliament as the single unitary voice of the "people" (instead of local confederated communities).[16]

In this regard, Lockean philosophical language and the generic liberal principles embedded in it could be combined convincingly with both approaches to the political order – decentralist and state building – fighting for supremacy in early America. Moreover, even the loyalist opponents of the American Revolution used Lockean arguments to counter the ideas that Americans were disenfranchised by the British Parliament (Bailyn 1967). Hence, the ambiguous Lockean liberal creed allowed for a smooth, albeit gradual, transition from one territorial framework of the political order (colonial, early revolutionary) to the other (post-1787) without a great disruption of the basic liberal consensus in American society.

Conclusion

Two major reinterpretations of the traditional ideological sources of American early politics follow from our analysis. First, the traditional, Hartzian claim about hegemonic Lockeanism should be replaced by a more elastic combination of liberalism and one feature that can be tentatively called "medieval localism." This offers, in Freeden's vocabulary, a rather peculiar "decontestation" of liberty, which attaches to early American decentralist liberalism's "core" concept of liberty the key adjacent concept of localist self-government, medieval in its origins.[17] Specific practices of this localist self-government were key perimeter concepts in this liberalism.

From this, the second conclusion follows: this specific, traditional mode of decontesting liberty in eighteenth-century America (by including medieval localism) was challenged not only by the imperial authorities but also by domestic nationalist elites eager to build the American nation-state on the ruins of the former colonial political architecture. In this sense, it is very precarious to talk about *the* early American political tradition or *the* ideological origins of the American Revolution, as historians of ideas have routinely done for at least a century. There are instead at least two competing major traditions in revolutionary America. One was "medieval libertarianism" as described here: historically and genealogically older, but not hegemonic. The other – a newer, modernizing liberalism – was that of a mercantilist nation-state, which saw in the decentralized patchwork of traditional political structures an obstacle to enlightened centralized governance.

Notes

1 See, for example, Zuckert 1996, 2002; Dworetz 1990; and Hamowy 1979.
2 This is emphasized by Bailyn (1967, 73–74) and Wood (1969, 23–28, 181–96), among others.
3 See Brunner 1992.
4 Clarke (1964, 11) writes: "All [members of Parliament] must consent to leave of absence for members, to amended judgements in cases of difficulty and *to grants of taxation* [emphasis added]."
5 This is a very bitter pill to swallow for many modern scholars who attempt incessantly to project the modern notions of the "state" and "civil society" back into the medieval institutions and avoid the inescapable conclusion that a medieval king did not represent a Weberian "government." They assume that the king has always been an absolute ruler, and that all seemingly democratic and representative institutions of the Middle Ages were created just as "consultative bodies," used by the "government" (the king) to facilitate his "policy making." However, if this were the case, it would be difficult to explain why the king would insist that local representatives should have *plena potestas* from their communities, if they were just called in for

consultations. For such attempts to project anachronistic modern notions of "state" and "government" into the English Middle Ages, see Monahan 1987 and Maddicott 2010. For the refutation, see Brunner 1992 and Kaminski 2002.

6   It is highly significant that the medieval sources do not talk about "taxation" but rather about "help and aid," "subsidies," "grants," and so on, underlying the voluntary and contractual nature of the financial revenue the king was obtaining from his subjects.

7   A series of tax rebellions in England against the centralizing policies and high taxation needed for military build-up under the Tudors testify to this. The sixteenth century was a golden age of tax rebellions in England, for example, Kett's Rebellion in 1549, the Wyatt Rebellion in 1553, the Pilgrimage of Grace in 1536, and so on (Tilly 1975, 22–23). These rebellions were the last stand of localist authorities against the advancing and consolidating modern state. Similar phenomena could be observed in France, Spain, and other continental countries (ibid.).

8   For a good analysis of the systems of representation in England and the American colonies in the eighteenth century, see Wood 1969, 162–97, and Jensen 1968, 7–70.

9   As, for example, Andrews (1924), Kaufman (2009), and Bailyn (1968) show that the power of colonial government was very weak, especially when compared with the power of central government in the Canadian colonies. The main reason was that the colonial authorities, led by the governors, did not have much of a power of patronage, which made a Walpole-style "influence" on popular legislatures very difficult to exert. Thus, although in theory (law) the governor and his hand-picked upper chambers had great deal of power, in practice their power was very limited. For this, see especially a detailed analysis in Bailyn (1968, 70–105).

10 Fisher (1989, 198), in his famous book, concurs: "When the Puritans came to America, this ancient system of government by town meetings, selectmen and fundamental laws became the basis of local government in New England."

11 This would later become the foundation of the famous conception of the "fusion of powers" in the Westminster-style democracies: simultaneous control of the legislature and executive by the current majority. However, the seeds of this mature conception lay in those early debates about short elections.

12 For wide-ranging discussions on how the concepts of political sovereignty came into being in England, see Kantorowicz 1957 and Skinner 1989.

13 See this chapter, pp. 24–26.

14 In most cases, this tradition was not identified as medieval by the colonists, but simply as "American," or, alternatively, as "ancient" or "Gothic."

15 See Bailyn 1967, 170.

16 Locke's centralism and his Hobbesian view of the state are treated in great detail in Jankovic 2019, especially ch. 4.

17 Giving localist self-government adjacent conceptual status rather than deeming it a core concept may seem to demote it from a central position in this liberalism. But as Freeden (1996, ch. 2) argues, adjacent concepts serve to qualify and "decontest" core concepts in crucial ways, such that no account of this liberalism's core concept of liberty can be accurately provided without extensive attention to how its adherents thought about liberty through the decentralist lens. This lens was produced as a result of various American colonies' experiences with experiments in localist self-governing practices, as discussed in this chapter. These practices fit as "perimeter concepts" in a Freedenite analytical reconstruction of this liberalism.

References

Andrews, Charles. 1924. *The Colonial Background of the American Revolution.* New Haven, CT: Yale University Press.

Bailyn, Bernard. 1967. *The Ideological Origins of the American Revolution.* Cambridge, MA: Harvard University Press.

—. 1968. *The Origins of American Politics.* New York: Alfred A. Knopf.

Boutton, Nathaniel, ed. 1877. *Miscellaneous Documents Relating to New Hampshire.* Concord, NH: Edward E. Jenks Printer.

Brewer, John. 1989. *The Sinews of Power: War, Money and English State, 1688–1783.* London: Unwin Hyman.

Brunner, Otto. 1992. *Land and Lordship: Structures of Governance in Medieval Austria,* translated and with an introduction by Howard Kaminsky and James van Horn Melton. Philadelphia: University of Pennsylvania Press.

Clarke, Maude V. 1964. *Medieval Representation and Consent: A Study of Early Parliaments in England and Ireland.* New York: Russell and Russell.

Dworetz, Steven. 1990. *The Unvarnished Doctrine: Locke, Liberalism and American Revolution.* Durham, NC: Duke University Press.

Edling, Max. 2003. *A Revolution in Favor of Government: Origins of the U.S. Constitution and the Making of the American State.* New York: Oxford University Press.

Edwards, John G. 1942. "Taxation and Consent in the Courts of Common Pleas, 1338." *English Historical Review* 57: 473–78.

—. 1958. "Commons in Medieval English Parliaments." Creighton Lecture for 1957. London: King's College

Ertman, Thomas. 1994. "The Sinews of Power and European State-Building Theory." In *An Imperial State at War: Britain from 1689 to 1815,* ed. Lawrence S. Stone, 33–51. London: Routledge.

Fischer, David H. 1989. *Albion's Seed: Four British Folkways in America.* New York: Oxford University Press.

Freeden, Michael. 1996. *Ideologies and Political Theory.* Oxford: Oxford University Press.

—. 2003. *Ideology: A Very Short Introduction.* New York: Oxford University Press.

Hamowy, Ronald. 1979. "Jefferson and the Scottish Enlightenment." *William and Mary Quarterly,* Volume 36, 3rd series.

Hartz, Louis. 1955. *The Liberal Tradition in America: An Interpretation of American Political Thought since the Revolution.* New York: Harcourt Brace.

Jankovic, Ivan. 2019. *The American Counter-Revolution in Favor of Liberty: How Americans Resisted the Modern State 1765–1850.* New York: Palgrave Macmillan.

Jensen, Merril, ed. 1967. *The Tracts of the American Revolution.* Indianapolis, IN: Bobbs-Merrill Company.

Jensen, Merril. 1968. *The Founding of a Nation.* New York: Oxford University Press.

Kaminsky, Howard. 2002. "The Noble Feud in the Later Middle Ages." *Past and Present* 177 (1): 55–83.

Kantorowicz, Ernst. 1957. *The King's Two Bodies: A Study in Medieval Political Theology.* Princeton, NJ: Princeton University Press.

Kaufman, Jason. 2009. *The Origins of Canadian and American Political Differences.* Cambridge, MA: Harvard University Press.

Madicott, John. 1981. "Parliament and the Constituencies 1272–1377." In *The English Parliament in the Middle Ages,* ed. R.G. Davies and Jeffrey H. Danton, 61–87. Philadelphia: Pennsylvania University Press.

–. 2010. *The Origins of the English Parliament, 924–1327*. Oxford: Oxford University Press.

Madison, James. 1865. *Letters and Other Writings of James Madison*. Volume 1, *1769–1783*. Philadelphia: J.B. Lippincott.

Monahan, Arthur P. 1987. *Consent, Coercion and Limit: The Medieval Origins of Parliamentary Democracy*. Montreal and Kingston: McGill-Queen's University Press.

Peters, Samuel. 1875. *General History of Connecticut*. New York: D. Appleton and Company.

Post, Gaines. 1943. "Plena Potestas and Consent in Medieval Assemblies: A Study in Romano-Canonical Procedure and the Rise of Representation 1150–1325." *Traditio* 1: 355–408.

Publicola [pseud.]. 1776. *To the Electors of New York*. New York: Broadsides.

Reid, John Philip. 1989. *The Concept of Representation in the Age of the American Revolution*. Chicago: University of Chicago Press.

Skinner, Quentin. 1989. "The State." In *Political Innovation and Conceptual Change*, ed. T. Ball, J. Farr, and R.L. Hanson, 90–131. Cambridge: Cambridge University Press.

Smith, William, ed. 1782. *History of the Province of New York, from the First Discovery to the Year 1782*. New York: Wilcox.

Tilly, Charles, ed. 1975. *The Formation of National States in Western Europe*. Princeton, NJ: Princeton University Press.

Tocqueville, Alexis de. 1969. *Democracy in America*, trans. George Lawrence. New York: Doubleday. First published in 1835–40.

–. 1998. *The Old Regime and the Revolution*, ed. François Furet and Françoise Mélonio, trans. Alan S. Kahan. Chicago: University of Chicago Press. First published in 1856.

Wood, Gordon S. 1969. *The Creation of the American Republic 1776–1787*. Chapel Hill: University of North Carolina Press.

–. 1982. "Conspiracy and the Paranoid Style: Causality and Deceit in the Eighteenth Century." *William and Mary Quarterly* 39, 3 (July): 401–41.

–. 2011. "Federalism from the Bottom-Up." *University of Chicago Law Review* 78 (2): 705–32.

Zubly, John Joachim. [1769] 1972. *Revolutionary Tracts*. New York: Reprint Company.

Zuckert, Michael. 1996. *Natural Rights Republic*. South Bend, IN: University of Notre Dame Press.

–. 2002. *Launching Liberalism*. Lawrence: University Press of Kansas.

2

Canadian Development Assistance and Mediated Geopolitics

KATHERINE REILLY

When Canada celebrated its twenty-fifth annual International Development Week in February 2015, I had the honour of chairing a panel about Canadian international development. I particularly wanted to ask the panelists about the upcoming Canadian federal election. Foreign policy had become an important issue during the campaign, and I wanted to know if my colleagues were concerned about the extent to which Canadian aid policy dialogue focused on questions of prosperity and security. To my surprise, they saw no need to think about development any differently. In fact, one participant asserted that "good development policy *should* contribute to *our* [Canada's] prosperity and security."

Canada had not always taken this approach. Until a decade ago, the country followed a Pearsonian strategy of middle-power multilateralism on the international stage, and development assistance was seen as a means to promote equal access to global trading blocs and political institutions. This made strategic sense for a small country with international reach, and it was consistent with Canada's development agenda of humane internationalism (Chapnick 2013; Black 2014) and global citizenship (Gaventa and Tandon 2010). A commitment to helping others reflected the deeply held beliefs of many Canadians and reinforced Canada's image as a friendly nation on the global stage.

Perhaps I should not have been so surprised. Ten years of Conservative government under Prime Minister Stephen Harper saw Canada withdraw from its post–Cold War liberal democratic compromise and adopt a unilateral and market-oriented approach to international relations (Chapnick 2012). Meanwhile, the work of Canadian development institutions came to reflect the ideological agendas of the Conservative Party of Canada and its project to disrupt the natural centre of political compromise in the country (Ibbitson 2015). Federal development institutions were reorganized around conservative values, including the promotion of Canadian security and prosperity, and the "public of record" on Canadian international development issues was radically restructured.

This restructuring involved re-mediating[1] communications channels between the federal government and the development community. In this chapter, I argue that this "re-mediation" was an effort to control both the flow and the content of communications between these parties. This was done to assert influence over a transnational ideological space that was strategic for the legitimation of conservative ideology and agendas. We can think of this as an example of *mediated geopolitics*, which I define as *mediating knowledge or views on the historical potential of geopolitical activities.* If we think of development interventions as political attempts to shape international futures, then the mediation of communications related to these interventions can be used to influence people's vision of what that future could be – the historical potential of those interventions.

This approach offers us a different way to think about cross-border conceptual travel: rather than looking at how concepts travel within and across national borders, it highlights efforts to channel ideas that shape patterns of insertion into global circuits of extraction, production, and exchange. In turn, this offers us new perspectives on geopolitics itself, which has emerged as a more contingent enterprise in a globally networked and multipolar world.

In what follows, I offer historical background and justification for this work before elaborating on the idea of mediated geopolitics. I then offer specific examples of how the Harper government used mediation to influence ideological flows within the Canadian international development space. I explore how new patterns of mediation worked to transform, and in some cases undermine, pre-existing channels of idea production and circulation. In the concluding section, I offer some thoughts about whether and how efforts to control ideological flows have purchase at the level of ordinary people. I also reflect on what has happened in the development assistance community since the 2015 election victory of Liberal leader Justin Trudeau.

Harper's Big Break and New Approach to Development Assistance

Prime Minister Harper's Conservative government undertook a major overhaul of Canada's approach to foreign affairs between 2006 and 2016. Foreign affairs, the military, the diplomatic service, international development, and humanitarian assistance all underwent fundamental organizational shifts, including in their relationships with each other. They came under much tighter oversight by the Prime Minister's Office, and foreign affairs and the military were prioritized. The Canadian International Development Agency (CIDA) was eliminated, and development assistance was made the mandate of a newly created Department of Foreign Affairs, Trade and Development (DFATD).

On the policy front, Harper emphasized trade and military engagement and eschewed Canadian participation in multilateral institutions, including the United Nations. He allowed Canada's seat on the UN Security Council to go to Portugal, for example, and was instrumental in undermining the Kyoto Protocol on climate change. Discursively, the Harper government spent heavily on commemorating the two hundredth anniversary of the War of 1812, and also financed and then celebrated the discovery of the remains of the Franklin expedition, which became mired in ice floes in the Canadian Arctic in 1846 while charting a course through the Northwest Passage. These activities symbolized a new official discourse that emphasized Canada's participation in wars and expeditions, and Canada's history of moral fortitude.

The Conservative government called the new approach to foreign affairs "Canada's principled foreign policy." Writing for the *Globe and Mail*, political commentator John Ibbitson (2014a) called the new approach to foreign policy "The Big Break," saying that "under the Harper government, Canada has experienced the most radical shift in foreign policy since the Second World War." Joseph Brean (2015), writing for the (conservative) *National Post*, offered the following characterization:

> Foreign affairs is no longer dominated by memories of blue-helmeted peacekeeping in Cyprus, nor does it put much stock in the United Nations talking shop where deceit and diplomacy meet and mingle. Rather, it is revealed in the aggressive, uncompromising stand taken against Russian President Vladimir Putin in Crimea; the precision air campaigns in Libya and against Islamic State in Iraq; the shuttering of Canada's embassy in Iran and the encouragement of Iranians to overthrow their "puppet masters."

These changes suggested that Canada's sixty-year Conservative-Liberal bipartisan commitment to liberal internationalism in foreign affairs had come to an end. Liberal internationalism, broadly speaking, is an approach to international relations that sees mutual benefit in pursuing economic and political interdependence through multilateral diplomacy, international organizations, and cooperation (Nossal 2013). In this view, international development work contributes to stability in an interdependent system by building capacity, alleviating suffering, responding to disasters, and generating goodwill. During the Cold War and in the post–Cold War period, liberal internationalism enabled Canada to punch above its weight in international affairs, and also offered protection from the excesses of others.

Did Harper undo Canada's foreign policy compromise? Some might argue that Canada continued to be a liberal internationalist country under Harper, given his continued focus on free trade and support for morally driven military interventions. Others argue that Canada did not become realist *enough*. "Getting along with others" was replaced with "doing what's right despite what others may think," but this was a far cry from "thinking strategically and pragmatically about Canadian foreign policy" (Paikin 2013).

Those in the middle ground say that Canada became much more unilateral and results-oriented in its foreign policy, which focused primarily on ensuring Canadian prosperity and security, investing less in sustaining the multilateral institutions that maintain the international system, including through humanitarian work (Cohen 2013; Heinbecker 2013). Canada continued to pursue free trade, but did so through bilateral agreements with strategic partners, even if this contradicted broader international commitments. Canada's free trade agreement with Peru was widely criticized, for example, as a means to promote Canadian mining operations at the cost of human rights and environmental security in poor regions of a developing country.[2]

In addition, Ibbitson (2015) argues that a *new* bipartisan compromise was created for Canadian foreign policy: "This Boy Scout of nations has become a brawler, maybe even a bit of a bully, and the Liberals and NDP seem fine with that." He observes that the Conservatives came to power on the basis of fundamental changes in the Canadian electorate, including the growing economic and political influence of Western Canada and the conservative leanings of recent waves of Canadian immigrants (Flanagan 2011). As a result of these changes, politicians across the spectrum have no choice but to adapt to conservative foreign policy trends because they reflect the new political reality (Ibbitson 2014b, 16).

We should expect aid policy to reflect a shifting international context for both humanitarian assistance and international development work (Goldfarb et al. 2013). Where 90 percent of global poverty was once concentrated in low-income countries with weak state capacity, today over 75 percent of absolute poverty is concentrated in middle-income countries with stable governments (Sumner 2012). Meanwhile, poverty is closely tied to global issues such as climate change and migration. Arguably, these issues demand greater international collective action, as in the case of the United Nations' new Sustainable Development Goals (SDG).

But instead of engaging United Nations efforts to reorient the liberal order, the Harper government chose to act unilaterally. It pursued targeted and strategic international development efforts, with the idea of making Canadian dollars stretch further and the goal of scaling up small unilateral interventions into programs with payoffs for Canadian industry. It also focused on actions that reflected "Canada's principled foreign policy" agenda. The Canadian development apparatus underwent major revisions with the objective of mandating results-oriented work, scaled-up impacts (Hartmann and Linn 2008), and greater efficiency.

The mandate to make international assistance "more efficient, focused, and accountable" was first announced in the 2007 Aid Effectiveness Agenda (CIDA 2007). Canada's development work was refocused on twenty priority countries selected according to their "alignment with Canadian priorities, need, and their ability to use aid effectively" (GAC 2016). In many cases, these were targets for free trade agreements (Colombia, Peru, Honduras, Ukraine, Vietnam, the Caribbean, Philippines, Senegal, Tanzania). New priorities were also established for Canadian development work: food security, economic growth, democracy, security, and children and youth.

This agenda was clearly reflected in Harper's official speeches, such as two given in Dakar, Senegal, in 2012.[3] In the first, at a roundtable event, Harper expressed his support for the transition from "relations previously focused on development assistance" to relations "increasingly focused on trade and investment" between Canada and Senegal. He went on to promote Canadian industries:

> I should also mention specifically that Canadian companies have particularly solid expertise when it comes to investments in this country and in this part of Africa, obviously. One of our strengths is the mining industry. But we also have obviously expertise in various extractive sectors as well as infrastructure, transportation and education, and of course, we place a fair

emphasis, our Government, and I know industry does as well, on corporate and social responsibility.

The following day, in a speech before the president of Senegal, Harper expressed his pleasure at visiting a "longstanding development partner of Canada" and exchanging ideas with "Canadian firms doing business here." He went on to describe his visit to a local vocational centre:

> Because of Canada's development assistance, young people here have been able to work on Senegal's national geomatics plan, and in fact, we've just signed an agreement in this area. This type of initiative not only helps Canadian businesses to identify opportunities, it also creates long-term jobs for the people of Senegal. And it is in this spirit of cooperation that we can achieve concrete results for our two countries. Today I have the great pleasure, we have the great pleasure of signing together and of course announcing that we have concluded negotiations towards a foreign investment protection and promotion agreement. This historic agreement will make it easier for Canadians to do business in Senegal and will help increase trade between our two countries.

Here we see a clear example of how development assistance was put at the service of Canadian prosperity.

Similar initiatives were carried out in Latin America. For example, at a business summit held during the Summit of the Americas in 2012, Harper emphasized the importance of the resource extraction industry to the Canadian economy:

> We know the good a government can do for the industry through prudent policy decisions. Looking to the future, we see increased Canadian mining investment throughout the Americas, something that will be good for our mutual prosperity and is therefore a priority of our Government.

He went on to discuss two development programs financed by CIDA designed to "share our expertise in this area because, as part of our Americas strategy, we are striving to promote prosperity, democracy and security throughout our hemisphere." In total, "Canada's foreign aid strategy has experienced a noticeable move along a spectrum from morality to national self-interest. This move has been punctuated by recent increases in support for projects directly tied to the activities of Canadian mining companies" (Dziewanski 2013).

The 2007 Aid Effectiveness Agenda also stated that "the Government of Canada will increase its engagement with the private sector in order to leverage its resources and expertise to help alleviate poverty and increase prosperity" (GAC 2016). This mandate was apparent, for example, in the AgResults program that Canada set up with the G20. The program offered a financial incentive to private entrepreneurs who developed food security innovations. Canada put up 40 percent of the initial investment, which Harper described as proving "Canada's demonstrated leadership in financing innovative development initiatives internationally."

Similarly, Harper's signature international development initiative, the Muskoka Initiative on Maternal, Newborn and Child Health, was announced at a meeting of the G8 in 2010 as a strategy for mobilizing financial resources. The initiative hinges on establishing a clear and measurable target that can attract the support of other international organizations and key donors, thus freeing government from its sole responsibility for financing development efforts. Harper met with Bill Gates on several occasions to discuss the initiative, and was quoted as saying that the Gates Foundation "brought a kind of a business-oriented rigour" and a "focus on results [and] achievements" to this issue.

These public/private partnerships drew criticism on two fronts. First, detractors point out that Canada's total commitment to poverty reduction, as measured in official development assistance (ODA), dropped from 0.34 percent in 2011 to 0.24 percent in 2014 (McLeod Group 2014, 2). Canada was leveraging smaller amounts of aid to attract resources from other actors, including private sector actors, and this meant that it would focus only on specific, measurable development outcomes that could galvanize a wide base of support. Second, the Conservative government was faulted for lacking leadership on women's reproductive rights, given that it was focusing on contraception and children's health but refused to support abortion. When asked about this issue during a CBC television interview in May 2014, Harper said that "we're trying to rally a broad public consensus behind what we're doing, and you can't rally a consensus on that issue ... in this country" (Do 2014). In other words, Harper was unwilling to show leadership on an issue that might go against the grain of key conservative values or offend potential private sector donors.

In sum, the Harper government channelled its values and commitments through its development policy activities and used them to advance Conservative agendas. There is nothing immediately unusual about this; it is normal for governments to channel their priorities through their policy apparatus. But I would like to argue that the changes Harper wrought in

Canadian foreign policy and Canadian development policy reflect a much larger shift, not just in ideological content but also in the strategies used to enact those ideological commitments.

Mediated Geopolitics and Ideological Flows

For the Harper government, achieving a fundamental ideological shift in and through development policy required more than just establishing new policies: a long-standing development establishment needed to embrace a new vision for and approach to development work. Judging from my experience at the twenty-fifth anniversary of International Development Week, the regime achieved some measure of success. What interests me is how this was accomplished.

With its Big Break, the Harper government shifted Canadian development work much more firmly in the direction of geostrategic activity. Of course, development policy always reflects and enacts geopolitics, even when the work is humanitarian in nature. It reflects assumptions about how historical progress ought to manifest, asserts a vision about how best to achieve imagined outcomes, and enacts this vision through projects. But clearly under the Harper regime, Canadian development work became much more overtly geostrategic by seeking to reorganize Canada's international engagements away from traditions and practices of liberal internationalism and towards results-oriented programming that served Canada's self-interest.

The Big Break was also geostrategic in a second sense. Recall that the Harper government came to power on the basis of changes to the Canadian electorate. Canada's Conservative coalition included a large bloc of immigrants who often form diaspora communities that maintain strong business and personal ties with their communities of origin. Meanwhile, the development community is also inherently transnational given that it establishes long-term collaborations with international and global partners. In this sense, a geostrategic reorganization of Canada's international engagements also entails a geostrategic reorganization of the media that organize flows of information between the Canadian government and its "public of record" on development issues, which is itself transnational in nature.

Re-mediating information flows was necessary to influence how existing members of the Canadian development community, including both members of the bureaucracy and the wider policy community, conceived of the historical potential of development work such that they would support the Harper government's larger agenda. If the Harper government could influence how the development community understood the historical potential of Canadian development work, this would leverage development policy as one valuable means of resituating the natural centre of Canadian politics.

With this in mind, I understand the changes that have taken place in the Canadian development community to be a form of *mediated geopolitics*, as defined above, on page 42. This conceptualization takes us beyond older discourse-centred accounts of geopolitics and into the territory of network-centric accounts of geopolitics.

Discourse-centric accounts of geopolitics focus on statesmanship and territorial strategy, and theorize how struggles to control resources (including ideational resources or media infrastructure) explain world politics (e.g., Nye 2004).[4] More nuanced accounts explore these struggles in light of interactions between the rules and resources structuring international interactions, and the capabilities and actions of key agents to control or leverage those resources.

Challenges to these "dominant" accounts draw on feminist standpoint theory (Gilmartin and Kofman 2004), situated knowledges (Rose 1997), and discourse analysis (Ó Tuathail 1996). These various strands of "critical geopolitics" highlight the constructed nature of the international system, particularly the role of discourse in normalizing dominant geopolitical constructs, including the above-mentioned struggle to control or leverage media resources.

There has been a tendency to organize the tension between dominant and critical geopolitical narratives into neo-Gramscian accounts of hegemony in the world system. For example, a contemporary textbook contrasts the dominant geopolitical discourses issued by statesmen [sic] as part of their territorial strategy with the situated knowledges that enact and represent contingent, localized spatial politics. For example:

> States still practice statesmanship; in that sense we are still offered "all seeing" interpretations of the world by political leaders and opinion makers. But their "situated knowledge" has been increasingly challenged by others in "situations" different from the clubs and meeting rooms of politicians and business leaders. As a result, geopolitical knowledge is seen as part of the struggle as marginalized peoples in different situations aim to resist the domination of the view of the powerful. (Flint 2012, 35)

This passage makes a stark separation between state actors and "marginalized peoples." This overlooks the tendency of neoliberal states to traverse this

gap in two ways: (1) by forming relationships with "publics of record" in specific issue areas, as in the case of the international development community
in Canada, and (2) by attempting to leverage partnerships with private sector
actors, diaspora communities, experts, and civil society to achieve government
ends. These relationships are strategically important both for the achievement
of outcomes and for the legitimation of the state vis-à-vis its citizenry.

The passage also masks the complexity of geostrategic negotiations in a
world that is organized along much more complicated lines. Geostrategic
engagements happen through varied and overlapping spaces and scales of
strategic importance.[5] These can be thought of more productively in terms
of ongoing and contested (re)insertions of nations and subnational group-
ings into circuits of global extraction, production, and exchange. Actors are
unlikely to enter into these strategic activities alone, and the formation of
geostrategic spaces of engagement will reflect complex calculations about
legitimation, power, and influence.

How can we understand the operation of power within these policy communities, and their relationship, in turn, with the wider Canadian society
that the government is strategically targeting for electoral purposes? For
critical scholars, ideology and discourse have long been understood to play
an important role in securing consent (Hall 1992). Following this approach,
we could study Harper's "dominant discourses" and how these worked to
create a "new normal" for development partners, who then transmitted this
vision to Canadian citizens.

But the cultural hegemony thesis has come under extensive criticism by
post-hegemony scholars in recent years (Lash 2007), particularly the idea
that power mobilizes discourses to discipline and/or obtain consent. Instead
post-hegemony scholars argue that, in a heavily mediated world, the normal-
ization of ideas takes place through immanent communications. In this view,
the dominant culture arises out of the performance of horizontal social networking and immaterial labour in mediated social spaces. Within infinitely
networked spaces, there is no recourse to an outside legitimating power that
puts its stamp on the "truth." Instead, power resides in *how* communications
platforms channel processes of meaning making; so it is the nature of the
networking itself – the cultural habits that one adopts through always-on
communications – that functions as an apparatus of discipline and coercion.

This perspective draws our attention to how mediation directly *enacts*
the historical potential of geopolitical activities, bypassing the need to
secure agreement. While I accept this thesis, I also join with those who
question the totalizing vision it advances (Jarrett 2014), and take up Nick

Couldry and Andres Hepp's views (2016) on this issue. Their constructivist approach focuses on "platforms which, for many humans, literally *are* the spaces where, through communication, they enact the social" and "the achieved sense of a social world to which media practices *contribute*" (ibid., 2–3; emphasis added). I also note that "mediation works to disguise or deflect from social conflict, while making the work of mediation unnoticed, naturalized" (Livingstone 2008, 13).

In total, mediation has grown in power vis-à-vis discourses as an explanation of social outcomes, but it is not singular or deterministic in its ability to produce those outcomes. Policy reflects the assumptions of an ideological stance, and so it will always be possible to identify the normalizing qualities of political discourses. All the same, there is an important difference between producing representations that normalize an ideology and mediatizing information flows in ways that influence ideological transformations. I want to focus on the latter, particularly on how this mechanism works to restructure and reorient geostrategic agendas.

This is especially notable where development work is concerned, since development is already wrapped up in the question of how to shape social change. The channels of idea formation available to us directly influence the horizons of geopolitical possibility, causing us to enact particular types of futures. It is here that the Harper government has had it largest impact: with its reorganization of the channels of information flow, the development community's sense of the possible has been quietly restructured in ways that are amenable to conservative values.

Re-Mediating Canadian Development Assistance

The reorganization of Canadian international development work by Harper's Conservative government has been widely observed and discussed in various publications.[6] During an eight-year period, the liberal internationalist development apparatus formed in the late 1960s and early 1970s was dissolved and replaced with a new apparatus more in line with Harper's "Big Break."

At the core of this shift was an effort to dissolve the federal government's long-standing partnership model for international development. Canada has a vibrant and diverse network of small charitable and volunteer organizations that connect Canadian communities to different localities around the world. An example is World Neighbours Canada (WNC), a small volunteer-run charitable non-governmental organization (NGO) based in the rural community of Oliver, British Columbia. For twenty-five years, WNC has raised money to support basic sanitation, water, cooking, and agricultural

programs in a handful of rural communities in Nepal, Guatemala, and
Honduras. Organizations such as these had long been represented to the
federal government through the Inter-Council Network (ICN), a national
umbrella group that brings together eight regional and provincial coalitions,
and worked closely with the partnership branch of CIDA, as well as a loose
group of national-level humanitarian, charitable, policy advocacy, and civil
society actors with offices in Ottawa and other major cities.

The Harper government moved to replace this policy community with
programs that mobilize specialized groups to achieve specific geostrategic
objectives. Signs of the impending changes emerged well before the elimi-
nation of CIDA in 2013. Several prominent Canadian development policy
organizations, including the North-South Institute, Kairos, the Canadian
Council for International Cooperation (CCIC), and the Inter-Council Network, experienced substantial funding cutbacks soon after the Conservatives took office in 2006. Early on, efforts to reorient development work
were handled through existing bureaucratic channels. For example, Can-
ada-watchers will remember the infamous "not" that International Cooperation Minister Bev Oda wrote into a CIDA document that recommended
Kairos "should" receive new funding.

As the reorganization of the sector advanced, organizations began to experience greater constraints both on what they could say and on the channels
through which they could say it. The first impacts were felt by formally designated charitable organizations. Under Canadian law, charities can use only
10 percent of their resources for advocacy work, none of which can be partisan in its bearing. This had long been interpreted to mean that groups could
oppose government policy, but not back a specific candidate in an election.
Under the Harper regime, however, advocacy work of *any* kind, at home or
abroad, by Canadian organizations *or* their international partners, was constrained. Charitable public interest organizations such as Amnesty International Canada were audited by Canada Revenue Agency to see whether they
were engaging in political activities or advocacy. This was widely interpreted as
a way to silence criticism of the broad-based policy and institutional changes
taking place across the sector (Deeby 2014). It also caused charitable organizations to rein in critical engagements with communities to focus instead on
more targeted forms of outreach and program implementation.

Meanwhile, under the Harper government, the ICN and its councils were
starved of funding, as were their members, forcing them to reconsider their
core mandate and reorganize their activities. This situation had a profound
effect on how ICN's membership formed relationships with the Canadian

public (ICN 2014). Public engagement on international development issues had begun to receive federal funding in the 1970s. Community-level education campaigns carried out by university development programs and international development NGOs were seen as a way to engage "ordinary" Canadians in the country's liberal and humane internationalist agendas and foster global citizenship.

Under Harper, work on this issue was largely defunded. This pushed development organizations to rely on less expensive social media campaigns to get the word out about their work. Social media is more cost-effective, but it is biased towards transactional forms of communication (ICN 2013), making it much less amenable to sustained, in-depth dialogue about international issues. These organizations found themselves pressured to pursue very specific agendas that were more results-oriented. And targeted social media campaigns became essential to justifying federal government support, presenting an image of success to the general public and fending off attacks by conservative media pundits. Members of this sector argue that "transactionalization" contributed to the breakdown of community-based channels for political mediation around international issues (theorized by Couldry, Livingstone, and Markham 2007) and that this generated a culture of apathy around liberal and humane internationalism (ibid.). What is more, the new social media channels masked the effects of changes in mediation by making it seem as though public outreach work was continuing as before.

Meanwhile, the federal government created new mechanisms to convene development partners that emphasized short-term strategic partnerships over long-term relationships. The AgResults program and the Muskoka Initiative on Maternal, Newborn and Child Health are key examples. Highly targeted cost-sharing initiatives offered the federal government a way to mobilize private money around a strategic goal that could be leveraged to advance domestic industry and foreign policy goals. The goals were carefully selected to align with conservative values. This put a set of parameters around how development actors could understand and enact the historical potential of development work.

This type of work was in turn supported by the Canadian International Development Platform (http://cidpnsi.ca/), which provides the evidence base necessary to identify and organize results-oriented initiatives. This project came into being during Tony Clement's presidency of the Treasury Board Secretariat, and was developed by the North-South Institute via its new home at Carleton University in Ottawa. The Treasury Board is charged with accounting for the federal government's fiscal commitments.

Clement understood that open government data about aid flows, foreign direct investment, trade, migration, and remittances would anchor Harper's commitments to efficiency and effectiveness in foreign affairs. The platform supports evidence-based analysis on international development issues, and is thus aligned with results-oriented work; it also supports analysis of links between its five focus areas, thus facilitating greater alignment between aid, trade, investment, migration, and remittances. As the project's lead investigator, Aniket Bhushan (2016), explains, it doesn't make sense for Canada to support a development program to help garment workers in Southeast Asia and at the same time uphold trade policies that disadvantage that industry. This is true, of course, but this new information system organizes these different agendas in such a way that they can all pull together to advance Canadian interests. In this we can see how an information system embodies and can subtly shift larger ideological commitments.

Finally, in the area of humanitarian aid, the Harper government sought to enhance channels for private donations, which had the effect of reinforcing the transactionalization of Canadians' relationship with international issues. In the wake of a major humanitarian disaster, such as Typhoon Haiyan in the Philippines, the government pledged to match every dollar raised by registered Canadian charities with a dollar of federal money. Charities have made active use of social media and text-based campaigns to encourage donations. Critics point out that this has restructured the Canadian public's relationship with global concerns. Rather than attempting to engender broad public understanding about global inequality, the emphasis is on momentary crises that can be addressed with material outlays. Consider the implications of this shift for work on climate change: the focus is on recovery services after a natural disaster rather than building up the kind of resilience that would prevent climate-related displacements.

What is more, the public remains uninformed about the nature of the matching funds. Specific charities do not automatically receive matching dollars from the federal government, but must apply for funding through a competition. This gives the federal government greater leverage over the programming decisions of applicants. Given the federal government's commitment to aid effectiveness, large humanitarian organizations that mobilize large relief efforts are prioritized in these competitions. So large "appeal mechanisms" like Canada's Humanitarian Coalition (CARE Canada, Oxfam Canada, Oxfam-Quebec, Plan Canada, and Save the Children Canada) are strategically placed to capture funding from federal matching programs, in effect leveraging the efforts of smaller organizations to increase their remit.

This in turn reinforces a tendency to engage with complex global issues in very instrumental or transactional ways.

The Humanitarian Coalition is also better positioned to manage the funding application process, which was reorganized around a new results-based management system during the Harper years. This model is designed to structure reporting and evaluation procedures so that program implementation can be more closely monitored after funds are delivered. This mechanism makes humanitarian assistance more highly targeted because funding applications must demonstrate how applicants will use money to achieve specific objectives mandated by the funding agency. Smaller charitable organizations with less administrative capacity find themselves sidelined from funding opportunities, which only further verticalizes the organization of humanitarian assistance in Canada. This reduces diversity in policy communities, and the new informational channels tie the work more tightly to federal government agendas.

The overall effect of this program of reforms was to undermine spaces of community dialogue and mobilization around global issues that, in their very forms of mediation, reflected the ideal of liberal internationalism. They were replaced with highly efficient and transactional media channels and evidence-based forms of decision making that could support targeted global initiatives. These reflect a culture of efficiency and results orientation that aligned with the Harper government's overall approach to foreign affairs. Canadians became disengaged with global issues in all but the most immediate ways, creating a discursive void that the Harper government could fill with the idea that development should serve Canadian prosperity and security.

The effects of these changes were certainly not lost on Canada's international development policy community. It began to search for ways to fight back against the apathy generated by transactional forms of engagement, while also countering the narratives being advanced by Harper. In 2015, ICN began to explore British work on development narratives (Darnton and Kirk 2011). Development organizations in the United Kingdom observed widespread public apathy towards development work, particularly after the 2008 financial crisis. In response, they searched for ways to frame development issues that connected with closely held values. Subsequent comparative work was commissioned by the Gates Foundation in Europe through the Narrative Project, which aimed to generate public support for government-funded foreign aid as a solution to global poverty. In 2015, Engineers Without Borders Canada and the Inter-Council Network worked with the Gates Foundation to run a Canadian poll with similar objectives.

These initiatives work by identifying "swings": undecided people who are open to being convinced on a specific set of issues. For example, the Narrative Project found that swings with particular characteristics are more likely to support development charities if they are told that development makes people more independent and self-reliant (Narrative Project 2014). This information is then used to carry out "discourse shaping" by identifying the *factors* that mediate public *attitudes* towards aid policy, the types of *mediation* that can be used to influence those attitudes, and the *terrain* that can be created and occupied through this work. Through these efforts, Canadian development organizations are engaging in their own processes of mediation in an attempt to reorient Canadian ideals about the historical potential of development work.

In summary, this case shows how mediation can contribute to an "achieved sense of a social world" that reflects either a more liberal or more realist approach to international affairs. It also demonstrates a variety of forms of mediation – channelling of information flows, information management, new ways of convening membership in groups, and social mediation. The case further demonstrates that mediation and discursive acts interact with each other in interesting ways, as when the transactionalization of public engagement in global affairs opens up space to assert new discourses about global issues, or when discourse shaping is used to create new mediated terrain for the realization of development agendas. This calls into question deterministic accounts of geopolitics that draw exclusively on communications infrastructure, or discursive power, or mediation of human activity as an explanation for historical outcomes, and opens up the possibility of more nuanced accounts of cross-border ideological flows and their effects.

Conclusion: The Legacy of Mediated Geopolitics

Harper did not win the 2015 federal election. The Liberal Party under Justin Trudeau came from behind to form a majority government. Observers are left wondering if Harper achieved fundamental change in Canada. Did Harper's new foreign policy myth become entrenched in the Canadian consciousness? Have Canadians embraced a strategic approach to international affairs? In a 2014 review of polling data, Trudeau's campaign adviser on foreign policy, Roland Paris, argued that Canadians continue to support the United Nations (a proxy for multilateralism), to emphasize Canada's role as a peacekeeper, and to experience pride in our military (Paris 2014). He concluded that despite Harper's best efforts, Canadians remain liberal internationalists at heart. But John Ibbitson (2015) offers a different interpretation:

> Opponents rage against this new Canada ... [and] point to polls that suggest conservative values are not Canadian values. But the critics are wrong ... We are a country that reflects the rise in population, power and influence of the West ... That is why the two men seeking to replace Stephen Harper as prime minister have embraced his agenda ... Both men know that, if they are to shatter the Conservative coalition of immigrant and Western voters, they must cater to the values and concerns of that coalition. Whatever happens in the election, the Harper legacy will be with Canada for a very long time.

More than three years into Trudeau's mandate, what can be said about Harper's legacy? From the outset, Trudeau indicated that he wanted to "restore constructive Canadian leadership in the world" and "support the deeply held Canadian desire to make a real and valuable contribution to a more peaceful and prosperous world" (Trudeau 2016). He committed an additional $112.8 million to Canada's aid budget. He also renamed DFATD "Global Affairs Canada," signalling his intention to beef up an office that was chronically under-resourced by Harper. This would seem to suggest a wholesale return to liberal and humane internationalism.

But the re-mediation of the relationship between the Canadian development policy community and the federal government has seen both groups take up new ways of channelling information flows. Efforts to make federal dollars stretch further and achieve greater impact have pushed actors to pursue more transactional forms of communication with the Canadian public to gain support. It isn't clear to me that Canadian values have fundamentally changed. The results of the election do not seem to bear this out. I also do not agree that the new Liberal government is necessarily constrained by the emergence of new and more conservative voting blocs in Canada. But I do believe that a broad uptake of mediated geopolitics across the development community in Canada has clearly emerged since 2006, in ways that support more conservative, market-oriented orientations to Canadian international development and reorient the community's shared sense of its realistic long-term objectives and vision.

By creating new channels through which information about development issues flows through the policy community, and also reorienting how that community interacts with Canadian society, the federal government had been able to reorient the work of these actors towards the geostrategic concerns of the state, and shift their vision of the historical potential of the work. The effects of these changes may be Harper's most important legacy for the development community in Canada.

Notes

1 I am referring to a fundamental issue for communications scholars: whether and how communications media (film, newspapers, images, Internet, databases, etc.) intervene in interpersonal or larger societal patterns of communication and with what outcomes. This was the central question asked by Harold Innis ([1951] 2008), for example.
2 For example, the Council of Canadians, Common Frontiers, and MiningWatch Canada (2009) issued a press release titled "Canadians Ask Federal Government to Halt Ratification of Canada-Peru Free Trade Agreement in Light of Peruvian Police Massacre of Indigenous Protesters" on June 11, 2009.
3 Quotes from Prime Minister Harper's speeches are taken from the unpublished archive of speeches compiled by Peter M. Ryan of MacEwan University in Edmonton. See Ryan 2015 for details.
4 See Nye 2004.
5 I subscribe to Erik Swyngedouw's definition of scale (1997, 169): "the embodiment of social relations of empowerment and disempowerment and the arena through and in which they operate." This constructivist approach to the idea of scale is further illuminated in the work of Marston (2000). By referring to spaces *and* scales, I mean that there are spaces in and through which globalization or transnationalism operates, and that they are ordered into patterns of structural relations that are accessible to some people and not others.
6 See, for example, extensive analysis by the McLeod Group: "Policy Briefs on International Development Issues," http://www.mcleodgroup.ca/mcleod-group-resources/policy-briefs/.

References

Black, David R. 2014. "Humane Internationalism and the Malaise of Canadian Aid Policy." In *Rethinking Canadian Aid*, ed. Stephen Brown, Molly den Heyer, and David R. Black, 17–34. Ottawa: University of Ottawa Press.
Bhushan, Aniket. 2016. "Canadian International Development Platform. Canada and the Developing World in 2016: Is Canada Back?" Public lecture at SFU Harbour Centre, June 23.
Chapnick, Adam. 2012. "A Diplomatic Counter-Revolution: Conservative Foreign Policy 2006–11." *International Journal* 67: 137–54.
–. 2013. "Refashioning Humane Internationalism in 21st Century Canada." *OpenCanada.org*, September 16.
CIDA. 2007. "Canada's Aid Effectiveness Agenda: Focusing on Results." Canadian International Development Agency, http://www.acdi-cida.gc.ca/INET/IMAGES.NSF/vLUImages/AidEffectiveness/$file/FocusingOnResults-EN.pdf.
Cohen, Andrew. 2013. "Canada, the World's New Contrarian." *Ottawa Citizen*, April 2.

Couldry, Nick, and Andres Hepp. 2016. *The Mediated Construction of Reality*. Cambridge: Polity Press.

Couldry, Nick, Sonia Livingstone, and Tim Markham. 2007. *Media Consumption and Public Engagement: Beyond the Presumption of Attention*. New York: Palgrave Macmillan.

Council of Canadians, Common Frontiers, and MiningWatch Canada. 2009. "Canadians Ask Federal Government to Halt Ratification of Canada-Peru Free Trade Agreement in Light of Peruvian Police Massacre of Indigenous Protesters." Press release. https://miningwatch.ca/news/2009/6/11/canadians-ask-federal -government-halt-ratification-canada-peru-free-trade-agreement.

Darnton, Andrew, and Martin Kirk. 2011. *Finding Frames: New Ways to Engage the UK Public in Global Poverty*. London: Bond for International Development.

Deeby, Dean. 2014. "Canadian Charities Feel 'Chill' as Tax Audits Widen into Political Activities." *Toronto Star*, July 10.

Do, Trinh Teresa. 2014. "Harper Won't Fund Abortion Globally Because It's 'Extremely Divisive.'" *CBC News*, May 29.

Dziewanski, Dariusz. 2013. "Is Canada's Foreign Aid Just about Looking Good?" *Huffington Post*, January 2.

Flanagan, Tom. 2011. "The Emerging Conservative Coalition." *Policy Options*, June 2011, 104–8.

Flint, Colin. 2011. *Introduction to Geopolitics*. New York: Routledge.

GAC (Global Affairs Canada). 2016. "Development Priorities: Aid Effectiveness Agenda: The Heart of Canada's International Assistance." Global Affairs Canada, https://international.gc.ca/world-monde/issues_development-enjeux_developpement/ priorities-priorites/aidagenda-planaide.aspx?lang=eng.

Gaventa, John, and Rajesh Tandon. 2010. "Citizen Engagements in a Globalizing World." In *Globalizing Citizens: New Dynamics of Inclusion and Exclusion*, ed. J. Gaventa and R. Tandon, 3–32. New York: Zed Books.

Gilmartin, M., and E. Kofman. 2004. "Critically Feminist Geopolitics." In *Mapping Women, Making Politics*, ed. L.A. Staeheli, E. Kofman, and L.J. Peake, 113–25. New York and London: Routledge.

Goldfarb, Danielle, et al. 2013. "Starting a New Conversation about Aid." *OpenCanada.org*, June 21. https://www.opencanada.org/indepth/starting-a-new -conversation-about-aid/.

Hall, Stuart. 1992. "Cultural Studies and Its Theoretical Legacies." In *Cultural Studies*, ed. L. Grossberg, C. Nelson, and P.A. Treichler, 277–94. New York: Routledge.

Hartmann, Arntraud, and Johannes F. Linn. 2008. "Scaling Up: A Framework and Lessons for Development Effectiveness from Literature and Practice." Wolfensohn Center for Development Working Paper 5. Washington, DC: Brookings Institution.

Heinbecker, Paul. 2013. "It's Not Just the Drought Treaty. Canada Is Vanishing from the United Nations." *Globe and Mail*, April 1.

Ibbitson, John. 2014a. "How Harper Transformed Canada's Foreign Policy." *Globe and Mail*, January 31.

–. 2014b. *The Big Break: The Conservative Transformation of Canada's Foreign Policy*. CIGI Working Paper 29. Waterloo, ON: Centre for International Governance Innovation (CIGI).

—. 2015. "How Harper Created a More Conservative Canada." *Globe and Mail*, February 6.

ICN (Inter-Council Network). 2013. "How Change Happens: Resources for Developing a Theory of Change." Vancouver: Inter-Council Network. http://globalhive.ca/hubs/how_change_happens.pdf.

—. 2014. "Exploring Public Engagement Effectiveness in Canada 2011–2014: Summary Report." Vancouver: Inter-Council Network. http://www.globalhive.ca/PDF/ICN_CA_Report_Sep1.pdf.

Innis, Harold A. [1951] 2008. *The Bias of Communication*. 2nd ed. Toronto: University of Toronto Press.

Jarrett, Kylie. 2014. "The Alternative to Post-Hegemony." *Culture Unbound* 6: 137–57.

Lash, Scott. 2007. "Power after Hegemony: Cultural Studies in Mutation?" *Theory, Culture, and Society* 24 (3): 55–78.

Livingstone, Sonia. 2008. "On the Mediation of Everything: ICA Presidential Address 2008." *Journal of Communication* 59 (1): 1–18.

Marston, Sallie A. 2000. "The Social Construction of Scale." *Progress in Human Geography* 24 (2): 219–42.

McLeod Group. 2014. "A Development Policy for Canada." Policy Brief 1. Ottawa: McLeod Group.

Narrative Project. 2014. *The Narrative Project: A Battle between Belief and Reason*. Presentation deck available at http://www.slideshare.net/jamesdnorth/the-narrative-project-overview-deck-july.

Nossal, Kim Richard. 2013. "The Liberal Past in the Conservative Present: Internationalism in the Harper era." In *Canada in the World: Internationalism in Canadian Foreign Policy*, ed. Heather A. Smith and Claire Turenne Sjolander, 21–35. Don Mills, ON: Oxford University Press.

Nye, Joseph. 2004. *Soft Power: The Means to Success in World Politics*. New York: Public Affairs.

Ó Tuathail, Gearóid. 1996. *Critical Geopolitics: The Politics of Writing Global Space*. London, UK: Routledge.

Paikin, Zach. 2013. "Canada's Foreign Policy Needs a Dose of Realism." *iPolitics*, May 8. http://ipolitics.ca/2013/05/08/canadas-foreign-policy-needs-a-dose-of-realism.

Paris, Roland. 2014. "Are Canadians Still Liberal Internationalists? Foreign Policy and Public Opinion in the Harper Era." *International Journal* 69 (3): 274–307.

Rose, Gillian. 1997. "Situating Knowledges: Positionality, Reflexivities and Other Tactics." *Progress in Human Geography* 21: 305–20.

Ryan, Peter M. 2015. "Strategic Access to the PMO: Diversity and Lobbyists in the Prime Minister's Speeches, 2004–2014." Presented at the 84th Annual Congress of the Humanities and Social Sciences, University of Ottawa.

Sumner, Andy. 2010. "Global Poverty and the New Bottom Billion: What if Three-Quarters of the World's Poor Live in Middle-Income Countries?" IDS Working Paper 349. Sussex, UK: Institute of Development Studies.

Trudeau, Justin. 2016. Minister of Foreign Affairs Mandate Letter. Ottawa: Office of the Prime Minister. http://pm.gc.ca/eng/minister-foreign-affairs-mandate-letter.

3

Right-Wing Populism, Conservative Governance, and Multiculturalism in Canada

DAVID LAYCOCK AND STEVEN WELDON

During the fall 2015 Canadian federal election campaign, Prime Minister Stephen Harper surprised observers by announcing that his Conservative government would not permit Muslim women to wear the niqab during their citizenship ceremonies. This move gave the Conservatives a temporary boost in the polls but was not enough to win the election (Conservative Party of Canada 2015). The new Liberal government cancelled the Conservative ban of niqab use in citizenship ceremonies shortly after coming to power. So perhaps we should just see Harper's niqab ban as a cynical election ploy and forget it?

In this chapter, we argue that exploring this calculated campaign move can enhance our understanding of populism in Canada, but not because it revealed a core ideological commitment among populist conservatives in this country. Unlike right-populist politics in much of Europe and the United States (Akkerman 2012; Norris and Inglehart 2016; Edsall 2017), anti-immigrant and anti–visible minority themes have been significant "perimeter concepts" but not central to populist conservatism in Canada since at least 2000. Such themes became less central still following the creation of the Conservative Party of Canada (CPC) in 2004. And despite the survival of populist anti-statism and populist plebiscitarianism in the new party (Laycock 2012),[1] populist nativism is unlikely to set the agenda for the party in the foreseeable future.[2] Having worked hard after 2004 to include immigrant communities in its electoral coalition, having benefited from a substantial visible minority vote in its 2008 and 2011 electoral victories, and needing to re-establish a "minimum winning coalition" (Flanagan 2011) that includes many ethnic minority citizens' votes, the Conservative Party can't afford to "do a Trump" and let its vocal nativist minority define its public appeal (Press Progress 2016; Wherry 2016). In Freeden's terms (1996), the Conservative Party can't remain a viable contender for national power while fashioning anti-immigrant themes and white nationalist nativism into key adjacent or even core concepts within its ideology, as has President Donald Trump in his morphological makeover of American Republican Party ideology.

This chapter demonstrates that while some contents and concepts of Canadian right-wing populism have migrated northward from the United States, circumstances unique to Canada have required populist conservatism to approach multiculturalism in ways that set it apart from right-wing populisms in the rest of the Western world. The Conservative Party's populism was more strategic about developing a politics of exclusion, because its principal goal was not excluding visible minorities but degrading the welfare state. As numerous studies have shown, the reverse is true for most right-wing populisms in Europe, while "white nationalism" vies with Tea Party anti-statism for policy and ideological pre-eminence in Trump's administration.

If advancing its central goal of degrading the welfare state seemed to require the targeting of Muslims on occasion as a means of expanding its electoral base, the Conservative Party did so. Degrading the welfare state was an adjacent concept within the structure of Harper's conservative ideology, instrumental to neo-Hayekian core concepts of liberty and a natural market order (Freeden 1996, ch. 8). Encouraging nativism was a rather desperate electoral tactic, not a basic ideological rationale for such action. Nonetheless, the party's use of this wedge politics tactic does point to a fragility in public support for Canadian multiculturalism often overlooked by commentators (Kymlicka 2010; Taub 2017). Addressing this fragility allows us to make better sense of both populist conservatism and multiculturalism in Canada.

Following some initial comments on the nature of populism's encounters with multiculturalism, we broadly characterize Canadian multiculturalism and indicate how significant attitudinal opposition to immigration and multiculturalism provides a basis for its manipulation by partisan and other forces. We then examine right-populist objections to egalitarian aspects of Canadian multiculturalism since 1986.

Our aim is to answer one question and explore another. First, in ideological terms, what is distinctive about the recent right-wing populist version of Canadian multiculturalism? Second, what are the prospects for nativist promotion of openly anti-immigration, anti-multicultural policies within conservative populism in Canada?

Regarding the first question, we will argue that the Conservative Party's efforts to push Canadian society off one of its key normative commitments to multiculturalism can be properly understood only as part of a broader Conservative agenda of undermining Canadian citizens' and governments' commitments to the welfare state. The common normative denominator targeted by the Conservative Party under Stephen Harper was a liberal egalitarian conception of equality. This has been overlooked by influential commentators, who treat the party's multiculturalism as a continuation of post-1970 Liberal and Progressive Conservative governments' multiculturalism (Bricker and Ibbitson, 2013, 2018). We contend, by contrast, that since North American conservatism has targeted this liberal egalitarian conception of equality with special urgency since the 1970s, a new Canadian Conservative Party that took many of its ideological bearings from south of the border adopted this goal as well. Pursuit of this goal on both sides of the border has often been indirect, through campaigns for tax cuts, deregulation of the state/market interface, and social welfare "entitlement reform," but displacing liberal egalitarian equality with a market-friendly understanding of both liberty and equality is the normative objective underpinning these and many other "new right" policy objectives (Laycock 2001).

In strategic terms, the Conservative Party under Harper's leadership worked to increase the range of "wedge politics" issues by developing an asymmetrical political polarization that favoured a party best at exploiting political vulnerabilities within Canada's extended experience with multiculturalism. Later in the chapter, a brief analysis of 2015 Canadian Election Study data allows us to explore openings for a more American or European version of populist conservatism's reaction to multiculturalism.

Clarification of the relationships between populism, multiculturalism, and equality allows us to see how the Canadian experience with multiculturalism incorporates two distinct liberal ideas of equality that lead in different directions, with contrasting political implications and applications. The genius of recent right-populism in Canada has been to advance its central agenda by exploiting the ambiguity regarding equality within Canadian multiculturalism.

Populism, Multiculturalism, and Equality

For Cas Mudde and Cristobal Kaltewasser (2012, 8), populist ideology posits a basic social division between "the people" and "elites," the moral purity of the people versus a corrupt elite, and holds that politics ought to express the general will of the people. While this minimalist definition has much to recommend it, explaining how we disagree with their approach raises important issues for the study of populist parties' dealings with multiculturalism.

Mudde and Kaltewasser's focus on the moral axis of populist politics tends to analytically exclude strategic aspects of these politics from analysis of populist ideology. Doing so overlooks the intertwining of political strategy and invocation of "the people" in all populisms. Examining the strategic dimension of populist politics helps us to understand modern right-populist adoption of plebiscitarian agenda setting and discursive exclusion of selected groups from "the people," which gained new prominence in Donald Trump's campaign for the American presidency. In Canada over the past thirty years, right-populist reaction to multiculturalism has evolved in a complex interplay of ideological and strategic political dimensions.

Mudde and Kaltewasser (2013) draw a valuable distinction between exclusive and inclusive populisms' drawing of boundaries between "the people" and "the elite." This distinction moves us analytically and empirically beyond a Eurocentric framing of all populism as extremely nativist and anti-immigrant, and acknowledges left-populism as a politically relevant species of populism. The politics of inclusion and exclusion are central to debates over multiculturalism and immigration, so focusing on their dynamics builds a valuable bridge between studying populism and appreciating its navigation of any particular multicultural environment. But Mudde and Kaltewasser's application of this distinction inclines them to overlook clues found in leader, party, and movement discourse that can suggest that populist politics is often effective because its appeals blur the line between inclusion and exclusion in complex ways.

This complex blurring occurs across what Mudde and Kaltewasser (2013) identify as the mutually constituting material, political, and symbolic dimensions of populist discourse and governing practice. As we argue below, the Canadian case illustrates that exclusion can be material, and both politically and symbolically informal rather than simply formal and/or obvious. Such a complex exclusion turns, at the ideological level, on how key concepts like equality and popular sovereignty are utilized in constructing social and political antagonisms, and can be a by-product of a strategically deployed plebiscitarian leadership style.

For Mudde and Kaltewasser (2013), three core concepts are "necessary and sufficient conditions of populist ideology": "the pure people, the corrupt elite and the general will." This means that "actors or parties that employ only an anti-elitist rhetoric should not be categorized as populist" (ibid., 151). We agree with the latter claim but take issue with their depiction of the "populist core." In Michael Freeden's approach to ideology analysis, distinguishing between strategically rhetorical claims and ideological core concepts is part of determining how a logic of ideological structuring operates (Freeden 1996, ch. 3). By focusing so much on exclusively populist core concepts, Mudde and Kaltewasser reduce our analytical traction on much populist activity in modern parties, such as Canada's Conservative Party. In effect, we are saying that populist politics matters well beyond the activities and appeals of the most obviously anti-elitist parties and politicians.

As we will see, the Conservative Party of Canada is not purely or even predominantly populist, but it nonetheless makes analytical sense to speak of its populist conservatism – or its conservative populism. The latter construction is in fact more appropriate in the current context, for several reasons. Mudde and Kaltewasser (2013) draw on Freeden to contend that unlike more comprehensive ideologies of liberalism, conservatism, and socialism, populisms are "thin ideologies" that must rely on a more comprehensive ideology for basic ideological moorings, and many concepts and policies.[3] This is consistent with Freeden's depiction of "thin" ideologies, but in Freeden's understanding of such ideologies, such a reliance means that no populism's ideological core is complete with just these three core concepts. Mudde and Kaltewasser's framework devotes insufficient attention to how part of the populist ideological core is unavoidably imported from the more comprehensive ideology on which it relies. A right-wing populist core will have a substantial proportion of recognizably conservative core concepts, even if what most obviously sets it apart from its competitors is the insistence on its advocacy for "the people" and a strident attack on elites.

Donald Trump's appeal, for example, obviously has something to do with populism. His attack on a "corrupt elite" is clear enough, and he seems to be saying something about both a "pure people" and their General Will when assuring his base that he will "make America great again" for them. But we cannot make sense of his slogan or his policies with just this conceptual toolkit. Versions of these ideas are indirectly invoked with reference to other ideas, such as a golden age of middle-class, white America, America and "the West" under attack by anti-Christian forces (Klimmage 2017), a virulent white nationalist nativism, and the unquestioned value of business rationality and conspicuous consumption. Trying to stuff all of his appeals and ideas into three distinctly populist conceptual holders in the core of his ideology to salvage a claim that Trump's populism is consequential to his campaign or presidency does not seem the best analytical path here.

It is more appropriate, we contend, to acknowledge two broad features of Trumpian ideology. The first is that not all important parts of his appeal and policy agenda must fit into or be reckonable in terms of his core concepts; in Freeden's terminology, these are often best understood as "adjacent" or "perimeter" concepts (see the Introduction to this volume). The second feature is that key elements in the Trumpian ideological structure, like his idea of "real America," or the idea that expertise is valid only if it advantages the short-term interests of corporate America, are conservative in the recent Republican Party tradition, and serve core conservative concepts like minimizing change and a market-defined "natural order" (Freeden 1996, ch. 8). Everything from his large corporate and income tax cuts to his radical reduction of environmental regulation indicates that whatever his uniqueness as a political leader, and whatever the extent of his threat to democratic institutions and norms, populist ideas inside and outside the core of his ideology "serve" conservative purposes more than vice versa.

This general point extends to our Canadian case. The dominant ideological orientation of the Conservative Party of Canada is a neoliberal conservatism, with a morphological core that draws on both conservative and classical liberal ideas about liberty, equality, and a natural market order, and on social conservative ideas about a naturally Christian and patriarchal social order. But when he engineered the creation of the Conservative Party in 2003, Stephen Harper understood that gaining power would require keeping some of the populist ideological content and strategically crafted appeal of its predecessor, the Reform Party, as well as large components of its economic and social conservative ideological core. Simply put, there is no realistic chance that a simple marriage of convenience between Hayekian conservatism and social conservatism can attract a winning electoral coalition in Canada.

Well before he achieved the merger of a right-wing populist party with a centre-right brokerage party, Stephen Harper had learned from Reform Party leader Preston Manning and Reform/Conservative Party strategic adviser Tom Flanagan that elements of populist appeal and policy moderation would each be required for a conservative party to contend for power in Canada. A frontal attack on the version of multiculturalism embedded by federal and provincial governments since 1971 would doom his party to perpetual opposition party status. However, rhetorical elite bashing and accepting some of the symbolic inclusion of past Canadian multiculturalism could yield plurality victories in Canada's single member plurality electoral system.

We should not confuse these strategic accommodations to Canadian political culture and the competitive dynamics of the federal party system with a fundamental change to Conservative Party ideology. These accommodations were, in morphological terms, largely at the level of perimeter concepts, with some refashioning of adjacent concepts. Even a merger with the more moderate Progressive Conservative Party did not alter the ideological core of the new, Harper-led party.

The Conservative Party of Canada thus developed a hybrid conservative-populist ideological core. The concepts of "the pure people, the corrupt elite and the general will" were modified within the core, or downgraded to less central roles in Conservative ideology, in the service of a Hayekian and social conservative–inspired long game of undermining the welfare state (Laycock 2001). Incorporating a reconstituted understanding of multiculturalism as an adjacent concept within the party's ideological morphology, in a way that modified its once Anglo-Saxon Protestant core conceptualization of "the people," was essential to Conservative Party success. As we show below, this involved a complex combination of "inclusive" and "exclusive" populist appeals.

Canadian Multiculturalism since 1971

Until the 1960s, almost all of the non-British and non-American immigration to Canada was European. In 2011, 21 percent of Canada's population was foreign-born, compared with 13 percent in Germany and the United States.[4] The proportion of households in 2011 with English mother tongues in English Canada's two largest cities was under 50 percent, though English predominates in many but not all suburbs. Demographically, urban Canada is unmistakably multicultural.[5]

The needs of the Canadian economy have dominated Canadian immigration policy (Tepperman 2017). Under the Harper government, priority was given to applicants willing to invest at least $350,000, those with a working language of English or French, and those filling skills shortages in the Canadian labour market (Ibbitson 2014). In a normal year, 5 percent of Canadian immigrants are refugees; in 2016 it was around 10 percent, less than one-third of recent European levels (Aiyar et al. 2016).

Objectives and Policy Anchors

Between 1971 and 2006, Canada's "multicultural integration" approach to multiculturalism blended government programs that consciously developed respect for immigrant cultures with programs that integrated immigrants socially, economically, and politically (Banting 2014, 67–68). Efforts at developing respect for diversity extended to the public school system and the CBC, both of which stress the multicultural fact and its normative foundations. Affirmative action programs in federal and provincial public sector hiring enhanced "employment equity" for immigrants who have become permanent residents or citizens (ibid., 71–72). And the federal and provincial governments funded programs for Canadian civil society organizations to provide counselling to newcomers (ibid., 73). Federal program spending in this area was modest before 2006, and had declined to less than $15 million by 2013 (Canadian Press 2013).

Canadian federal and provincial governments have explicitly celebrated diversity since 1971, as "part of a state-led redefinition of national identity ... to build an identity more reflective of Canada's cultural complexity" (Banting 2014, 74). Recent research on immigrants' attitudes towards their adopted Canadian community shows that they are very positive compared with immigrants to Europe and the United States (Wright and Bloemraad 2012). Various critics have painted less attractive pictures of Canadian governments' pre-2006 underlying rationales for and impacts of immigration and multicultural integration policies (Haque 2012; Abu-Laban 2014), but they do not deny that "official multiculturalism" before the Harper government was formally premised on ideological foundations quite distinct from those that emerged during his government.

Some efforts to discuss multiculturalism in Canada incorporate attention to policies for and public views of First Nations peoples. We do not follow this approach in this chapter, for two reasons. First, First Nations peoples do not see themselves as appropriately understood in the same analytical discourse as recent arrivals to Canada. And second, our primary point of comparative reference, European experience with immigrant-based multiculturalism, includes no indigenous minorities comparable to Canada's First Nations.

Constitutional Anchors of Multiculturalism and Equality

The redefinition of Canadian national identity since the late 1960s is reflected in key constitutional changes introduced by Pierre Trudeau's Liberal government in 1981. Most obviously, Section 27 of the Canadian Charter of Rights and Freedoms states that the whole Charter "shall be interpreted in a manner consistent with the preservation and enhancement of the multicultural heritage of Canadians." Less obvious, but more important, the Charter's equality commitments in Section 15 have important implications for policy design affecting ethnic minorities in Canada. Section 15(1) protects all citizens against discrimination "based on race, national or ethnic origin, colour, religion, sex, age or mental or physical disability." But Section 15(1) is an abstract protective device. With a minimalist or formal conception of multicultural equality, it neither mandates nor sanctions particular types of government intervention in the market economy or other aspects of civil society where discrimination might occur.

The Charter's Section 15(2) presents a liberal egalitarian normative justification for state measures to mitigate a wide range of social inequalities. It clarifies that Section 15(1) "does not preclude any law, program or activity that has as its object the amelioration of conditions of disadvantaged individuals or groups including those that are disadvantaged because of race, national or ethnic origin, colour, religion, sex, age or mental or physical disability."[6] Canadian courts have interpreted Section 15(2) to mean that affirmative action hiring and other measures aimed at overcoming group-based disadvantages, in the workplace and the larger socio-political arena, are consistent with the constitutionally sanctioned core understanding of Canadian equality. And though they have remained within what Ian Angus (Chapter 5) refers to as the "mode of liberal individualism," the courts have made it clear that included among the groups assisted by this constitutional provision are women, LGBT individuals, the elderly, and the disabled, as well as ethnic minorities, including recent immigrants claiming refugee status (Hurley 2007; Blinch 2016).

Since the late 1980s, right-populists and conservatives in Canada have seen the courts' interpretation of equality as a massive obstacle to implementation of their anti-statist and/or anti-egalitarian agendas, and as an attack on traditional family and Christian values. Most of the ideological firepower for this critique, including its invocation of "states' rights" arguments and themes from the American "culture war" over women's rights and gay rights, came from the conservative movement in the United States (Laycock 2005b; Farney 2012). To counter the liberal egalitarian view of equality as justifying substantial state intervention, the Reform Party and leading lights in the later Conservative Party of Canada followed American conservatives in proposing "equality under the law," with no "special rights" for specific groups, and no warrant for state intervention in labour markets or other redistribution of resources and opportunities (Laycock 2001, 2005b).

There should thus be no surprise that during its tenure in federal government from 2006 to 2015, the Conservative Party of Canada attempted to recast multiculturalism based on a formal conception of equality and to delegitimize an expansive, state-intervention–validating conception of substantive equality. Using Freeden's approach to mapping ideological action, we can say that this attempted redefinition of multiculturalism and delegitimizing of substantive equality occurred through strategic use of both adjacent and perimeter concepts. The main thrust of adjacent conceptualization occurred in relation to multiculturalism and equality. A variety of perimeter concepts were expressed through Conservative government policy initiatives. As we will see, the latter included the new citizenship guide, changes to immigration policy, and the notorious "Zero Tolerance for Barbaric Cultural Practices Act."

Public Opinion towards Multiculturalism, Immigration, and Refugees

Will Kymlicka (2010, 7) has argued that

> Canadians view immigrants and demographic diversity as key parts of their identity. Compared to every other Western democracy, Canadians are more likely to say that immigration is beneficial ... and more likely to support multiculturalism and to view it as a source of pride.

Recent surveys and analysis complicate this rosy picture. A July 2017 Ipsos-Reid survey on attitudes towards immigration questioned 17, 903 residents in twenty-five countries. Forty percent of Canadian respondents said that immigration was causing their country to change in ways they did not like, somewhat below British (43 percent), Swedish (44 percent), German (45 percent), and Spanish (46 percent) respondents but well below those in most other European countries. When asked whether immigration has had a positive impact on their country, Canadians led most Europeans by a large margin, and were very slightly ahead of UK and US residents. However, the proportion of those who agreed that immigration has had a positive impact was still only 38 percent (Ipsos-Reid 2017). In September 2016, the Angus Reid Institute found that 68 percent of Canadians believed that "minorities should do more to fit in with mainstream Canadian society."

Charles Breton's analysis of Canadian attitudes towards immigration and ethnic minorities argued that Canadians are *not* fundamentally onside with their governments' multicultural policies, especially those that involve an activist state redistributing state revenues. His analysis of 2011 data found that 74 percent disagreed (47 percent strongly) that "ethnic minorities should be given government assistance to preserve their customs and traditions," 60 percent wanted immigration to be more difficult, and 48 percent saw "all those different cultures" as a threat to Canadian values. In marked contrast, 83 percent of respondents supported giving "ethnic minorities ... the same political rights as the Canadian people" (Breton 2015, 367–69). And an analysis of 2011 Canadian Election Study data by Dietlind Stolle and her colleagues revealed that "when confronted with concrete policies and real benefits, the average Canadian seems to be relatively hesitant to support financial grants [to ethnic organizations], but more willing to make public space available [to these groups]" (Stolle et al. 2016, 344–45).

All of this suggests that "Canadians ... do not support a basic tenet of multiculturalism: government financially supporting ethnic minorities" (Breton 2015, 368). Even if Canadian national identity does not have what Breton calls "the exclusionary potential of many of its European counterparts" (376), a relatively state-centric (while still liberal individualist) Canadian multiculturalism has less public support than is often assumed, and this can be exploited by politicians committed to rolling back the state.[7]

Right-Populism and Multiculturalism since 1986

The Reform Party of Canada

When the Reform Party of Canada was created in 1986, it attracted western regionalists, anti-statists, free marketers, direct democracy enthusiasts, opponents of a strong federal government, and social conservatives. In 1992, Reform was the only party to oppose the Charlottetown constitutional reform package, designed to accommodate Quebec's concerns about the preservation of its distinctive community. The Reform Party led a successful referendum campaign against what it called a back-room deal among self-serving politicians and "special interests," and emerged as the leading populist, anti–old party political force. It broke into the federal party system in the 1993 federal election, taking fifty-two seats in Parliament and becoming the only substantial opposition party left in English Canada (Laycock 2001; Flanagan 1995).

The Reform Party's right-wing critique of taxes, fiscal deficits, state intervention, and the welfare state all helped to push the Liberal government towards welfare state retrenchment and austerity measures. Successful right-wing provincial parties and English Canadian media support for fiscal conservatism and tax cuts complemented Reform Party efforts to steer public policy to the right. The Reform Party's visceral opposition to the welfare state prevented it from offering a version of the "welfare chauvinism" typical of European right-populist parties.

The Reform Party's limited regional appeal led to a rebranding in 2000 as the Canadian Reform Conservative Alliance Party. Shortly after Stephen

Harper became Alliance leader in 2003, he engineered a merger of the
Canadian Alliance and the Progressive Conservative Party to form the Conservative Party of Canada. From 2006 to 2015, his party formed two minority governments and one majority government by appearing to be more
centrist than its activists.

Like the new right elsewhere, the Reform Party opposed expansion of
equality rights under the banner of "no special rights for special interests"
and opposition to elite power. Like the American new right, Reform defined
elites as part of or benefiting from a recently expanded welfare and regulatory state. The conservative definition of elites turned a generic populist
opposition to elite power into a critique underwritten by a distinctively
right-wing political economy and understanding of "representational failure" (Laycock 2005a). This opposition to state elites and their beneficiaries
was undertaken against the backdrop of constitutional reform in the early
1980s that had legitimized state intervention on behalf of women and ethnic
minority groups.

The Reform Party's opposition to constitutionalized rights for ethnic
minorities occasionally erupted in politically awkward opposition to immigration or visible minorities (Harrison 1995; Laycock 2001).[8] More fre-
quently, it was expressed as a demand for "private multiculturalism" and
abolition of federal programs that support multiculturalism. In the 1993
election campaign, the Reform Party proposed leaving "individuals and
groups free to preserve their cultural heritage using their own resources"
(Reform Party of Canada 1993, 6–7).[9] Federal politicians, bureaucrats, and
ethnic community leaders supportive of state expenditures to promote multicultural integration, ethnic cultural development, and public respect for
ethnic diversity were portrayed by the Reform Party as "elites" insisting on
"special rights" not enjoyed by ordinary Canadians (Laycock 2001).

Official Reform Party opposition to governments' efforts to build multiculturalism was not openly nativist. Party leader Preston Manning successfully marginalized hard-edged nativist and racist activists and candidates,
understanding that multiculturalism had been woven into Canadian identity
through conscious federal and provincial government program design since
the late 1960s. The 1982 Canadian Charter of Rights and Freedoms had, in
effect, constitutionalized the normative basis of this interweaving, legitimiz-
ing what Hayekian conservatives, social conservatives, and right-wing populists saw as an ominous pattern of egalitarian overreach by the postwar state.

Reform Party leaders wanted to delegitimize and then eliminate this
overreach, not just with regard to ethnic minorities but across all aspects

of social and economic redistribution, in support of their core ideological conceptual commitments to a natural market order and a Hayekian understanding of liberty.[10] Their political challenge was to oppose and undermine a comparatively demanding conception of multicultural equality while not appearing to reject equality or multiculturalism per se.

The Conservative Government, Right-Populism, and a Redefined Multiculturalism

When Stephen Harper's Conservative Party won the 2006 federal election, it seemed that he had wrought a substantial ideological change in his party in order to win support from a centrist electorate in a single member plurality electoral system. Earlier Reform and Canadian Alliance proposals for radical tax cuts, program cuts, transformation of state structures, and promotion of direct democracy had been replaced, in the 2006 election manifesto and campaign, with a series of incremental policy changes.[11] And it seemed that the Conservatives had stepped into line with the "pan-Canadian consensus" on multiculturalism (Pennings and Van Pelt 2006).

This story of ideological transformation confuses perimeter concepts in the party's ideology for its ideological core. And it misses the careful calculation regarding multiculturalism involved in taking the new party to power. Harper and his key advisers understood that acquiring and maintaining power required a new strategy with regard to the numerous ethnic minority voters in the major cities in Ontario and Quebec. These cities had been electoral wastelands for the Conservatives' Reform and Canadian Alliance predecessors between 1988 and 2004. So the party muffled its activists' previously open disdain for multiculturalism and began recruiting numerous visible minority candidates for upcoming elections. This was realpolitik strategy rather than substantial ideological transformation, and it involved a careful recalibration of the Reform Party's exclusionary conceptualization of "the people."

The Conservative Party still had to assure its old Reform voters and activists that their concerns about visible minority immigration and multiculturalism since the 1960s, as directed by both Liberal and Progressive Conservative governments, would not be ignored. Yet such reassurances for party faithful had to be somehow provided without alienating existing visible minority immigrant communities.

Balancing this new, ethnic minority–friendly image with assurances to the party's non-immigrant base was a big challenge. Harper's success was aided by his adoption of a plebiscitarian model of relations between party members, MPs, and the party leader. In this model, the leader exercises overwhelming power over his party members, activists, and MPs (Harris 2014; Laycock 2012), despite their prior endorsements of grassroots democracy. This is close to Weber's account of plebiscitarian leadership and representation (Green 2010). Opportunities for member influence on the party's direction were replaced by "direct, unmediated, and one-way communication ... from the center to the members/supporters" (Katz and Mair 2009, 761).

Harper's plebiscitarian populism was a good fit with the Conservative approach to multiculturalism. Party members and activists were tightly scripted from the Prime Minister's Office, which exercised an obsessive degree of message control over MPs, cabinet, and all government officials, including diplomats (Martin 2010; Harris 2014; Bourrie 2015). Plebiscitarian leadership messaging framed political conflict in terms of populist antinomies of "the people" (or "hard-working taxpayers") and "special interests."

This invocation of the classic populist antagonism between the people and elites occurred not just in the frequent email fundraising messages to party donors and in speeches by the prime minister to party faithful. It also appeared in numerous government press releases, budget speeches, and Speeches from the Throne between 2006 and 2015 (Laycock 2012). To expand its voter base enough to gain and hold power, the party needed to do more than claim to represent "the people"; it also needed to keep the boundaries of this category discursively ambiguous. Harper's old Reform Party supporters needed evidence that they were the "real people," and ethnic minority voters needed to feel valued by the new Conservative Party.

The old Reform Party base was very loyal to Harper and the Conservative Party (Gidengil et al. 2012), so expanding the Conservative electorate to include ethnic minority voters became the top priority. This involved attendance by the prime minister and multicultural minister at ethnic group events, symbolic apologies for pre–Second World War federal government acts of racial discrimination, and a campaign – using a revised citizenship guide – to encourage recent immigrants to accept true "Canadian values."

The politics of continual wedge issue creation strengthens plebiscitarian leadership and populist appeal, with the leader fighting for the people against its enemies. On matters of immigration and multiculturalism, the Conservative government created wedges by discursively constructing "good immigrants" and "un-Canadian" immigrants, appealing in different ways to both the party's base and its new visible minority supporters.

Multiculturalism and Immigration: Balancing
Right-Populism and a "Minimum Winning Coalition"

With Jason Kenney as minister of citizenship and immigration (2008–13) and then minister for multiculturalism (2013–15), the Harper government attempted to redefine the Canadian model of multiculturalism. Its messaging regularly attributed a self-reliant anti-statism and conservative social values to Canadian immigrants. As Kenney quipped in 2010, "these new Canadians ... are the personification of Margaret Thatcher's aspirational class. They're all about a massive work ethic" (Friesen 2010).

The Conservative government made it clear that "good immigrants" would embrace Canada's historical values, including affection for the British monarch (Abu-Laban 2014), and work hard to integrate themselves into the Canadian mainstream. This was presented with a conservative twist in the Conservative government's revised citizenship guide as "celebrating our different cultural traditions, but not at the expense of sharing common Canadian traditions" (Citizenship and Immigration Canada 2012).

A subtle but far more revealing aspect of the new guide was the absence of any reference to the Charter of Rights and Freedoms. This sent a clear signal to old Reform Party activists that a Conservative Canada would steer clear of equality rights supportive of gender and sexual identity and affirmative action for ethnic minority citizens. Following the American Republican Party's militant opposition to similar rights and policies, Reform Party activists and intellectuals had strenuously opposed such rights and their policy extensions (Laycock 2005b). By intentionally ignoring the core constitutional foundation of ethnic minority rights in Canada in its new citizenship guide, the Conservative Party steered new citizens away from associating their Canadian–ness, and Canadian multiculturalism, with an egalitarian ethos and activist state (Citizenship and Immigration Canada 2012).

The citizenship guide's emphasis on "social cohesion" and "real" Canadian values was an indirect nod to Reform Party voters' concerns about multiculturalism. It reassured them that on the Conservative Party's watch, Canada would not be taken over by foreign languages and cultures. In effect, Kenney and other Conservatives were saying that the values and lifestyles of the Canadian majority would be re-established as the unquestionably dominant norm, even if the level of visible minority immigration did not decline, and even if a superficial acceptance of cultural diversity was retained.

In its overhaul of immigration policy, the Conservative government placed more emphasis on "economic immigrants," eliminated "family class immigrants," shifted refugee resettlement costs to private agencies or the

United Nations High Commissioner for Refugees, and denied landed refugee applicants government-financed health care coverage (Zilio 2016). This demonstrated that good immigrants would not need to rely on the state for social services.

The Conservative government practised symbolically inclusive multicultural politics shrewdly. It offered formal government apologies for past Canadian government injustices to the Chinese and South Asian communities, which had substantial symbolic value to these large immigrant communities even with a tiny outlay of government funds (Friesen 2013). Harper and Kenney appeared at countless ethnic minority group events that offered partisan advantage, while dramatically underspending established program funding allocated for events designed to "promote intercultural understanding, respect for democratic values or civic memory and pride" (Canadian Press 2013). The government gave minor cabinet posts to several visible minority MPs, and its backbench included numerous Chinese-Canadian and Indo-Canadian MPs from "ethnic ridings." Though it had a smaller proportion of visible minority candidates than the Liberal Party in the 2015 election, at 13 percent the Conservative Party was tied with the social democratic New Democratic Party. In the thirty-three federal constituencies where visible minority citizens made up over 50 percent of residents, the Conservatives presented twenty-five visible minority candidates, the highest proportion among the parties (Griffith 2016).

Equality and "Exclusive" Populism

Such incorporation of ethnic minority citizens into party and Parliament is unheard of among European right-populist parties. Combined with its massive ethnic outreach efforts (Bricker and Ibbitson 2013), the Conservatives appear to count as the only case of "inclusive populism" among right-wing populisms in the contemporary West.

But inclusion is not just a matter of bringing group representatives inside the party tent. As Mudde and Kaltewasser (2013) argue, inclusion and exclusion in populist parties occur along material, political, and symbolic dimensions. These dimensions converge in party policy, party ideology, and party candidate selection, which can be assessed in combination to position a party along a continuum. To illustrate, consider three aspects of inclusion, all involving particular kinds of equality: (1) equality of national and religious access; (2) equality of effective civic integration; and (3) equality of socio-economic advantage. These aspects point to a range of party/government policy relevant to immigration and multicultural integration experience that traverses elements of material, political, and symbolic inclusion/exclusion.

Equality of national and religious access
Can anyone enter the country and pursue permanent resident or full citizenship status as easily as all others? Or is it harder, legally or in practice, for some foreigners to successfully immigrate? The Conservative government overhauled immigration legislation to distinguish between "safe" and "not safe" national sources of immigrants, with over forty countries on the latter list. The government also made it harder to enter Canada as a permanent resident, requiring proof of employment before admission to Canada (Muerrens 2015).

In the 2015 election campaign, the Conservative Party contended that only "persecuted minority" Syrian refugees should be brought to Canada. As one commentator said, "Harperspeak is to earnestly proclaim that he gives refugee preference to 'the most needy' minorities. To most Canadians that sounds reasonable. To Muslims from countries where they are the majority, they know it's meant to exclude them. To Harper's Christian fundamentalist base, it is code for 'people like us'" (Sears 2015).

Equality of effective civic integration
The most obvious aspect of civic integration is incorporation of immigrants from ethnic minorities into electoral politics, through party nominations as candidates. Less obviously, civic integration involves access to processes of social and political life. Here one asks whether any groups are prevented from using, or made to feel uncomfortable when using, these processes. The example that stands out here, to be discussed later, is the Conservative Party and government's treatment of Muslim Canadians and prospective Muslim immigrants as the dangerous, anti-woman (CBC News 2015a), un-integrable "other" (Abu-Laban 2014; Griffith 2015).

Equality of socio-economic advantage
Finally, if immigration programs give priority to those who are well educated or who can invest large sums of money in the host country's economy, or to those who are fluent in the host nation's official languages, they are effectively biased against those with low or modest incomes, lower education or job market skills, and language skills. If a small proportion of immigrants are refugees, and the government deprives some refugees of health care coverage, the bias in favour of well-off immigrants increases. Core Conservative Party voters may then be less likely to see immigrants as expensive wards of

an undesirable welfare state. This reduces the level of effective multicultural inclusiveness in populist conservatism and, to a lesser extent, in centrist Canadian liberalism.[12]

These assessments suggest how the Conservative Party's orientation to equality and civic integration was intended to marginalize the welfare state, and help us to understand the degree of multicultural inclusion it intended, which was more symbolic than political, and less material than either political or symbolic.

Denying health care to refugee claimants is a telling example of how right-populist exclusion works to undermine multicultural equality because it served two complementary purposes. First, it assured the party base that the government would not spend their tax dollars on undeserving refugee applicants. Second, it sent a signal to recent and potential immigrants that under Conservative governments, refugee applicants do not deserve social services unless they run a gruelling gauntlet. Here we find a hint of welfare chauvinism, but just a hint, because the Conservative government reduced funding for many social services for "real" Canadians as well.

Exclusion was also strongly communicated in 2015 with the Conservative's Zero Tolerance for Barbaric Cultural Practices Act.[13] This legislation was named to "cultivate the belief that Muslim immigrants are a threat to Canada" (Lenard 2015). Much other Conservative government policy conveyed a sense of who was included in and would benefit from a multicultural Canada. The Office of Religious Freedom was established in 2011 by Stephen Harper and led by the dean of a small evangelical Christian college. This was intended not only to placate evangelical Christians but also to gain support from minority groups of Canadian Muslims while marginalizing the larger Sunni and Shiite groups by painting them as friendly to terrorism (Siddiqui 2013; Kirkup 2015).

The Conservative Party has linked Muslims to terrorism since it took office in 2006 (Abu-Laban 2014). It stepped up this rhetorical campaign once it won a majority government, and made it a frequent theme in the 2015 election campaign (CBC News 2015f). Data from the 2015 Canadian Election Study suggested that this tactic was relatively successful. Respondents who believed the government should suspend citizens' rights in order to "crack down on terrorism" were disproportionately those who disliked or really disliked Muslims in Canada, and who supported a lower level of immigration.[14]

Nonetheless, it would be a mistake to see Conservative Party efforts to promote exclusion based on ethnicity or religion as the central feature of its discursive structuring of the people and its enemies. As we argued earlier, this was partly a matter of adjacent conceptualization, and mostly a matter of perimeter conceptualization, in the overall Conservative Party morphology. The primary boundary of exclusion in Canadian right-populist conservatism was created by detaching the idea of substantive equality, requiring significant state intervention within a moderately generous welfare state, from the dominant narrative about multiculturalism and diversity. This is rarely a part of right-populism in Europe, where "welfare chauvinism" attracts many working class and lower-income voters (Schumacher and van Kersbergen 2016).

The Conservative Party's 2011 election victory relied on a major increase in big-city visible minority community support for Conservative candidates, with 31 percent of racial minority voters supporting the Conservatives, versus 9 percent support within this category for the Canadian Alliance in 2000 (Bricker and Ibbitson 2013). In 2011, long-time party campaign architect Tom Flanagan argued that ethnic minorities in English Canada had replaced Quebec voters as a necessary part of the Conservative Party's "minimum winning coalition" (Flanagan 2011). It is difficult to imagine a strategist for Donald Trump, Marine Le Pen, or Geert Wilders making similar recommendations.

The Balancing Act Fails

Before 2015, growing signs of Conservative government hostility towards Muslim Canadians were overshadowed by the government's many efforts to bring Asian Canadian communities within the Conservative voter pool. On the eve of the 2015 federal election, it even seemed that Conservative support in these communities might help them remain in power (Loewen and Rubenson 2015).

The Conservative government introduced and passed legislation in 2011 that banned niqabs during citizenship ceremonies. In June 2015, just before the election campaign, it promised legislation to override a March 2015 Federal Court declaration that this niqab ban was unconstitutional. But even having its Indo-Canadian minister of multiculturalism defend the government's actions could not disguise their exclusionary right-populist character (CBC News 2015g).

After trailing in the polls through an extended election campaign, Conservative strategists decided to rally Canadians against Muslims threatening Canadian values, thus creating what they hoped would be a power-saving electoral wedge between the Conservatives and the three English Canadian opposition parties. So they revived the issue of the niqab ban and established a "Barbaric Cultural Practices Hotline" (Keenan 2015; Radwanski 2015). The prime minister deployed "dog-whistle politics" (Sears 2015) in a leader's debate by referring to "old stock" Canadians, who he claimed were receiving lower-quality health care than "bogus refugee claimants" before his government had declared pending claimants ineligible for medical care (CBC News 2015b). The Conservative decision to play wedge politics with multiculturalism was certainly not the only reason that the party lost to Justin Trudeau's Liberals (Pammett and LeDuc 2016), but doing so ended badly for Harper's Conservatives.

Conservative Equality, Right-Populism, and Multiculturalism

Enhancing the Conservative Party's electoral chances had, over a decade, required clever strategy and non-trivial ideological compromises, but at the adjacent and perimeter levels of its ideological structure. What Ken Boessenkool and Sean Speer (2015) rightly characterize as the Hayekian core of Stephen Harper's political understanding and commitments were not compromised by these ideological adjustments.

By 2015, the Conservative Party had increased its ethnic minority support while transforming immigration and changing the tenor and ideological significance of multiculturalism. The party accomplished each of these in ways that disassociated multiculturalism from its previously strong links with the welfare state and equality rights agendas. However, by giving priority to thinly veiled racism in their 2015 practice of electoral wedge politics, the Conservatives showed that they were desperate to win at all costs. After the prime minister had described the niqab as "anti-woman," well known Canadian philosopher Charles Taylor accused him of "playing along with an unfortunate tendency, an Islamophobic tendency, in North America [which is] a direct danger to our security and terrible for our society" (CBC News 2015e). Even conservative commentators contended that denying Muslim women the right to dress as they wish when taking a citizenship oath trampled both religious freedom and the Canadian norm of cultural tolerance (Orwin 2015).

Both the niqab debate and the public debate over refugee eligibility for medical care featured the prime minister driving a wedge between "real Canadians" and "the other," to animate anti-Muslim and anti-immigrant sentiment among voters. Such politically desperate discursive recasting of the people and its enemies undermined his government's ten-year campaign to show that they really did support multiculturalism.

While it was not directly linked to the Conservative Party's main ideological objectives, the Muslim-demonizing strategy was based on an electorally motivated populist majoritarianism. Public opinion research commissioned by the Prime Minister's Office had revealed the electoral upside of calling niqab-wearing Muslim women "un-Canadian" (Beeby 2015).[15] It was also based on what the party leadership knew about its "base": since Reform Party days, the party base had been considerably less accepting of visible minority immigration than supporters of other English Canadian parties. The gap was illustrated in the 2015 Canadian Election Study survey, which showed that 55 percent of Conservative voters supported a ban on Muslim women covering their faces in public, compared with 34 percent of Liberal voters.[16]

Shortly before the election, Harper was so pleased with what his pollsters told him about the public's response to his niqab ban that he proposed a ban on niqab use by all federal civil servants (CBC News 2015d; Naumetz 2015). But this good Canadian/un-Canadian division was widely seen as an indication that the Conservatives would not know where or how to stop in their efforts to exploit intolerance (Plant 2015). A seasoned political consultant opined that

> Stephen Harper is ... a garden-variety right-wing populist ... with distinctly Canadian features. By processing anger and prejudice through the filter of Canadian values, he has created a more acceptable face of populism. Donald Trump would attack veiled Muslim women as terrorists in disguise, Harper's code is that we need to ensure that they observe Canadian values. (Sears 2015)

In Conservative Party hands, plebiscitarian populist leadership involved centrally scripted appeals to various ethnic communities and privileged representation to those on the desired side of various discursive and ideological divides. Unlike right-populists in Europe, Canada's right-populists successfully recruited members and candidates from visible minority groups and avoided a simple "immigrant/real citizen" dichotomy. But as we have seen, Conservative Party success owed much to superficial "political inclusion" tactics that disguised its symbolically and politically exclusion-creating rejection of the liberal egalitarian version of social citizenship interwoven in Canada's distinctive form of multiculturalism.

When the right-populist appeal was on track, the boundary of exclusion was determined by groups' support for or antagonism towards the welfare state. Support for the welfare state made a group a "special interest," which in turn performed discursive functions of exclusion and conflict structuring. This was foundational for Canadian right-populism, and until the last election campaign it was the primary determinant of Conservative Party strategy towards immigration and multiculturalism.

Since the 2015 election, Justin Trudeau's Liberal government has returned, ideologically and symbolically if not much materially, to a liberal egalitarian foundation for multiculturalism based on the Charter of Rights and Freedoms. This shift from the Harper government's attempt to undermine such egalitarianism included a symbolically striking standard of inclusion in Trudeau's first cabinet (CBC News 2015c). It had gender parity, a First Nations female lawyer as minister of justice, a decorated Sikh military veteran as minister of defence, and a first-generation Afghan Canadian woman as minister for democratic institutions. With the first cabinet shuffle, a naturalized Somali refugee became Canada's minister of immigration.

Canadian Attitudes towards Multiculturalism and the Welfare State and the Prospects for Nativist Populist Conservatism

How successful was the Conservatives' attempt to detach the welfare state from multiculturalism? We can look more closely at this with data from the 2015 Canadian Election Study, which asked a series of questions on attitudes towards minorities and support for the welfare state. The short answer is that the Conservatives appear not to have been very successful.

Looking at Figure 3.1, which shows data from the 2015 Canadian Election Study, we see that welfare state support tracks closely with attitudes towards immigrants. Those in favour of welfare state expansion are also more positively oriented towards immigrants. Moreover, support for the welfare state and immigration remain high across Canada – over 75 percent of respondents indicated that income inequality is a big problem in Canada, and just over 75 percent believed that more should be done to reduce the income gap in Canada. Of this 75 percent, 50 percent supported the current level of immigration, while 32 percent thought *more* immigrants should be accepted.[17]

The lack of welfare chauvinism in Canada is also evident in the controversy over the niqab. As Figure 3.2 shows, although a strong majority of Canadians supported banning Muslim women from wearing the niqab in public, those who favour expanding the welfare state are less likely to support such a ban. Respondents who want to reduce the welfare state are nearly 50 percent more likely to support the ban than those who want to expand it. Interestingly, however, those who want to maintain the welfare state have a different pattern in terms of their attitudes towards immigration generally and banning the niqab. For banning the niqab, their attitudes are similar to

Figure 3.1 Attitudes towards welfare state and support for immigrants in Canada

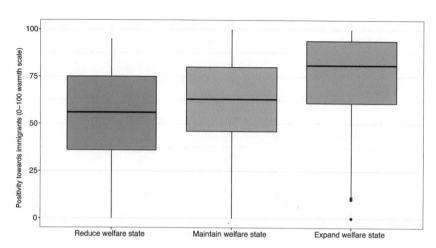

Source: Fournier, Cutler, Soroka, and Stolle. 2015.

Figure 3.2 Attitudes towards welfare state and banning the niqab

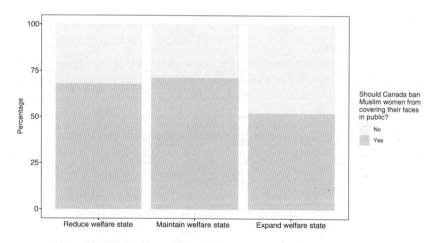

Source: Fournier, Cutler, Soroka, and Stolle. 2015.

those who want to reduce the welfare state, but for immigration generally, this group is closer to those who want to expand the welfare state.

More research needs to be done here, but on the face of it, there is little evidence that the efforts of Stephen Harper and the Conservative Party to sever multiculturalism from the welfare state in Canada were a success. It is possible that these efforts will pay dividends in future elections, especially if the Conservatives continue to push this narrative. Some party activists would like to bring immigration even more to the forefront, especially Muslim immigration, and prominent Conservative Party MP Maxime Bernier formed the People's Party of Canada in September 2018 to pursue a combination of classical laissez-faire liberal, anti-multicultural and immigration reduction objectives. The longer Donald Trump is America's president, the more emboldened right-wing Canadian conservatives may be to use right-populist political framing to achieve nativist objectives. We also do not yet know how much of the Harper government's policy legacy on both multicultural integration and federal support for the welfare state will be altered by the Trudeau Liberal government. So it is too soon to tell how much the Conservative government succeeded in altering the policy and program infrastructure of Canadian multiculturalism, even if it did not succeed in its project of ideologically redefining multiculturalism in terms of opposition to the welfare state.

Acknowledgments

We gratefully acknowledge the assistance of Vanessa Loders, who provided us with preliminary data analysis of the 2015 Canadian Election Study data discussed in this chapter. We also thank Charles Breton, who provided data analysis of this same CES data for an earlier version of this chapter. David Laycock thanks Yannis Stavrakakis of Aristotle University in Thessaloniki, Greece, and Johannes Pollak, of the Institut für Höhere Studien in Vienna, Austria, for hosting his early presentations of the paper on which this chapter is based. And we thank participants in an April 2017 European Consortium on Political Research workshop on "The Influence of Radical Right Populist Parties on Policy-making in Europe," held in Nottingham, UK, for their helpful feedback on a more recent version of our co-authored paper.

Notes

1 Plebiscitarian politics involves highly dominant leaders who present all of their decisions as mandated by their previous election or, in some instances, by plebiscites held by the leader to secure a formal approval for a prior decision the leader does not expect to be overturned by voters or party members. This authoritarian leadership style treats party members or voters as passive recipients of leader's decisions, although authorization of these by "the people" is always claimed by the plebiscitarian leader. See Green 2010 for a good discussion of how this was formulated by Max Weber, and see Katz and Mair 2009 for its application to contemporary European political parties. Stephen Harper's plebiscitarian leadership style is discussed later in this chapter.

2 This is true for a host of reasons, most of which are well explained by Emma Ambrose and Cas Mudde (2015).

3 In the aftermath of the Brexit vote in the United Kingdom, Freeden (2017) contended that the lack of conceptual cohesion and issue reaction-driven character of right-wing populism in Europe renders its local variants emaciated, not just conceptually and structurally "thin."

4 For detailed 2016 census data on Canada's foreign born population, see https://www150.statcan.gc.ca/n1/pub/11-627-m/11-627-m2017028-eng.htm. For 2017 Canadian, German, and American figures, see http://www.pewglobal.org/interactives/international-migrants-by-country/.

5 For additional census data on Canada's urban demographic, see https://www12.statcan.gc.ca/census-recensement/2016/dp-pd/hlt-fst/lang/Table.cfm?Lang=E&T=32&Geo=00.

6 For the full text of the Charter, see http://laws-lois.justice.gc.ca/eng/Const/page-15.html.

7 Some recent research by the Bertelsmann Foundation argues that integration of Muslim minorities in Europe has gone considerably better than public opinion data on immigration and multiculturalism would suggest (El-Menouar 2017).

8 As interpreted by the courts after 1985, the Charter has supported minority language educational rights and growing demands for financial compensation, land, and self-government by Canada's Aboriginal communities.

9 The Reform Party *Blue Sheet* (1995, 5) supported "the principle that individuals or groups are free to preserve their cultural heritage using their own resources," while the Canadian Alliance *Policy Declaration* (2000, #38) stated that "multiculturalism is a personal choice and should not be publicly funded."

10 Stephen Harper told an audience of American conservatives in 1997 that "the first fact" they needed to know about Canada was that it is "a Northern European welfare state in the worst sense of the term, and very proud of it."

11 For Reform, Canadian Alliance, and Conservative Party federal election platforms from 1988 to 2006, see http://www.poltext.org/.

12 These selective and unavoidably exclusionary criteria for immigrants (not refugees) had been adopted by the federal Liberal government before 2006, and have been retained by the Trudeau Liberal government since 2015.

13 For the full text of the Zero Tolerance for Barbaric Cultural Practices Act, see https://laws-lois.justice.gc.ca/eng/annualstatutes/2015_29/.

14 From the 2015 Canadian Election Study Post Election Survey data, cross tabulation of agreement with "The government should be able to crack down on suspected terrorists, even if that means interfering with the rights of ordinary people" (pes11_48b) with answers to (1) "How do you feel about Muslims living in Canada?" (pes11_21) and (2) "Do you think Canada should admit more immigrants, fewer immigrants, or about the same as now?" (pes11_28).

15 The poll can be viewed at http://epe.lac-bac.gc.ca/100/200/301/pwgsc-tpsgc/por-ef/privy_council/2015/047–14-e/tables.htm.

16 Data compiled by Charles LeBreton.

17 Fournier et al., 2015, Post Election Survey questions: Is income inequality a big problem in Canada? How much do you think should be done to reduce the gap between the rich and the poor in Canada? Do you think Canada should admit more immigrants, fewer immigrants, or about the same as now?

References

Abu-Laban, Yasmeen. 2014. "Reform by Stealth: The Harper Conservatives and Canadian Multiculturalism." In *The Multicultural Question: Debating Identity in 21st Century Canada,* ed. Jack Jedwab, 149–72. Montreal and Kingston: McGill-Queen's University Press.

Aiyar, Shekhar, Bergljot B. Barkbu, Nicoletta Batini, Helge Berger, Enrica Detragiache, Allan Dizioli, Christian H Ebeke, et al. 2016. *The Refugee Surge in Europe: Economic Challenges.* IMF Staff Discussion Note. N.p.: International Monetary Fund. https://www.imf.org/external/pubs/ft/sdn/2016/sdn1602.pdf.

Akkerman, Tjitske. 2012. "Comparing Radical Right Parties in Government: Immigration and Integration Policies in Nine Countries (1996–2010)." *West European Politics* 35 (3): 511–29.

Ambrose, Emma, and Cas Mudde. 2015. "Canadian Multiculturalism and the Absence of the Far Right." *Nationalism and Ethnic Politics* 21 (2): 213–36.

Angus Reid Institute. 2016. "What Makes Us Canadian? A Study of Values, Beliefs, Priorities and Identity." http://angusreid.org/canada-values/.

Banting, Keith. 2014. "Transatlantic Convergence? The Archaeology of Immigrant Integration in Canada and Europe." *International Journal* 69 (1): 66–84.

Beeby, Dean. 2015. "Poll Ordered by Harper Found Strong Support for Niqab Ban at Citizenship Ceremonies." CBC News, September 24. http://www.cbc.ca/news/politics/canada-election-2015-niqab-poll-pco-1.3241895.

Boessenkool, Ken, and Sean Speer. 2015. "How Harper's Philosophy Transformed Canada for the Better." *Policy Options,* December 1. http://policyoptions.irpp.org/2015/12/01/harper/.

Bourrie, Mark. 2015. *Kill the Messengers: Stephen Harper's Assault on Your Right to Know.* Toronto: Harper Collins.

Breton, Charles. 2015. "Making National Identity Salient: Impact on Attitudes toward Immigration and Multiculturalism." *Canadian Journal of Political Science* 48 (2): 357–81.

Bricker, Darrell, and John Ibbitson. 2013. *The Big Shift.* Toronto: HarperCollins.

–. 2018. "What's Driving Populism? It Isn't the Economy, Stupid." *Globe and Mail,* February 10. https://www.theglobeandmail.com/opinion/what-is-driving-populism-it-isnt-the-economy-stupid/article37899813/.

Canadian Press. 2013. "Millions in Multiculturalism Funding Going Unspent." CBC News, June 20. https://www.cbc.ca/news/politics/millions-in-multiculturalism-funding-going-unspent-1.1311570.

Canadian Reform Conservative Alliance. 2000. *Policy Declaration.* Ottawa: CRCA.

CBC News. 2015a. "Harper Says 'Overwhelming Majority' Agrees with Tories on Niqabs." CBC News, March 11. http://www.cbc.ca/news/politics/harper-says-overwhelming-majority-agrees-with-tories-on-niqabs-1.2990439.

–. 2015b. "Harper's 'Old-Stock Canadians' Line Is Part Deliberate Strategy." CBC News, September 18. http://www.cbc.ca/news/canada/montreal/harper-old-stock-canadians-debate-1.3233615.

–. 2015c. "Meet Justin Trudeau's New Liberal Cabinet." CBC News, November 4. https://www.cbc.ca/news/politics/trudea-cabinet-ministers-profile-1.3304176.

–. 2015 d. "Niqab Ban for Public Servants Would Be Considered: Stephen Harper." CBC News, October 6. https://www.cbc.ca/news/politics/stephen-harper-niqab-ban-public-servants-1.3258943.

—. 2015e. "Stephen Harper 'Dumb' to Say Niqab Is Anti-Women, Charles Taylor Says." CBC News, March 27. https://www.cbc.ca/news/politics/stephen-harper-dumb-to-say-niqab-is-anti-women-charles-taylor-says-1.3013427.

—. 2015f. "Terrorism Mailout from Conservative MP Lawrence Toet Called 'Preposterous.'" CBC News, March 11. http://www.cbc.ca/news/canada/manitoba/terrorism-mailout-from-conservative-mp-lawrence-toet-called-preposterous-1.2990095.

—. 2015g. "Tim Uppal Defends Bill to Ban Niqab at Citizenship Ceremonies." CBC News, June 24. http://www.cbc.ca/news/canada/edmonton/tim-uppal-defends-bill-to-ban-niqab-at-citizenship-ceremonies-1.3126212.

Citizenship and Immigration Canada. 2012. *Discover Canada: The Rights and Responsibilities of Citizenship*. Ottawa: Minister of Citizenship and Immigration. https://www.canada.ca/content/dam/ircc/migration/ircc/english/pdf/pub/discover.pdf.

Conservative Party of Canada. 2015. "The Hon. Chris Alexander and the Hon. Kellie Leitch Announce Measures to Stop Barbaric Cultural Practices Against Women and Girls." Conservative Party of Canada, https://www.conservative.ca/the-hon-chris-alexander-and-the-hon-kellie-leitch-announce-measures-to-stop-barbaric-cultural-practices-against-women-and-girls-2/.

Edsall, Thomas. 2017. "The Peculiar Populism of Donald Trump." *New York Times*, February 2. https://www.nytimes.com/2017/02/02/opinion/the-peculiar-populism-of-donald-trump.html?action=clickandcontentCollection=opinionandmodule=NextInCollectionandregion=Footerandpgtype=articleandversion=columnandrref=collection%2Fcolumn%2Fthomas-b-edsall.

El-Menouar, Yasemin. 2017. *Muslims in Europe: Integrated but Not Accepted?* Gütersloh, Germany: Bertelsmann Foundation. https://www.bertelsmann-stiftung.de/fileadmin/files/BSt/Publikationen/GrauePublikationen/Study_LW_Religion-Monitor-2017_Muslims-in-Europe_Results-and-Country-Profiles.pdf.

Farney, James. 2012. *Social Conservatives and Party Politics in Canada and the United States*. Toronto: University of Toronto Press.

Flanagan, Tom. 1995. *Waiting for the Wave: The Reform Party and Preston Manning*. Toronto: Stoddart.

—. 2011. "The Emerging Conservative Coalition." *Policy Options*, June 2011, 104–8.

Fournier, Patrick, Fred Cutler, Stuart Soroka, and Dietlind Stolle. 2015. The 2015 Canadian Election Study. [dataset]

Freeden, Michael. 1996. *Ideologies and Political Theory*. Oxford: Oxford University Press.

—. 2017. "After the Brexit Referendum: Revisiting Populism as an Ideology." *Journal of Political Ideologies* 22 (1): 1–11.

Friesen, Joe. 2010. "Jason Kenney: The 'Smiling Buddha' and His Multicultural Charms." *Globe and Mail*, January 29.

—. 2013. "Chinese Head-Tax Redress Funds Clawed Back." *Globe and Mail*, February 27. http://www.theglobeandmail.com/news/politics/chinese-head-tax-redress-funds-clawed-back/article9101632/.

Gidengil, Elisabeth, et al. 2012. *Dominance and Decline: Making Sense of Recent Canadian Elections*. Toronto: University of Toronto Press.

Green, Jeffrey. 2010. *The Eyes of the People: Democracy in an Age of Spectatorship*. New York: Oxford University Press.

Griffith, Andrew. 2015. "The Conservative Legacy on Multiculturalism: More Cohesion, Less Inclusion." *Policy Options,* October 29. http://policyoptions.irpp. org/2015/10/29/the-conservative-legacy-on-multiculturalism-more-cohesion-less-inclusion/.

–. 2016. "Visible Minority Representation in the 2015 Election." *Policy Options,* March 5. http://policyoptions.irpp.org/2016/03/05/big-shift-or-big-return-visible -minority-representation-in-the-2015-election/.

Haque, Eve. 2012. *Multiculturalism within a Bilingual Framework: Language, Race, and Belonging in Canada.* Toronto: University of Toronto Press.

Harper, Stephen. 1997. "Speech to Council for National Policy," Montreal, June. Reprinted in the *Globe and Mail,* December 15, 2005. https://www.theglobeandmail. com/news/national/text-of-harpers-speech/article1131985/.

Harris, Michael. 2014. *Party of One: Stephen Harper and Canada's Radical Make-over.* Toronto: Viking.

Harrison, Trevor. 1995. *Of Passionate Intensity: Right-Wing Populism and the Reform Party of Canada.* Toronto: University of Toronto Press.

Hurley, M. 2007. "Charter Equality Rights: Interpretation of Section 15 in Supreme Court of Canada Decisions." Ottawa: Library of Parliament, Parliamentary Research and Information Service, Government of Canada.

Ibbitson, John. 2014. "Conservatives Changed the Nature of Canadian Immigration." *Globe and Mail,* December 16. https://www.theglobeandmail.com/news/politics/ how-conservatives-changed-the-nature-of-canadian-immigration/article22101709/.

Ipsos-Reid. 2017. *Global Views on Immigration and the Refugee Crisis.* https://www. ipsos.com/en/global-views-immigration-and-refugee-crisis.

Katz, Richard S., and Peter Mair. 2009. "The Cartel Party Thesis: A Re-statement." *Perspectives on Politics* 7 (4): 752–66.

Keenan, Edward. 2015. "When Stephen Harper Refers to 'Barbaric Culture,' He Means Islam – an Anti-Muslim Alarm That's Ugly and Effective because It Gets Votes: Edward Keenan." *The Toronto Star,* October 5. http://www.thestar.com/ news/canada/2015/10/05/when-stephen-harper-refers-to-barbaric-culture-he -means-islam-an-anti-muslim-alarm-thats-ugly-and-effective-because-it-gets -votes-edward-keenan.html.

Kirkup, Kristy. 2015. "Bill C-51 Hearings: Diane Ablonczy's Questions to Muslim Group 'McCarthy-esque.'" CBC News, March 13. http://www.cbc.ca/news/ politics/bill-c-51-hearings-diane-ablonczy-s-questions-to-muslim-group -mccarthyesque-1.2993531.

Klimmage, Michael. "It's Time to Take the Idea of the West Back from the Populists." *Washington Post,* June 8. https://www.washingtonpost.com/news/democracy-post/ wp/2017/06/08/its-time-to-take-the-idea-of-the-west-back-from-the-populists/ ?utm_term=.f9e4e231a029.

Kymlicka, Will. 2010. *The Current State of Multiculturalism in Canada and Research Themes on Canadian Multiculturalism 2008–2010.* Ottawa: Citizenship and Immigration Canada.

Laycock, David. 2001. *The New Right and Democracy in Canada: Understanding Reform and the Canadian Alliance.* Don Mills, ON: Oxford University Press.

–. 2005a. "Visions of Popular Sovereignty: Mapping the Contested Terrain of Contemporary Western Populisms." *Critical Review of International Social and Political Philosophy* 8 (2): 125–44.

–. 2005b. "Reconfiguring Popular Sovereignty in Post-Charter Canada: The View from the Canadian New Right." In *Constitutional Processes in Canada and the EU Compared,* ed. John E. Fossum, 225–58. ARENA Report 8/05. Oslo: Centre for European Studies, University of Oslo.

–. 2012. "Populism and Democracy in Canada's Reform Party." In *Populism in Europe and the Americas: Threat or Corrective to Democracy?,* ed. Cas Mudde and Cristobal Rovira Kaltewasser, 46–67. New York: Cambridge University Press.

Lenard, P. 2015. "What Future for Canada's Immigration Policy?" *Policy Options,* September 9. http://policyoptions.irpp.org/fr/magazines/september-2015/election-2015/what-future-for-canadas-immigration-policy/.

Loewen, Peter, and Daniel Rubenson. 2015. "Loewen: Support for Conservatives' Niqab Ban Is Deep and Wide, Even among Immigrants." *Ottawa Citizen,* October 9. http://ottawacitizen.com/opinion/columnists/loewen-support-for-conservatives-niqab-ban-is-deep-and-wide-even-among-immigrants.

Martin, Lawrence. 2010. *Harperland: The Politics of Control.* Toronto: Viking.

Mudde, Cas, and Cristobal R. Kaltewasser. 2012. *Populism in Europe and the Americas: Threat or Corrective for Democracy?* New York: Cambridge University Press.

–. 2013. "Exclusionary vs. Inclusionary Populism: Comparing Contemporary Europe and Latin America." *Government and Opposition* 48 (2): 147–74.

Muerrens, Stephen. 2015. "Immigration after the Conservative Transformation." *Policy Options,* October 16. http://policyoptions.irpp.org/2015/10/16/immigration-after-the-conservative-transformation/.

Naumetz, Tim. "Ministers Had No Objection to Niqabs in Public Service Last March." *Hill Times,* October 10. https://www.hilltimes.com/2015/10/10/ministers-had-no-objection-to-niqabs-in-public-service-last-march-2/33710/43710.

Norris, Pippa, and Ronald Inglehart. 2016. "Trump, Brexit and the Rise of Populism: Economic Have-Nots and Cultural Backlash." Paper presented at the American Political Science Association Annual Meeting, September 1–4, Philadelphia.

Orwin, Clifford. 2015. "Stephen Harper's Veiled Attack on Religious Freedom." *Globe and Mail,* February 18. https://www.theglobeandmail.com/opinion/stephen-harpers-veiled-attack-on-religious-freedom/article23044095/.

Pammett, Jon, and Lawrence LeDuc. 2016. "The Fall of the Harper Dynasty." In *The Canadian General Election of 2015,* ed. Jon H. Pammett and Christopher Dornan, 357–80. Toronto: Dundurn.

Pennings, Ray and Michael Van Pelt. 2006. "Replacing the Pan-Canadian Consensus." *Policy Options,* March 2006. Archived without pagination at http://policyoptions.irpp.org/magazines/the-prime-minister/replacing-the-pan-canadian-consensus/.

Plant, Geoff. 2015. "According to Stephen Harper, There Are Two Types of Canadians." *Globe and Mail,* October 12. https://www.theglobeandmail.com/news/politics/according-to-stephen-harper-there-are-two-types-of-canadians/article26776388/.

Press Progress. 2016. "Kellie Leitch's Campaign Manager: Jason Kenney Weakened Immigration Controls." *Press Progress,* November 14. https://pressprogress.ca/kellie_leitch_campaign_manager_jason_kenney_weakened_immigration_controls/.

Radwanski, Adam. 2015. "Harper's Culture War Appears to Have Defined Tory Campaign." *Globe and Mail,* October 6. http://www.theglobeandmail.com/news/national/harpers-culture-war-appears-to-have-defined-tory-campaign/article26694760/.

Reform Party of Canada. 1995. *Blue Sheet: Principles, Policies & Election Platform.* http://www.poltext.org/sites/poltext.org/files/plateformes/can1993r_plt_blue_sheet_en_12072011_125204.pdf.

Schumacher, Gijs, and Kees van Kerbergen. 2016. "Do Mainstream Parties Adapt to the Welfare Chauvinism of Populist Parties?" *Party Politics* 22 (3): 300–12.

Sears, Robin. 2015. "Stephen Harper's Dog-Whistle Populist Politics." *Toronto Star,* October 5. https://www.thestar.com/opinion/commentary/2015/10/05/stephen-harpers-dog-whistle-populist-politics.html.

Siddiqui, Haroon. 2013. "Stephen Harper's Real Agenda on Religious Freedom." *Toronto Star,* February 24. http://www.thestar.com/opinion/editorialopinion/2013/02/24/stephen_harpers_real_agenda_on_religious_freedom_siddiqui.html.

Stolle, Dietlind, Allison Harell, Stuart Soroka, and Jesse Behnke. 2016. "Religious Symbols, Multiculturalism and Policy Attitudes." *Canadian Journal of Political Science* 49 (2): 335–58.

Taub, Amanda. 2017. "Canada's Secret to Resisting the West's Populist Wave." *New York Times,* June 27. https://www.nytimes.com/2017/06/27/world/canada/canadas-secret-to-resisting-the-wests-populist-wave.html.

Tepperman, Jonathan. 2017. "Canada's Ruthlessly Smart Immigration Policy." *New York Times,* June 28. https://www.nytimes.com/2017/06/28/opinion/canada-immigration-policy-trump.html?andmoduleDetail=section-news-3andaction=clickandcontentCollection=Opinionandregion=Footerandmodule=MoreInSectionandversion=WhatsNextandcontentID=WhatsNextandpgtype=article.

Wherry, Aaron. 2016. "How Do You Screen Beliefs? The Troublesome Task of Testing for 'Anti-Canadian Values.'" CBC News, September 4. https://www.cbc.ca/news/politics/wherry-leitch-values-1.3746846.

Wright, Matthew, and Ingrid Bloemraad. 2012. "Is There a Trade-off between Multiculturalism and Socio-Political Integration? Policy Regimes and Immigrant Incorporation in Comparative Perspective." *Perspectives on Politics* 10 (1): 77–95.

Zilio, Michelle. "Liberals Restore Refugee Health Benefits Cut by Previous Government." *Globe and Mail,* February 18. http://www.theglobeandmail.com/news/politics/liberals-cancelling-controversial-cuts-to-refugee-health-care/article28797720/.

4

Not Merely Playing
Game Theory's Subversive Proclivities

LAURENT DOBUZINSKIS

Game theory has travelled across many disciplinary and cultural boundaries. It is arguably more influential than ever today, but is also the object of much criticism and hand wringing. Thus, it is an ideal case study for looking into the more general question of how a paradigm flowing across various boundaries affects the areas into which it spills, and also for considering how this process of diffusion can reshape the agent of change itself. Profoundly influenced by cultural references they inherited from Mitteleuropa, its founders – John von Neumann and Oskar Morgenstern – ended up as central figures of the American scientific establishment. Embodying elements drawn from mathematics and economics, game theory has moved into military planning, political science, philosophy, and, more unexpectedly, evolutionary biology. It has even made forays into the humanities, the media, and popular culture. Although some scholars use it as merely one more tool in their methodological toolkit, others have applied it with more zeal to question the conventional wisdom of their respective disciplines.

In the end, however, being applied to so many very different problems, game theory has become the Proteus of the social sciences. Under some guises, it looks radically different from what its founders envisioned. But it is not merely a way of tackling specific research problems. Sometimes subtly, sometimes less so, game theory challenges several crucial epistemological beliefs, notably about the sense in which mathematics is relevant to the social sciences, and what it means to act rationally. Others have gone as far as to claim that it undermines the political culture of liberal democracies.

My goal in this chapter is to provide an overview of these developments and to address the sometimes virulent positions adopted by critics and defenders of what Jon Elster (2008) has described as "the most significant advance in 20th Century social sciences."[1] I wish to underline the immense potential of game theory as an intellectual ferment, as a way to pose profound questions by using deceptively simple concepts. But I do concede that there are risks in doing so: the corrosive epistemological, cultural, and political implications of this protean analytical device ought to be kept in mind. Game theory is essentially a way of coming to grips with the meaning of strategic thinking, but can itself be used strategically.

It is the nature of the ends served by the uses of game theory that matters. There are, of course, many criteria that can be applied to the evaluation of these goals. In this chapter, I subscribe to a broadly defined "liberal" conception of political economy; if pushed, I would confess to sharing Ken Binmore's "whiggish" sympathies (Binmore 2005, 185). From that angle, game theory serves the analytical purposes of free (playful?) inquiring agents intent on questioning utopian or naïve views of what politics can achieve. Hence it poses no inherent threat to a liberal democratic way of life where such imaginative inquiry can flourish; in fact, it can enhance our understanding and ongoing re-evaluation of its strengths and potentials.

However, game theory can also be deployed in questionable and potentially perverse ways that betray a cynical view of moral issues and political arrangements. "Scientistic" misuses of the theory and a myopic emphasis on self-interest in the construction of political issues can delegitimize a liberal democratic order, and here I find some common ground with heterodox critics of liberal political economy. There is always the possibility, however, that as a more sophisticated understanding of recent trends in game theory begins to inform public debates, a way out of this impasse can be found.

In this chapter, I first look back at the origins and founding principles of (classical) game theory, then I retrace the peregrinations of game theory across disciplinary boundaries to assess its varied impacts on the fields it has "invaded." I consider how far it has moved from its origins and what it means for our understanding of rationality. Finally, I elaborate on my remark above concerning the significance of strategic thinking for practical politics.

Origins and Founding Principles

The contemporary literature on game theory offers varied and sometimes contradictory interpretations, thus presenting even more reason to go back to its roots. There are excellent works on the history of game theory

(Leonard 1995, 2008, 2010; Dimand and Dimand 2002; Giocoli 2003, 2009; Erickson 2015) that show how it has been shaped by a series of ongoing and sometimes tortuous debates about cross-cutting methodological and discipline-specific issues. But there is general agreement that it originated with the publication in 1944 of John von Neumann and Oskar Morgenstern's *The Theory of Games and Economic Behavior* ([1944] 2004). One of the stated purposes of this seminal work was "to find the mathematically complete principles which define 'rational behavior' for the participants in a social economy, and to derive from them the general characteristics of that behavior" (ibid., 31). Another milestone in the history of game theory was, of course, the publication in 1951 of John Nash's article outlining what became known as the "Nash equilibrium" in non-cooperative games. Before examining these major achievements, I will briefly examine some of their more or less distant antecedents.

Strategic thinking is an essential aspect of life in a social setting. People make choices knowing full well that others do the same; some of these merely involve deciding among practical issues (e.g., choosing a spouse or forging alliances with neighbouring groups), others involve moral challenges. I pragmatically take this as an experiential "given." Therefore, it is not surprising that one finds examples of game-theoretic reasoning in the Bible or the Talmudic tradition (Aumann 2002; Brams 2011, ch. 2). And of course all successful military leaders, going back to Pericles or Hannibal, have devised winning strategies (although the term itself in its modern connotation did not emerge until the beginning of the nineteenth century). Niccolò Machiavelli famously strategized about war and politics in *The Prince*. Jean-Jacques Rousseau's allegory of the dilemma faced by hunters who have to choose between cooperating in hunting a deer or going off individually after a rabbit is the origin of the much-discussed "stag hunt" game. (The latter seems to have dethroned Prisoner's Dilemma as being the most relevant to political philosophy and public policy because it brings to light the crucial importance of trust in establishing stable social relations [Skyrms 2004].) But in a sense Rousseau was the first critic of the application of game theory to politics: in the *Social Contract*, he takes great pains to explain that the "General Will" can emerge only when voters vote sincerely, listening exclusively to their conscience. Strategic voting can only result in the qualitatively inferior – at least in Rousseau's eyes – sum of individual interests (or "particular wills").

While Rousseau's contribution was only accidental, as it were, the Enlightenment philosopher who came the closest to articulating a game-theoretic

outlook on political economy was David Hume; his explanation of how
social conventions evolve strongly evokes contemporary models of repeated
games and coordinated equilibria with which contemporary game theorists
are familiar (Vanderschraaf 1998). Also Michael Chwe (2013) argues that
Jane Austen had a keen understanding of strategic thinking and, in particular, of how it is often used by less powerful individuals who exploit the "clue-
lessness" of those who hold power over them.

Antoine-Augustin Cournot (1838) was the first economist to systematically use mathematics to analyze economic problems. In his analysis
of monopolies and duopolies, Cournot did not make use of the concepts
deployed by game theorists (e.g., expected utilities and mixed strategies)
but he can still be regarded as one of the early precursors of strategic modelling in economics who anticipated the Nash equilibrium. Nash's genius is to
have thought of his equilibrium as a solution to *all* non-cooperative games.

The turn of the last century was a crucial time in the history of mathematics, logic, and the philosophy of science, with groundbreaking innovations at the crossroads of these disciplines by John von Neumann and Oskar
Morgenstern, who serendipitously met in the United States. Two streams
of apparently unrelated inquiries were captivating mathematicians and
philosophers in Mitteleuropa: set theory and the game of chess (Leonard
1995, 733; Ferreiros 2016, 12–13). The mathematician Ernst Zermelo's work
placed him at the confluence of these streams; he began to think of chess
as a set-theoretic problem. He deliberately bracketed out the psychological
aspects of the game.[2] In a paper published in 1912, Zermelo proved by following what is today called "backward induction" that it is always the case
that one of three "solutions" exists: either white has a winning strategy, or
black has a winning strategy, or "each of the two players has a strategy guaranteeing at least a draw" (Maschler et al. 2013, 3).

None of this was unfamiliar to von Neumann, who knew Zermelo and
had studied under David Hilbert, one of the most influential mathematicians of that era, known for his championing of Georg Cantor's set theory
(although his students, more than he, were the ones who moved the theory
forward). However, von Neumann worked on a much more ambitious problem: finding a solution to *all* zero-sum games. In a paper he presented to the
Göttingen Mathematical Society in 1926, von Neumann laid down a proof
for the so-called minimax theorem. All two-person zero-sum games have
either a pure (minimum of the maximum gains/maximum of the minimum
gains, i.e., the "saddle point") or mixed (i.e., randomized) winning strategy.[3]
Interestingly, as Leonard (1995, 734) notes, "with the minimax theorem, the

prevailing probabilistic view of the world in physics was being reflected in von Neumann's theory of human interactions."

Von Neumann pursued other, unrelated problems for a decade, then returned to the mathematical problems in the late 1930s. The focus of *Theory of Games and Economic Behavior* on economics is largely attributable to Morgenstern, however. The long introductory chapter bears the imprint of Morgenstern's idiosyncratic views on economic theory. Morgenstern was highly critical of practically all schools of thought in economics: "he vilified authors such as Hicks, Hayek, Keynes, and Samuelson, rejected the works of the business cycle theorists, and failed to get along with any of his colleagues at the Princeton Economics Department" (Giocoli 2003, 230). Before he moved to the United States, his research program united two seemingly irreconcilable schools of thought. The first was Austrian economics. Morgenstern attended Ludwig von Mises's seminar in Vienna and worked as an assistant to Hans Mayer.[4] From both he acquired the typically Austrian scepticism towards Walrasian general equilibrium. Austrian economists (then and now) are opposed to using mathematics to study what they consider irreducibly complex economic problems.

In his book *The Limits of Economics* (1937), Morgenstern expressed his critical opinions about the relevance, or lack thereof, of statistics in economic analysis. But – and this is the second facet of his research program – Morgenstern was very much influenced by the epistemological views of the mathematician Karl Menger, whom he met in the 1930s. Karl Menger strongly argued in favour not only of the axiomatization of mathematics but also of a similarly formalist approach to the study of social phenomena (Giocoli 2003, 233). Morgenstern's mathematical skills were limited but when the opportunity arose, he teamed with von Neumann in the hope of setting economics on a sound mathematical footing (i.e., set theory), while unmooring it from the neoclassical paradigm and its unreflective use of mathematical tools. The outcome of their common efforts (*Theory of Games and Economic Behavior*) covers a wide range of topics in a somewhat disjointed manner: zero-sum games, the concept of expected utility, and cooperative games. While game theory in its early stages was often associated with military applications largely co-terminous with lethal zero-sum games, about half of the book is about cooperation and coalition formation.

The second momentous step in the history of game theory took place in the early 1950s: first in his 1950 PhD dissertation and then in an article published in 1951, John Nash proposed a solution to all non–zero-sum non-cooperative games. The Nash equilibrium (NE) consists of the best response of each player to each other's strategies; in some games, there will be two or more such equilibria (e.g., "chicken"). Nash was not an economist, nor could he rely on a co-author such as Morgenstern who could alert economists to the significance of a new mathematical theorem. Therefore, although it turned out that the Nash equilibrium was far more relevant to the social sciences than von Neumann's works, it took quite some time for scholars to perceive the significance of this concept. Even members of this group of mathematicians were a little confused. As related by Paul Erickson (2015, 130), when Arthur Tucker came up with the now famous "Prisoner's Dilemma,"[5] opinion among them was divided between those who realized that it was a typical example of a game with an obvious Nash equilibrium (i.e., playing the dominant strategies Defect-Defect) and those who relied on von Neumann's work to argue that a coalition would form to play Cooperate-Cooperate. The latter is more attractive because it is pareto-efficient, but the coalition is unfeasible in the absence of enforcement mechanisms.

In the 1940s and 1950s, game theorists were mostly to be found at the Pentagon or the RAND Corporation, but this does not prove that game theory is inherently a child of the Cold War paranoia. It was more a consequence of the fact that mathematicians interested in game theory had few other options for pursuing their interests, considering the rather tepid response from social scientists to their new approach at the time (see below).

From this account, the epistemological tenor, let alone the ideological orientation of classical game theory, is ambiguous. Although some of its premises were anticipated in more literary forms, it belongs to applied mathematics. Set theory rather than a somewhat circumstantial association with war planning is truly the fundamental origin of game theory. Although this says something about the *epistemology* of classical game theory, nothing much can be said about its intrinsic ideological orientation. It is the uses to which the theory has been put, rather than the theory itself, that have an ideological connotation. Just as it makes little sense to speak of the ideological nature of genetics, even if eugenics was a reactionary project, game theory is difficult to pin down on an ideological spectrum, even if it has occasionally been harnessed for militaristic or elitist projects.

It remains true that an epistemological critique of game theory is legitimate, albeit challenging. Set theory is vaguely Platonist and the idea that essential aspects of the human experience, such as choosing between alternative ways of acting, can be reduced to mathematical problems for which there are universally valid "solutions" rests on rationalist premises. Rationalism has been criticized for its tendency to flatten personal, cultural, and social differences, and to ignore the value conflicts that stand in the way of an objective assessment of strategic options. It has been rebuked by both conservative liberals, such as Michael Oakeshott and Friedrich Hayek, and by progressive communitarians. Indeed, Hayek's critique of "scientism" and more specifically his scepticism about the use of mathematics in economic analysis account for the lack of enthusiasm towards game theory displayed by the followers of the Austrian school (Cachanosky 2010).

For their part, communitarian and feminist critics have zeroed in on methodological individualism. As long as game-theoretic models treat "players" as individuals without ties to their communities, and without an identifiable gender, critics argue that they will obfuscate more than they will explain. As Peregrine Schwartz-Shea (2002, 301) remarks:

> For feminist researchers and others interested in understanding the ways in which societies shape and are shaped by sex, gender, race, and similar factors, the continuing influence of game theory is troublesome. Because the game-theoretic individual has no (theorized) sex, much less gender or race, the substantive issues concerning sex/gender are, at best, invisible in such analyses.

In a similar vein, Sonja M. Amadae (2016, 3–61) faults game theory for being rooted in a "neoliberal subjectivity" that betrays a reductionist understanding of human agency characterized by "the commodification of all values," a rationalization of "cheating and free riding," and a "quasi-Darwinian worldview." It rejects the "logic of appropriateness" (ibid., xvii) embodied in older forms of classical liberalism. But if this logic rests on the no-harm principle, as Amadae claims, then recent trends in evolutionary game theory suggest that her description of amoral players locked in ruthless competition no longer fits contemporary advances in game theory. These trends are focused on the notion of reciprocity and evoke parallels with the Humean/Smithian notion of "sympathy" (I revisit this crucial insight in the next section).

In other words, the criticisms of game theory listed above hit their mark when they target classical game theory. But notwithstanding von Neumann's intention of setting aside all psychological considerations in the construction of a "theory of games," subjectivity has crept back into the game-theoretic models (Dufwenberg 2010). Consequently, game theory has moved beyond its classical framework to a new phase in its development. Modelling players who must reason in terms of mutual adjustments to each other's moves has alerted game theorists to the profound uncertainty inherent in most social interactions. At the theoretical level, this question has become central to the "epistemic program" in game theory, which "asks: what do different notions of rationality[,] and different assumptions about what players believe about what others believe about the rationality of players[,] imply regarding play in a game?" (Dekel and Siniscalchi 2015, 620; see also Perea 2014). The players from that perspective are not all-knowing rational automata but individuals seeking to find out what the identity of their opponents are; much like ordinary human beings, they are trying to learn something about their interlocutors.

Thus, to come back to Schwartz-Shea's point, if gender explains beliefs, then players in epistemic game theory should want to find out more about the gender of other players. At the empirical level, experimental game theory has revealed how players draw from a wide range of norms and beliefs when deciding how to respond to other players' moves. I am not trying to stretch the point by arguing that game theorists have become sophisticated anthropologists, but they have been led by the logic of their own models to consider a much wider range of motivations than was true of first-generation theorists.

Branching out into many disciplines has brought to light more sharply some of the limitations of game-theoretic models. In a dialectical manner, however, this march into unfamiliar terrains has also opened new pathways that make it more difficult to attach any simplistic epistemological or ideological label to post-classical game theory.

The Wandering Theory

Game theory made few inroads into the social sciences until the late 1970s, then took off in the 1980s. It would be tempting to associate this turn with what, for a lack of a better term, I will call "neoliberalism," even if I think that it homogenizes many distinct cultural and ideological trends. (As previously mentioned, this is what Amadae [2016] forcefully claims.) But I want to argue that if a reduction of liberalism to the logic of the market has indeed occurred, it is more in keeping with the assumptions and methods of Public Choice or Downsian models of voting behaviour (Downs 1957) than with game theory itself. Indeed, I hereafter point out that game theory has ended up undermining some of the basic assumptions of "mainstream" neoclassical economics and casting doubts on the extent to which "rational" political actors can escape the constraints imposed by political institutions, past practices, and so on. What follows is a rough, but I hope reasonably accurate, account of how game theory has unsettled established practices and familiar categories in the social sciences and philosophy.

Economists were intrigued at first, and they were certainly more interested in game theory than their colleagues in other disciplines. However, even in economics the new approach petered out. This is not difficult to understand in view of von Neumann and Morgenstern's very explicit goal of displacing the kind of mathematics that was then common practice in economics – not to mention that in 1944 many economists were not very proficient in mathematics. Scholars usually resist attempts to upset the cart.

Economists rather quickly lost interest in game theory for several reasons. Non–zero-sum games offer very limited possibilities for modelling market exchanges that are supposed to be mutually beneficial for all parties involved in the transaction. Cooperative games, on the other hand, had been presented by von Neumann and Morgenstern in a rather tentative manner and the "stable set" solution they formulated is more useful for understanding why coalitions are unstable than for making predictions.

But how can we explain the fact that they took so long to recognize the potentialities inherent in Nash's work on non-cooperative non–zero-sum games? As Nicola Giocoli (2003, 2) remarks, it is difficult to square the indifference economists showed towards the Nash equilibrium in the 1950s and 1960s with Robert Aumann's assertion that the "Nash equilibrium embodies the most important and fundamental idea of economics, that people act in accordance with their incentives." The answer proposed by Giocoli (2003, 3–10) is that economic methodology first had to transition from a view of the economy "as systems of forces" to one that posits "systems of relations." While the former made full use of conventional algebra, only the latter is consistent with set theory. It was as a result of their encounter with game theory that economists began to pose economic problems in set-theoretic terms. Mark Blaug spoke of a "formalist revolution" to account for this transformation (Giocoli 2003, 6).[6]

The transition to a more formalist approach was also facilitated by the so-called refinement program. The last obstacle that had to be surmounted to demonstrate the analytical power of game theory to economists – and other social scientists – was the perplexing existence of multiple equilibria. While from an ontological standpoint it might be reassuring to learn that social reality is not rigidly determined, from a more empirical perspective it is frustrating not to be able to explain what rational agents can be expected to do in a whole range of situations.[7] Is there a way to choose among theoretically possible equilibria? And how can game theory be used to model choices based on incomplete information, that is, when at least one of the players involved is not entirely certain about what game he or she is playing. Real-life economic agents are, after all, rarely all knowledgeable about the markets in which they operate.

What Giocoli calls the "refinement literature," which is mostly associated with the works of John Harsanyi and Reinhard Selten, addresses the problem of multiple equilibria and incomplete knowledge. The first can rather easily be done by describing games in their extensive form, which is more realistic and indeed eliminates unfeasible equilibria based on non-credible threats (Selten's subgame perfect equilibrium).[8] The second problem is where Harsanyi made his most decisive contribution, by proving that games of incomplete information (i.e., uncertainty about the game) can be transformed via Bayesian statistics[9] into the more manageable games of imperfect information (where at least one player does not know where he/she happens to be on the decision tree).

But even if the incorporation of Bayesianism into game theory was a significant transition, the most important departure from classical game theory occurred a decade or two later when game theory and behavioural economics converged. In all sorts of experimental settings, a new generation of game theorists came to the realization that the players do not have to conform to the archetype of *homo economicus* to find their own "solutions" to their games. Very often it is norms of reciprocity rather than strict rationality that structure their decisions.

A few political scientists became interested in game theory quite early on, but game theory has been a widely used analytical instrument in political science only since the 1980s, and even then the impact of game theory is more evident in American political science than elsewhere. A cursory look at the graduate curriculum in US and Canadian universities, or the paucity of articles in the *Canadian Journal of Political Science* using game-theoretic models, for example, reveal a marked contrast between the importance granted to formal theory in the former and its more marginal place in the latter. This can partly be explained by a long-standing resistance on the part of Canadian political scientists (arguably more explicit among English-speaking researchers) to intellectual currents imported from the United States. In the 1960s and 1970s, the Canadian political science community was largely hostile to "behavioralism," in no small measure because this approach was perceived to be a threat to a more distinctive Canadian style of studying politics.

The current opposition to "neoliberalism" among many Canadian social scientists, rather than anti-Americanism per se, stands as the most plausible reason for their scepticism towards game theory. They see it as closely tied to economics, and therefore as tarnished by the gradual shift of that discipline towards a neoliberal conception of the relationship between states and markets.[10] The fact that game theory has made considerable inroads into American political science is hardly the sort of argument that would convince them to think otherwise! However, the rest of this chapter should provide reasons for re-evaluating this preconceived idea.

The most vocal proselytizer of game theory among political scientists was William Riker, who was seduced by game theory in the 1950s because it promised to make political theory – until then a purely normative exercise, as he saw it – more rigorous and empirically testable. Riker (1962) made contributions to the study of coalitions and in 1992 was still defending the relevance of von Neumann and Morgenstern's work on coalitions. But when game theory finally took off in political science in the 1980s, it was mostly non-cooperative games that were examined.[11] Game-theoretic models have been used in all subfields of the discipline (e.g., to study legislatures and legislative committees in American government[12] as well as a whole range of problems relevant to comparative politics [Munck 2001]) but it is arguably in the field of international relations that its impact has been the most profound.[13] The case of the 1962 Cuban missile crisis alone is the subject of a vast literature.[14]

The first wave of game-theoretic papers consisted mostly of theoretical explorations; hypotheses were not systematically tested. This sort of research drew sharp criticism from Donald Green and Ian Shapiro (1994), who argued that the rational choice approach (not limited to game theory) had not delivered on its promise to produce testable results. For Green and Shapiro, many predictions turn out to be less than convincing, and, typically, rational choice authors add layers of ad hoc assumptions to make the data conform with the models. In the wake of this critique, political scientists began to pay more attention to hypothesis testing and deployment of game-theoretic concepts in analyzing large data sets in a more rigorous manner. Formal (i.e., deductive) and inductive methods became more complementary, and in this sense game theory has gained precision and empirical relevance but arguably lost some of its uniqueness.[15] This should not necessarily be seen as proof of limitations inherent in game theory, such as a reductionist conception of rationality or a fixation on the concept of equilibrium, but as an opportunity to transcend these limitations. I would argue that this is precisely what has happened.

A decisive step was taken when game theory was meshed with experimental methods. Borrowed from social psychology, these methods are now widely used in economics and political science and add considerable support to Herbert Simon's notion of "bounded rationality." As it turns out, individuals can still be "rational" when they take shortcuts to make decisions, relying on rules of thumb or known best practices instead of carefully weighing the costs and benefits of each feasible alternative. But this also means that they are susceptible to inevitable errors and biases. An even more significant move away from the construct of *homo economicus* took place when evolutionary game theory emerged out of the work that evolutionary biologists (e.g., Smith 1982) undertook when they applied game-theoretic models to the study of population dynamics. Evolutionary game theory dispenses with the notion of rational players altogether, substituting instead competition among strategies.

Not all of these theoretical and empirical explorations converge, but a unifying conclusion might be that institutional rules, cultural norms, and ideological frameworks are just as important for understanding strategic choices as sheer self-interest. It is not surprising, therefore, that many political philosophers have taken a strong interest in game theory. Here I can only highlight several explorations of the problem of justice that exemplify the versatility of game-theoretic concepts.

Kenneth Binmore is a prolific author whose ideas deserve attention because he is one of the most often cited architects of the new synthesis between game theory, philosophy, and evolutionary psychology. He has built upon this foundation to propose a path towards feasible reforms aimed at achieving a greater degree of social and political equality. This program is detailed in a technical style in his two-volume series *Game Theory and the Social Contract*, but is conveniently summarized in his *Natural Justice* (2005). Although sharing their goals of moving in the direction of a fairer and more egalitarian socio-economic and political order, Binmore is equally critical of Kantian moral theory (and of Rawls) and of the utilitarian theories of Jeremy Bentham or John Stuart Mill. He reproaches them for not paying sufficient attention to the *strategic* thinking all real-life people employ when choosing between different options in which they have a mutual stake. He also contends that previous thinkers could not have known what evolutionary psychology teaches us about the critical significance of *fairness* in our social impulses.

Binmore concludes from this evidence that most people are unlikely to act as pure altruists, but neither are they myopically selfish. They expect to be treated *fairly* by others and know that the same is expected from them. Reciprocity provides the mechanism that bridges self-preservation and other-regarding dispositions. It is indeed the focal point of a rapidly growing literature at the crossroads of social psychology, behavioural economics, and moral philosophy.[16]

This is not to deny that a casual survey of current affairs would provide many examples of callous disregard for human rights or rampant corruption. But the point here is that it would be a mistake to take this as a reason for modelling strategic interactions among the members of reasonably well functioning societies as being predisposed to violate social norms and institutional rules – rules that are in fact the outcome of previous trade-offs and rational bargaining, as David Hume famously argued. Binmore concludes that it is therefore not necessary to situate ghostly creatures behind a Rawlsian veil of ignorance in order to draft a new social contract because most citizens of liberal democracies interested in perfecting their institutions can be expected to bargain fairly and to enter into reciprocal commitments. But to maximize the chances of success for achieving such a project, he recommends a decentralized, bottom-up process of debate, experimentation, and learning. I would suggest that this recommendation is very apt when it comes to the increasingly popular idea of replacing some aspects of the welfare state with a guaranteed minimum income.

A similar emphasis on the local – indeed, in her case, the personal – context of efforts aimed at achieving justice can also be found in Ruth Lane's creative synthesis (2007) of Thomas Schelling's unorthodox take on game theory and approaches usually thought to be at the postmodern end of the epistemological spectrum. She argues that there are many important aspects of our lives that traditional state institutions cannot, and indeed should not, control or even attempt to improve. Individuals ought to be responsible for their actions – something she calls "self-government" (as in government of the self) but since we are immersed in a web of social relations, we must engage with others in achieving our goals, sometimes in conflictual, sometimes in cooperative ways. She claims that Schelling's demonstration of how social psychology can guide the judicious application of game-theoretic concepts, together with Ludwig Wittgenstein's existential "language games" and Michel Foucault's micropolitics, provide tools for better understanding the challenges individuals face in playing "the game of justice."[17] Strategy is not about winning at all costs but about choosing worthy friends and allies, knowing when to defend one's values and when to concede defeat, and being attentive to opportunities to engage with others in changing the parameters of the game.

All in all, game theory has served as a catalyst for transforming some of the most cherished verities in a number of disciplines. And far from imprisoning the social sciences in the straitjacket of conventional economic reasoning, it has opened up new vistas that social scientists – including economists themselves – have only begun to appreciate. In a nutshell, game theory has undermined the grip that the notions of rationality and self-interest had on classical economic thinking. On the other hand, it has served to remind social scientists in other disciplines of the risks that they run when they fail to ask which incentives and motivations are at play in any political situation.

Nothing Is Left Unchanged

The previous section hints at several ways in which game theory has played a disruptive role. In this section, I take stock of these developments and underline the extent to which game theory has emerged as a rich and complex analytical method that defies any simple depiction or ideological pigeonholing. Briefly:

- Game theory has been instrumental in bringing the problem of asymmetric information to the attention of economists, thereby opening new avenues of research on auctions design, competitive pricing, labour contracts, and so on. Conversely, it has stimulated an interest in "mechanism design" as a way of proposing institutional reforms for dealing with some of these issues.
- The realization that a Nash equilibrium is not always attainable has deepened our understanding of the complexity of social dilemmas in which possibilities for misunderstandings, failure to read "signals," and so on, abound.[18] Hence the importance of understanding what players believe, and how these beliefs may result in seemingly irrational moves on their part (which is the sort of problem that epistemic game theory tackles).
- Evolutionary game theory has been a catalyst for rethinking the meaning of rationality and for relaxing the assumption of methodological individualism. In this context, competition takes place among impersonal strategies rather than among self-interested individuals; these strategies can be likened to the institutional rules and cultural values that promote (or hinder) economic growth, social cooperation, trust, and so on. And these

strategies explain, at least in part, the differences in well-being and political stability among societies across time and space.
* Experimental methods have highlighted the importance of norms of fairness in the representations that agents make of the world they live in.

Recent trends in applying game-theoretic concepts to the "real world" of markets, political institutions, and even ecological systems show the extent to which the theory has moved in new directions. Contrary to received ideas, game theory in conjunction with social psychology and evolutionary biology has undermined the all too glib image of *homo economicus*. Today, game theory has become an umbrella under which diverse research programs coexist in a way that makes it difficult for the epistemologist to characterize it in a succinct manner without adding a string of qualifiers!

Conclusion: What Is Game Theory Good for, after All?

To recap, I have argued that game theory is multifaceted; it is compatible with a multiplicity of research programs. Scholars who value intellectual pluralism in research and policy debates, therefore, should welcome further progress in the exploration of the potentials inherent in the paradigmatic notions of non-cooperative and cooperative games.

But what about *practical* politics? Could Amadae (2016) be right in arguing that game theory has helped to legitimize a Darwinian view of competition in markets and electoral politics? Is it really part and parcel of a plan to undermine social policies aimed at promoting the common good? Has the "new political economy" discarded the harm principle upon which older forms of liberalism rested? As Sandra Peart and Daniel Levy (2005) have argued, political economy took a wrong turn long before the emergence of game theory, when the marginalist revolution discarded the Smithian notion of "sympathy." As I argued above, these accusations are in part disproved by advances in theoretical game theory. But could they be right about a vulgate of game theory that political strategists in government and political parties would eagerly apply? Is the climate of cynicism that prevails among voters not justified in part by the actual behaviour of partisan advisers for whom winning is the only goal?

In trying to answer such questions, one has to keep in mind that little is known about the extent to which the reasoning of the political "elites" have been directly or indirectly informed by game theory. While Amadae (2016) raises a barrage of criticism along these lines, her assertion that game theory is to blame for the ills of political institutions in Western democracies is just that – an assertion. The pathologies I have just alluded to are real, but finding the smoking gun that directly implicates game theory itself is a challenge that Amadae fails to meet.

I suggest that further investigation of this matter would have to proceed along two paths. The first involves an empirical problem: to what extent are the concepts and methods synonymous with game theory's actually being used to model the choices confronting policy makers, and to what extent are practical recommendations deduced from such models by policy analysts, party strategists, and so on? As far as policy making is concerned, there is good evidence that game theory is being used in some policy domains, such as the design of auctions for allocating common pool resources (Binmore and Klemperer 2002). On political decision making, the literature is slim (but see Mulé 2001) or more anecdotal than systematic (e.g., Bueno de Mesquita 2009), but future research may help fill this gap.

The other path is more challenging. It concerns the extent to which game-theoretic notions have penetrated the interpretive frameworks within which the political "elites" operate. Whatever can be written on this issue is necessarily somewhat speculative, therefore the view I am about to offer must be taken with the proverbial grain of salt. As far as speculative reflections go, Amadae's critique is worth pondering. Following up on her denunciation of the displacement of the "no harm principle" of Millian liberalism (Amadae 2016, 59) by the logic of "the end justifies the means," I concede that strategic thinking may have pushed the policy-making elites of Western democracies into a trap of this sort. In a world where feasible options are hedged on all sides by overlapping and reinforcing economic, social, and environmental constraints, they may have become convinced that the complex trade-offs they work out are the "best responses" to the moves they expect their domestic or foreign competitors to make.[19] Consequently, those who disagree with them can only have "irrational" objections that can be justifiably ignored. Neoliberalism is itself a way of making sense of the diminishing policy capacity of large centralized state institutions.

But it is not necessary to invoke neoliberalism to suppose that that the ruling elites operating within these institutions feel that those who are too ill informed to fathom the complexity of the games being played are not entitled to have their say in the matter. Centre-left parties do not seem to operate very differently in that respect. Unfortunately, this is just the kind of politics that "irrational voters" who do not benefit from globalization (Kaplan 2007), or who have not had the opportunity to pursue a college degree, or who see no need for multiculturalism in the rural communities where they live, and so on, find alienating. As is all too obvious, populist demagogues have found a way to capitalize on these frustrations.

The remedy is not to discard game theory altogether. The onus is on researchers who have pushed game theory in new directions to voice their concerns about such misinterpretations. They can remind us, for example, that experimental game theory shows that most people are guided by a sense of fairness, and that although self-interest is a powerful motivation, in most cases our "selves" turn out to be moderately altruistic. Or they can stress that the point about the Nash equilibrium is not that the "solutions" to social conflicts are preordained but that we may end "in a bad place" if we neglect to pay sufficient attention to institutional reforms that nudge preferences in the direction of acceptable social norms. That ought to be the contribution of game theory to liberal democratic practices. Far from being the vector for a coherent reductionist ideology, game theory can be used creatively to unravel many dogmas about politics and economics.

Notes

1 Paul Erickson (2015, 1), for his part, situates game theory "at the heart" of "a great sequence of debates, now lingering in their seventh decade, about the prospect for building a mathematical theory of rational decision-making that might not only revolutionize the study of human behaviour and social interaction, but that had the potential to rationalize decision-making in every area of human affairs."

2 In doing so, Zermelo set himself in opposition to what was probably the dominant hypothesis among philosophers and mathematicians interested in the theory of games, namely, that games are not reducible to pure mathematics because the psychology of the players in large measure explains the outcome. This position was advanced by the chess master and dilettante philosopher Emanuel Lasker with respect to chess, and the French mathematician Emile Borel with respect to card games. It is interesting to note that today the behavioural approach to game theory is rediscovering the importance of psychology.

3 In 1953, the French mathematician Maurice Fréchet tried to downplay the role played by von Neumann in pioneering game theory by insisting that Emile Borel had actually paved the way for him by introducing the contrast between pure and mixed strategies. In his reply, von Neumann (1953) insisted that when he wrote his 1928 paper he had not read Borel's 1921 paper. Moreover, von Neumann remarked that in that paper, Borel suggested that there may not be an equilibrium in a zero-sum game, whereas, of course, the minimax theorem proves the existence of such an equilibrium.

4 Mayer is rarely mentioned by Austrian economists; in fact, Friedrich Hayek dismissed him as a rather insignificant scholar, largely due to Mayer's rallying to the Nazis when they took power in 1938 and helping them to purge Jews and liberals from his department. And when the Soviets took over in 1945, he managed to keep his position. But, as Leonard (2010, 83–88) argues on the basis of a close reading of

his writings on economic theory, Mayer's views of market processes were not very different from those of Hayek and Mises.

5 Some authors prefer to write "prisoners' dilemma."

6 For a biting critique of this development, see McCloskey 2002.

7 All zero-sum equilibria have the same value but this is not the case in non–zero-sum games.

8 There is insufficient space here, however, to discuss the intriguing epistemological questions raised by the method of backward induction used to identify subgame perfect equilibria.

9 In a nutshell, Bayesian statistics is a method for estimating the credibility of an initial hypothesis in light of new evidence (e.g., if the probability associated with an alternative hypothesis becomes greater than that of the original hypothesis, then it makes sense to revise one's initial beliefs).

10 Needless to say, the point of this chapter is precisely that this is a superficial perception.

11 Textbooks about game theory for political scientists have become more and more mathematically sophisticated; compare in that respect Riker and Ordeshook 1973, Morrow 1995, and McCarty and Meirowitz 2007.

12 Articles on this and comparable subjects are not difficult to find in journals such as the *American Political Science Review* or the *Journal of Politics*.

13 Thomas Schelling ([1966] 2008) opened a pathway; for another example of early work in this field, see Snyder 1971.

14 One of the most often addressed questions is the extent to which the Kennedy administration and the Soviet leadership were involved in a game of chicken. For an overview, see Zagare 2014.

15 For a survey of the methodological issues at stake in this regard, see Morton 1999.

16 There is insufficient space here to cite all the relevant contributions, but see Bowles and Gintis 2002 for a short summary.

17 A willingness to debate critical theorists is also apparent in papers by Johnson (1991), Landa and Meirowitz (2009), and Saunders (2012).

18 Even in the case of repeated games, one cannot rule out the possibility that "some player never learns to predict his opponent's behavior" (Foster and Young 2001, 12850).

19 To name just a few constraints: massive public debts, sluggish economic growth, the aftermaths of the Great Recession, vast planetary movements of population, climate change, and so on.

References
Amadae, Sonja M. 2016. *Prisoners of Reason: Game Theory and Neoliberal Political Economy*. New York: Cambridge University Press.

Aumann, R. 2002. "Game Theory in the Talmud." *Research Bulletin Series on Jewish Law* (June 2002): 1–12.

Binmore, Ken. 2005. *Natural Justice*. Oxford: Oxford University Press.

Binmore, Ken, and Paul Klemperer. 2002. "The Biggest Auction Ever: The Sale of the 3G British Telecom Licenses." *Economic Journal* 112 (478): C74–C96.

Bowles, Samuel, and Herbert Gintis. 2002. "Homo Reciprocans." *Nature* 415 (10): 125–28.

Brams, Stephen J. 2011. *Game Theory and the Humanities: Bridging Two Worlds.* Cambridge, MA: MIT Press.

Bueno de Mesquita, Bruce. 2009. *Predictioneer: One Who Uses Maths, Science and the Logic of Brazen Self-Interest to Predict the Future.* London: Bodley Head.

Cachanosky, Nicolas. 2010. "Spontaneous Orders and Game Theory: A Comparative Conceptual Analysis." *Revista de Instituciones, Ideas y Mercados* 52: 52–88.

Chwe, Michael. 2013. *Jane Austen: Game Theorist.* Princeton, NJ: Princeton University Press.

Cournot, Augustin (1838) 1897. *Research Notes into the Mathematical Principles of the Theory of Wealth*, trans. N.T. Bacon. London: Macmillan.

Dekel, Eddie, and Marciano Siniscalchi. 2015. "Epistemic Game Theory." In *Handbook of Game Theory with Economic Applications*, volume 4, ed. P. Yoing and S. Zamir, 619–702. Amsterdam: Elsevier.

Dimand, Mary Ann, and Robert W. Dimand. 2002. *A History of Game Theory: From the Beginning to 1945.* London: Routledge.

Downs, Anthony. 1957. *An Economic Theory of Democracy.* New York: Harper.

Dufwenberg, Martin. 2010. "Game Theory." *Wiley Interdisciplinary Reviews: Cognitive Science* 2 (2): 167–73.

Elster, Jon. 2008. "When the Lottery Is Fairer than Rational Choice." Ideas.net, http://www.booksandideas.net/When-the-lottery-is-fairer-than.html.

Erickson, Paul. 2015. *The World the Game Theorists Made.* Chicago: University of Chicago Press.

Ferreiros, Jose. 2016. "The Early Development of Set Theory." In *Stanford Encyclopedia of Philosophy* (Fall 2016 Edition), ed. E.N. Zalta. https://plato.stanford.edu/entries/settheory-early/.

Foster, Dean P., and H. Peyton Young. 2001. "On the Impossibility of Predicting the Behavior of Rational Agents." *Proceedings of the National Academy of Sciences* 98 (22): 12848–53.

Giocoli, Nicola. 2003. *Modeling Rational Agents: From Interwar Economics to Early Modern Game Theory.* Cheltenham, UK: Edward Elgar.

–. 2009. "Three Alternative (?) Stories on the late 20th-Century Rise of Game Theory." *Studi e Note di Economia* 14 (2): 187–210.

Green, Ian, and Donald P. Shapiro. 1994. *Pathologies of Rational Choice Theory: A Critique of Applications in Political Science.* New Haven, CT: Yale University Press.

Johnson, James. 1991. "Habermas on Strategic and Communicative Action." *Political Theory* 19 (2): 181–201.

Kaplan, Bryan. 2007. *The Myth of the Rational Voter: Why Democracies Choose Bad Policies.* Princeton, NJ: Princeton University Press.

Landa, Dimitri, and Adam Meirowitz. 2009. "Game Theory, Information, and Deliberative Democracy." *American Political Science Review* 53 (2): 427–44.

Lane, Ruth. 2007. *The Game of Justice: A Theory of Individual Self-Government.* Albany, NY: SUNY Press.

Leonard, Robert. 1995. "From Parlor Games to Social Science: Von Neumann, Morgenstern, and the Creation of Game Theory 1928–1944." *Journal of Economic Literature* 33 (2): 730–61.

–. 2008. "Origins of Game Theory in Economics." In *New Palgrave Dictionary of Economics*, Second Edition, Vol. 3, ed. S.N. Durlauf and L.E. Blume, 562–67. Basingstoke, UK: Palgrave Macmillan.

–. 2010. *Von Neumann, Morgenstern, and the Creation of Game Theory: From Chess to Social Science, 1900–1960*. Cambridge: Cambridge University Press.

Maschler, Michael, Eilon Solan, and Shmuel Zamir. 2013. *Game Theory*. New York: Cambridge University Press.

McCarty, Nolan, and Adam Meirowitz. 2007. *Political Game Theory*. New York: Cambridge University Press.

McCloskey, Deirdre. 2002. *The Secret Sins of Economics*. Chicago: Prickly Paradigm Press.

Morgenstern, Oskar. 1937. *The Limits of Economics*, trans. V. Smith. London: William Hodge and Company.

Morrow, James D. 1995. *Game Theory for Political Scientists*. Princeton, NJ: Princeton University Press.

Morton, Rebecca C. 1999. *Methods and Models: A Guide to the Empirical Analysis of Formal Models*. Cambridge: Cambridge University Press.

Mulé, Rosa. 2001. *Political Parties, Games and Redistribution*. Cambridge: Cambridge University Press.

Munck, Gerardo. 2001. "Game Theory and Comparative Politics: New Perspectives and Old Concerns." *World Politics* 53: 173–204.

Nash, John. 1951. "Non-Cooperative Games." *Annals of Mathematics* 54 (2): 286–95.

Peart, Sandra, and David M. Levy. 2005. *The Vanity of the Philosopher: From Equality to Hierarchy in Postclassical Economics*. London: Routledge.

Perea, Andrés. 2014. "From Classical to Epistemic Game Theory." *International Game Theory Review* 16 (1): 144001 (22 pages). DOI: 10.1142/S0219198914400015.

Riker, William. 1962. *The Theory of Political Coalitions*. New Haven, CT: Yale University Press.

Riker, William, and Peter C. Ordeshook. 1973. *An Introduction to Positive Political Theory*. Englewood Cliffs, NJ: Prentice Hall.

Saunders, Ben. 2012. "Democratic Politics between the Market and the Forum." *Political Studies Review* 10: 23–35.

Schelling, Thomas C. (1966) 2008. *Arms and Influence*. New Haven, CT: Yale University Press.

Schwartz-Shea, Peregrine. 2002. "Theorizing Gender for Experimental Game Theory: Experiments with 'Sex Status' and 'Merit Status' in Experimental Games." *Sex Roles* 47 (7/8): 301–19.

Skyrms, Brian. 2004. *The Stag Hunt and the Evolution of Social Structure*. Cambridge: Cambridge University Press.

Smith, John Maynard. 1982. *Evolution and the Theory of Games*. Cambridge: Cambridge University Press

Snyder, Glenn. 1971. "'Prisoner's Dilemma' and 'Chicken': Models in International Politics." *International Studies Quarterly* 15 (1): 66–103.

Vanderschraaf, Peter. 1998. "The Informal Game Theory in Hume's Account of Convention." *Economics and Philosophy* 14: 215–47.

Von Neumann, John. 1953. "Communication on the Borel Notes." *Econometrica* 21 (1): 124–27.

Von Neumann, John, and Oskar Morgenstern. (1944) 2004. *The Theory of Games and Economic Behavior.* Princeton, NJ: Princeton University Press. Reprint of the 3rd edition, 1953.

Zagare, Frank C. 2014. "A Game-Theoretic History of the Cuban Missile Crisis." *Economies* 2: 20–44.

PART 2

IDEOLOGY IN THE POLITICS OF CIVIL SOCIETY

5

The Contribution of Rhetorical Analysis and Discourse Theory to the Study of Political Ideologies
The Cases of Multiculturalism and Environmentalism

IAN ANGUS

Political philosophy attempts to define the best political order for human beings without restriction. It must therefore, of necessity, give rise to the subsidiary discipline, which we might call "political theory," that is concerned with the best political order under given circumstances. For example, it may not have been good for human beings that they engaged in the domination of nature, but it is now impossible for us to think of politics as if such a historical commitment had not become a fate.

This classical distinction is perhaps most clearly drawn in the passage early in Plato's *Republic* where Socrates accedes to Glaucon's desire to investigate the luxurious city, which is the unjust city, and not the healthy city that would be the first concern of the philosopher (Plato 1997b, 372e, 1011). Investigation of the luxurious city incorporates the philosopher's judgment that the current given circumstances are unjust in a manner to be determined by the ongoing inquiry. Political theory, or what political approach is possible under such restricted unjust circumstances, is thus both distinct from political philosophy outright, or investigation of the just city, and dependent on it, since it will be shown how the current unjust circumstances result from the failure to realize philosophy, or justice. Thus, at the very beginning of philosophical reflection on politics, it is acknowledged that a pure discourse on the best regime for humans is not possible as such, that is, unaffected by the historical situation of injustice in which philosophical questioning is provoked.[1]

The study of political thought understood as the movement of political ideas among a population is distinct, at least initially, from political philosophy and political theory insofar as it is interested in the commitments that drive the actions of people involved in politics. In a certain sense, political thought is a further logical restriction not only from human universality to determinate historical circumstances but also from determinate historical circumstances to the actual play of political ideas within a given population in such circumstances. These commitments usually do not have the theoretical coherence of political philosophy, comprising more a field of concerns, attitudes, and dispositions that are brought into a defensible field-relationship in the light of the political issues posed in a given context.

With these distinctions in mind, I have previously defined political thought as follows:

> It is not about philosophical fundamentals, such as "what is the good society?" nor about specific struggles or critiques. It is an attempt to articulate some mid-level thoughts about the ethical, economic and political claims of socialism that might contribute to future debates. Also, it aims at coherence; that is to say, I don't attempt to mention everything that is important, but rather to follow out the implications of a couple of basic issues and articulate their inter-relation. In that sense, it is admittedly partial. Despite these limitations, it seems to me that contemporary attempts at coherent, if not comprehensive, socialist political thought are necessary for both a future theoretical synthesis and the sort of collations and compromises involved in a political platform. (Angus 2001b, 117–18)

Political thought is therefore a permeable domain influenced by other popular and commercial ideas, past defeats or victories, estimation of present prospects, and so forth. While influenced by powerful and authoritative ideas and their transmission by government and media, political thought is nevertheless a popular discourse permeable to outside influences that mutates over time, which can influence political institutions under certain circumstances. One major source of mutation and invention of political thought is social movements: more or less autonomous grassroots movements that propose new critical understandings of the current political situation and propose alternatives. Obvious examples are women's liberation/feminism, the LGBT movement, and the environmentalism/ecology movement. It is not too much to say that such movements represent the vibrancy of contemporary democracy versus its institutional atrophy (Angus 2001a).

Such movement-oriented vibrancy must be studied and understood in a different fashion than the history of political philosophy or institutional politics. One of its major features is the development and circulation of critical ideas within an ambit of personal commitment and urgency. In this chapter, I argue that the theoretical resources of rhetoric and discourse theory are important to understanding the workings of this domain, and rely on two major examples: multiculturalism and environmentalism. It is all too easy to forget the original vibrancy when an institutional closure has taken place, as I will argue is the case with multiculturalism. And it is always tempting to overlook the possibility of innovation in the face of new political challenges, as I will illustrate with one case of contemporary environmentalist discourse.

An Overview of Rhetoric and Discourse Analysis

In Aristotle's *Rhetoric*, rhetoric is defined in contradistinction to dialectic, or logic; dialectic is the process of discovery and presentation of truth, whereas rhetoric is concerned with persuasion. It is universal in the sense of not being bound to a definite class of objects but is oriented to action, or those things about which we deliberate – that is, persuasion is relevant to those things that we may or may not do. It is not relevant if our deliberation makes no difference to whether the things in question happen. It is, in this sense, indifferent to the question of truth. It is about how we are persuaded to act and not about whether the action is right in itself. While it may be true that humans have a natural propensity to truth, it is obvious enough that truth does not prevail by itself. One must be persuaded even to see and act upon the truth. A statement is persuasive because it persuades *someone* (Aristotle 1984, 1354a–1357a, 19–28). A classic example that illustrates this is the doctor who knows what will cure the patient; even the best doctor cannot cure a patient who refuses to take the medicine. Even when there is no doubt about the best course of action, rhetoric has a role to play. But when the best course of action is not known, or cannot be known, the role of rhetoric is greater still.

Aristotle claims that there are three kinds of persuasion: one pertaining to the personal character of the speaker, a second concerning putting the audience in a certain frame of mind, and a third directed to "the proof, or apparent proof, provided by the words of the speech itself" (Aristotle 1984, 1356a; see1358a, 25, 32) – in classical terminology, *ethos, pathos,* and *logos*. Clearly, rhetorical analysis is directed not only to the internal content of a speech but also to the situation in which the speech is made. Aristotle is, of course, thinking mainly about the oral speeches made in the public contexts that dominated ancient Greek life. It is an important moment in Plato's dialogue *Phaedrus* when Socrates catches Phaedrus hiding Lysias' written speech behind his cloak, so that they can discuss Lysias' words themselves and not Phaedrus' version of them (Plato 1997a, 228d–228e, 509). It is perhaps not too much to say that the study of rhetoric since that time has progressed more through the necessity to understand different situations of interlocutors and new media of communication than through the introduction of new types of content.

Discourse theory is a much more recent development of rhetoric that is oriented not so much to the effectiveness of particular speeches, through the metaphors that they use, for example, but to the structure of expressive forms themselves. To be sure, Aristotle had already classified persuasive speech into three kinds: forensic rhetoric deals with the past, and attempts to establish justice or injustice through the means of accusation and defence; epideictic rhetoric deals with the present and establishes honour and dishonour through praise and blame; deliberative rhetoric deals with the future in order to defend or attack a course of action through exhortation (Aristotle 1984, 1358b–1359a, 32–34). We can therefore say that the study of political thought according to Aristotle is a study of the persuasive effect of the speaker, audience, and logic in a deliberative rhetoric.

Discourse theory takes this focus on types of rhetoric further into *genres* of speech and writing. It is concerned with the structuring effect of a given *form of expression* in persuading the audience towards a given conclusion. If a film begins by panning up to a door, the door opening, the camera entering to show an empty hall, turning left and entering a room, to reveal a dead body lying on the floor, the audience immediately knows that this is a mystery genre and that the story will be successfully concluded when it is explained why that body is dead on the floor. Anything else along the way will rightly be regarded as either part of the process of discovery or as an entertaining aside not integral to the main plot. And, as has often been remarked about mysteries, they are structured by an intention to restore justice by the discovery of truth. Some very interesting stories have been told by playing with the limits of this initially simple genre with regard to the meaning and institution of justice and of truth, as well as of the process of discovery.

We are all quite competent in the rhetorical forms used in various genres of film nowadays, since film was likely the most effective and predominant medium of the twentieth century. While rhetorical analysis was initially focused on the internal character of a speech and its effectiveness as such, with the development of writing and, later, media such as television and film, it has become evident that the medium of expression itself contains certain affordances and constraints that tend towards distinct forms of persuasion. Marshall McLuhan is the most famous, but certainly not the only, significant name in this study. McLuhan's famous dictum that "the medium is the message" was intended to convey the idea that the forming character of the medium itself was what it mainly conveyed – that the structuring of human experience by a given medium was its most important social effect. I have suggested that this would be better phrased as "the message is the medium," which makes it clearer that what is conveyed is not the content but the medium itself (Angus 2000, 41–43). Taking this thought to its conclusion, one might conclude that the whole field of human experience is structured by the characteristics of, and interactions between, a plurality of media of communication – what is nowadays called a "media ecology" (Angus 2000, ch. 2; 1997, 57–68; 2005).

When a topic is of widespread public interest, there is what we may call a "field of discourse" that pertains to that topic. The borders of that field are not clearly defined; they shade off into related ideas and overlap with others. Multiculturalism, for example, is related to the issue of national identity and overlaps with that of immigration, and it does so differently in different countries based on their histories. A field of discourse is structured, at any given time and place, both by its edges, or boundaries, and internally through what I call its "axes of significance." These axes serve to uncover and structure a discursive space within which we can place different contributions to the debate. The structuring makes some things easy to say and be accepted while others are much more difficult and are often misinterpreted as versions of the easy positions. If one wants to say something that runs against the dominant structuring, one then has a motive for analyzing the structuring itself in order to open the way, make a bit easier to understand and accept, and then propose a more difficult and challenging position. Such analysis of a field of discourse is pragmatically grounded in the difference between the predominant discourse in a given time and place and the challenging contribution one wants to make. Thus, I would agree with Iris Marion Young's critique of deliberative democracy due to the vitality of greeting, rhetoric, and storytelling versus the reduction of communication to a one-dimensional rational discourse, and perhaps add that gesture and emotion are likewise significant (Young 1996).

In the discussion that follows, I aim to show how rhetoric and discourses feature in social movements, allowing their political thought to articulate and engage their activists as well as contest the political thought of their rivals. Discourse analysis will be further clarified by reference to the example of multiculturalism. In addition, discourses can overlap and there may be significant translations between them. I will illustrate this in my second example, which is drawn from the contemporary politics of the environmental movement.

Multiculturalism as a Field of Discourse
In the mid-1990s, I wanted to develop a theory of multiculturalism in the Canadian context that would challenge the hegemonic Protestant elite and not be simply a mode of liberal individualism – in other words, where ethnic identity would have *public* significance and where no identity would hold the centre (Angus 1997, ch. 6). Two ideas were dominant in the prevailing discourse.

The first idea was that ethnic identities and therefore multiculturalism were *in opposition to* national identity. This rhetorical form appeared in both academic analyses and the press. We may imagine it as a continuum with ethnic identity as one extreme and national identity at the other, so that one could approach one end only by distancing oneself from the other. The debate was structured around an alternative between identity and difference, or inclusion versus separateness. Clearly, such a phrasing made it very hard to argue for multiculturalism since it was conceptualized from the outset as divisive. Second, the most sophisticated theory of multiculturalism at the time, that of Charles Taylor, made the important breakthrough that a national identity could be characterized by a "deep diversity" such that a distinct group could belong to Canada *in a certain way* such that each would be Canadian *through* being members of their distinct communities (Taylor 1992).

While Taylor limited such deep diversity to the differences between French, English, and Aboriginal peoples, and explicitly denied it to multiculturalism in English Canada, it opened up the important idea that forms of belonging may be *on different levels of identification.* Nonetheless, Taylor's analysis carried over from hermeneutic philosophy the posing of intercultural interaction as a relationship between "us" and "them" such that there remained an implicit centring of an insider who is asked to cede some space to an outsider. In other words, it is possible for a discourse that has been criticized for excluding certain groups to include them in a restricted sense by acknowledging them in a manner that positions them as exceptions or special cases. In that way, the criticized exclusive discourse becomes more inclusive, while at the same time "centring" itself on a privileged insider. An "us" versus "them" posing of Canadian national identity contained exactly this problem that I wanted to criticize and surpass.

By pointing out and documenting these dominant ideas, the three significant structuring axes of the multiculturalist field of discourse in Canada that I called "the originality of the multicultural context" could be determined: the colonial history that was passed on to the hegemonic Anglo-Protestant elite, immigration, and the problematic character of national identity in a non-revolutionary New World state. These three axes opened the space within which the debate concerning multiculturalism took place. Most interventions could be placed as closer to one of these axes and as dealing more problematically with the other two. The two assumptions served to obscure the originality of this discursive space and thereby to reduce more complex interventions to positions determined by one of the axes.

This goes a long way towards explaining how and why interventions often talked past each other and, more importantly, towards defining what would be necessary to make a theoretical intervention that would address the nature of this space as such. I argued that ethnic and national identities must be conceptualized as pertaining to different domains of relevance such that everyone is both a member of a particular group and of an encompassing national one. Multiculturalism in this sense would be the universalization of a right to particular belonging within a pluricultural, unilingual context. Thus, an adequate response to the field of discourse as a whole would require a rethinking of the relationship between universal and particular belonging, identity and difference, and inclusion and separateness.

The point is that determining the problematic abiding assumptions in a field of debate can lead to a characterization of the field of discourse as a whole through its structuring axes, and that this characterization defines what will count as an adequate theoretical intervention. In this respect it mirrors the classic Platonic position regarding the subservience of rhetoric to philosophy: discourse analysis is motivated by a sense of the limits of current discourse, opens the space for a comprehensive analysis of the field of discourse, and terminates in a claim to truth. No one is guaranteed, of course, that the claim to truth will be accepted. As often as not, it is reduced by readers back to one of the prior insufficient positions within the field. But the presentation of the discourse analysis prior to the claim to truth aims to provide the attentive reader with a ladder out of the muddle of debate to a perspective on what structures such debates, and thereby to a claim that aims to address the whole field. Still, no one can be guaranteed attentive readers, especially in a preoccupied and impatient time (see Angus 2014 for a response to critics).

A field of discourse mutates over time due to the interventions that are made so that some interventions become classics. They become classics because a great many later interventions refer back to them and often repeat their formulations of the issue, such that subsequent reference eventually becomes near-obligatory. From our current perspective, the Multiculturalism Act (1988) is one such classic, not least because it has become law. In retrospect, we can observe three historical periods in the multiculturalist discourse. Before the act, a certain indeterminacy of language and reference prevailed such that one intervention referred to "a social philosophy for ethnicity" (Angus 1988) indiscriminately to cover government policy, social existence, politics, political theory, and philosophy, whereas later it became necessary to distinguish, at a minimum, sociological fact, government policy, and a philosophical ideal of social interaction, as well as interesting interactions between them (Angus 1997, 139). In a further development, R.J.F. Day has argued that it is characteristic of government ideology that the philosophical ideal is presented as if it were an accomplished fact (Day 2000, 6). After the Multiculturalism Act, multiculturalism came to refer primarily to government policy so that critics often ignored the wider discursive field from which the act had emerged. As it became policy, some coexistence of diversity and sameness became an accepted, mainstream part of Canadian society, and even of government legitimation, until the Conservative attack on this and other Liberal policies under the Harper regime from 2006 to 2015 (see Chapter 3).

At this point, a revised version of the original opposition between identity and difference resurfaced. A rhetoric of opposition on a continuum between multiculturalism and the nation suggested that we may have gone "too far" towards separateness. A *Globe and Mail* editorial of October 8, 2010, opined that "multiculturalism should be struck from the national vocabulary. Instead, Canada needs to refocus the debate, and have the courage to build a successful society around the concept of citizenship." Neil Bissoondath's slippery-slope argument that diversity inevitably becomes stereotyping, exoticism, and ghettoization was revived and treated as a classic statement (Bissoondath 1994, 110, 211–12).

The attack on multiculturalism is no longer limited to conservatives. Slavoj Žižek (1997) has argued that "the 'real' universality of today's globalization through the global market involves its own hegemonic fiction (or even ideal) of multiculturalist tolerance, respect and protection of human rights, democracy, and so forth." The current field of discourse comprises the traditional rhetorical continuum of opposition and also a radical rhetoric of rejection of the centring of cultural identities, which argues that multicultural inclusion is actually inclusion into a subordinate position dependent on a still privileged centring pole – whether this centring mechanism is understood to be either the state or the neoliberal economy. The critique of centring focuses on the multicultural as a quasi-official legitimating of minor identities while the centring structure is left untouched. Contemporary discourse hovers between the notions that multiculturalism is not real diversity but only a simulacrum hiding a centre, and the classic rejection of diversity for identity. A new critique and theoretical intervention would have to begin from these two assumptions.

New Alignments in Environmental Discourse

I now want to develop several other aspects of discourse theory through a focus on the contemporary instance of translation between the terms "Mother Earth," or Pachamama, and "ecology" that is, I think, of immense significance for the environmental movement. Given that a society contains an indefinite plurality of discourses that may overlap or conflict, contact and translation between discourses opens new possibilities for speech acts and may bring a new social actor into being.

Back in 1973, Arne Naess published an extremely influential paper called "The Shallow and the Deep, Long-Range Ecology Movement: A Summary," in which he argued for a "relational, total-field image" in which "organisms [are seen] as knots in the biospherical net or field of intrinsic relations" (Naess 1995, 6). Since then, the ecology movement has grown to become a permanent presence in Western debates concerning the environment. Naess was careful to point out that "insofar as ecology movements deserve our attention, they are *ecophilosophical* rather than ecological [because] ecology is a limited science which makes *use* of scientific methods" (Naess 1995, 8). The field of discourse of the environmental movement comprises three axes: ecology as a science, philosophy as a description of the human good, and a socio-political orientation that – since it was at odds with the institutional failure of state and capital to adequately represent ecological goods – became a social movement rather than a party or position. Thus, it is structured by the three axes of science, philosophy, and social movement.

In an address to the United Nations in 2007, titled "Let's Respect Our Mother Earth," President Evo Morales of Bolivia stated that indigenous people need to rediscover their roots in respect for Mother Earth, or

Pachamama, since they "have been called upon by history to convert our-selves into the vanguard of the struggle to defend nature and life" (Morales 2007). In recent years, this vanguard role has become apparent in the whole of the American continent and around the world, not least in British Columbia. It is based upon the remembering and recovery of an ancient tra-dition of place-based knowledge; the social practices that enable memory, deliberation, and action; and a political activism that spans reform of the treatment of Aboriginal people by the contemporary state to radical critique of colonialism. This field of discourse features axes of located knowledge, traditional practices, and social action.

The relations between deep ecology and indigenous renewal and defence of Mother Earth have by no means been without their conflicts. There are two reasons for this, I think. First, deep ecology begins from the inhabita-tion of humans of the whole earth and thereby tends to consider the whole earth its patrimony. This can come into conflict with the place-based knowl-edge and practice of Aboriginal claims, which suggest that not all are equally placed to appreciate what is at issue in a given locality. This is further com-plicated by the failure of the deep ecology movement to develop a critique of colonialism, and thereby too often to participate in it theoretically. Consider, for example, the 1985 influential collection *Deep Ecology: Living as if Nature Mattered*. This collection contains only one two-page section on "Primal Peoples and Deep Ecology," which ends by stating that "supporters of deep ecology do not advocate 'going back to the stone age' but seek inspiration from primal traditions" (Devall and Sessions 1985, 97). No comment is required. Thus, the two movements have proceeded for quite a while largely independently, occasionally in conflict, and at times with tactical alliances.

It seems to me that this situation has altered dramatically in approxi-mately the last decade and that the increasingly prevalent cultural transla-tion of the terms "ecology" and "Mother Earth" is both a consequence of and a motivator for the change. Further, the cultural translation is a node between two distinct discourses that is changing both and developing a new, composite social actor.

The "People's Agreement of Cochabamba" that resulted from the World Conference on Climate Change and the Rights of Mother Earth (2010) uses the term "Mother Earth" repeatedly but also refers to "capitalism" many times and once introduces the term "ecosystem" in the course of distinguish-ing between forests and monoculture, suggesting that "we require a defi-nition for negotiation purposes that recognizes the native forests, jungles and the diverse ecosystems on Earth." It has become increasingly common to see Aboriginal writers describe the place-based traditional knowledge of their people as ecosystemic. Marie Battiste and James [Sa'ke'j] Young-blood Henderson (2000, 42) define Indigeneous knowledge as "the expression of the vibrant relationships between the people, their ecosystems, and the other living beings and spirits that share their lands." Ed McGaa (2005, 130) consistently connects native knowledge to ecosystemic wisdom, in order to remind us that "when a society stops honouring the guidance of the Great Spirit, especially in ceremony, its people become excessively selfish and manipulative toward each other and Mother Earth." By suggesting that ceremony connects traditional knowledge to social practice, he shows that Western-style societies have no institution through which to mediate ecological knowledge with community action. And Linda Hogan (2009, 118) reminds us of the "spiritual fragmentation that has accompanied our ecological destruction."

Alongside the Aboriginal use of ecosystemic terminology, one can see also the increasing willingness of scientific ecologists to appreciate the pertinence of Aboriginal place-based knowledge. We may note that as far-seeing an ecologist as Stan Rowe stated in the 1990s that traditional ecological knowledge was of limited relevance because of a "fundamental cultural gap" between Aboriginal societies and Western, or settler, ones (Rowe 2006, 64).[2] But the new, third edition of the ecology textbook *Sacred Ecology* has been updated to show that "traditional knowledge as process, rather than as content, is what we should be examining. Also important is the issue of knowledge dialogue. Scholars have wasted too much time and effort on a science vs. traditional knowledge debate; we should reframe it instead as a science *and* traditional knowledge dialogue and partnership" (Berkes 2012, xxiii). As we may expect, the scientific paradigm is slow to adjust, but such an adjustment may be underway.

I am suggesting that the Aboriginal discursive space constructed by the axes of located knowledge, traditional practices, and social action has come to intersect with, and overlap, the discursive space of the ecology movement constructed by the axes of science, philosophy, and social movement. And I think we can say that the point of intersection is the cultural translation of ecosystem as Mother Earth. The ecological whole, often without Arne Naess's clear distinction between science and philosophy, is treated as equivalent to the sacred whole of Mother Earth that unifies the Aboriginal discourse. Such a translation between discourses is an example of conceptual travel, blending, and reciprocal modification that, in this specific case, amounts also to a cultural translation. It occurs through a translation that is constructed by, in the words of Ernesto Laclau and Chantal Mouffe (1985, 63), "the relation of equivalence established among them, in the context of their opposition to the dominant pole, construct[ing] a 'popular' discursive position." From this point of intersection, new issues arise that give rise to a more developed discourse and an increasingly overlapping space.

In particular, the form of knowledge in ecology can be productively compared to, and translated by, place-based Aboriginal knowledge. Of course, it remains a political question to what extent Aboriginal community action can come into productive relation with the social movement practices of the ecology movement. However, instances of productive collaboration have come into being – not least on Burnaby Mountain, where Simon Fraser University is located on the traditional territory of the Tsleil-Waututh nation, in the protest against Kinder Morgan's proposed pipeline expansion. Stephen Collis (2015, 25) has distinguished three participant groups: local residents and concerned citizens, First Nations, and environmental activists. So, we may well be witnessing the birth of a new social actor created and sustained by this intersection.

Now, I don't want to suggest that all is rosy and without conflict in this new discursive space. Aboriginal knowledge was traditionally characterized as folklore by the dominant science-based culture, and there have also been many cases of cultural appropriation of Aboriginal practices (Little Bear 2012, 519–20). But I am interested here in the possibility of a convergence and in the conditions required for it. Leroy Little Bear (2012, 526) has suggested that the storytelling of traditional Blackfoot knowledge "resonates with the definition of the 'humanities' in academia," so we may say that the first condition of a genuine cultural translation is the rejection of any assumption of primacy in one discourse over the other. As Deanna Reder (2012, 515–16) has said, "so long as one group's (one class's, one culture's, one individual's) humanity depends on the dehumanization of another's, no 'world humanity' is possible." This may be considered an advantage of a discourse-theoretical approach, insofar as all contributions are treated as stories and speech-acts; there is no assumption that one discourse is about "reality" in a manner that would discount other discourses a priori.

Therefore, the major condition for pushing ahead with this process of cultural translation is that it rejects "the colonial assumption that one discourse is the only *legitimate* basis for the adjudication of competing claims" (Angus 2008, 82). Insofar as it incorporates a critique of centralizing power, a critique of any situation in which the rules of interaction between groups, and their discourses, are monopolized by one of the groups or discourses, a cultural translation may produce a productive new discursive space for thought and action.

One of the ways in which this is being carried out is a new interrogation of the relationship between the Marxist theory of exploitation in capitalism and the colonial dispossession of peoples that creates the proletariat. Glen Coulthard (2014, 151–52) has argued that "Marx's thesis on primitive accumulation must be stripped of its rigidly *temporal* character; that is, rather than positing primitive accumulation as some historically situated, inaugural set of events that set the stage for the development of the capitalist mode of production through colonial expansion, we should see it as an ongoing practice of dispossession that never ceases to structure capitalist and colonial social relations in the present." The environmental movement was always ambivalent – or perhaps it is better to say that there were competing tendencies – on the question of capitalism. The present conjuncture opens the possibility not only of strengthening the environmentalist wing that centres on a critique of capitalism but also of radically rethinking the traditional Marxist assumptions upon which that criticism has generally depended.

Conclusion

What is at issue in the temporal and spatial mutation of political thought is not the theoretical content to which it refers, nor whether it legitimately applies an idea from the history of political philosophy and political theory, but the *cluster of ideas* that structure a discursive space framed by an ongoing social activism around a political issue. This discursive space leaves open room for various speech-acts, agreement and disagreement, internal mutation, and mutation through interaction with other discourses. There are no external rules for such mutations; they must be tracked from within the affordances and closures of the discourse itself.

The multicultural example in this chapter was intended to show how a discourse analysis could reveal dead ends in the current formulations in order to point to possible creative interventions. The Aboriginal-environmental example was meant to show how a cultural translation between discourses opens up new possibilities for both of them and for the construction of a new space; a new, composite social actor; and a rich development of thinking on its crucial themes. In my view, the motivation for using these resources for the analysis of popular political thought is to make an intervention in that thought. The theoretical resources of rhetoric and discourse theory are neither substantive nor compelling enough to orient a life or a community. They are secondary resources whose justification, in my view, is limited to the extent that they can understand creative political thought in the past and open possibilities for political intervention in the present and future.

There is thus a significant overlap between the approach that I have sketched, based upon rhetorical and discourse theory, and that which Michael Freeden (2015) calls "the morphological analysis of ideology." Both are concerned with analyzing the independent, or relatively independent, movement of political ideas in a population without reducing it, or especially declaring it incorrect, with reference to political theory or philosophy. This distinct domain of popular political ideas is what rules practical politics. It requires detailed, focused analysis on the structuring and movement of ideas, as well as correlative and clustering concepts, in order to bring out its specific features so that, unlike other approaches that attempt "to contain their importance and downgrade their intricacy by describing them as a series of simplified generalizations, often characterized by a single organizing concept, or that neglects the multitude of variants nesting under general headings," the specific historic-conceptual frame of popular political ideas comes into focus (Freeden 2015, 116–17).

Nevertheless, there is a significant disagreement concerning the purpose of this enterprise. As I have emphasized, the purpose of rhetorical and discourse analysis is to enable an *intervention* in the domain of political thought. Specifically, analysis of the *structuring* of political thought aims to allow an intervention that does not succumb to the existing structuring but purports to alter it. Such an intervention is a matter for politics, of course, and its success depends on many factors that may be estimated but not predicted. There is no category of intervention in Freeden's morphological conception, so that it must rest upon a general social-scientific justification. In his words, "the study of ideology involves decoding and interpretation, not its juxtaposition with truth" (Freeden 2015, 115). The purpose of such an activity is apparently *understanding* the movement of political ideas/ideologies in a given population. Thus, it seems to be a version of the sociology of knowledge.

It is no doubt correct that the analysis of political thought requires, in a certain sense, setting aside the question of truth, insofar as truth is associated with political theory or philosophy. Indeed, such a setting aside of truth is characteristic of the sociology of knowledge. "The morphological approach aligns itself to a methodology that obviates truth not by denying but by ignoring much of it" (Freeden 2015, 129). But, while the specificity of analysis requires setting aside the concept of truth as associated with political theory or philosophy, an *intervention* raises the question of truth again in a different manner. In my approach, the relation to truth is what *motivates the inquiry* into the structuring of political thought and *determines the form of the intervention*. So, while rhetorical and discourse analysis lets go of the question of truth in order to examine the actual structuring of political thought (as does morphological analysis), the intervention or proposal requires a claim to truth, or at least *greater* truth, in order to be meaningful. In this sense, my analysis rests on a *political* justification, not a social-scientific one. For this reason, my analysis emphasizes more the structuring of a predominant discourse rather than simply the movement and alteration of ideas, since the aim of the analysis is to unpack the sources of *stasis* in political options in order to allow an intervention that aims to shift the predominant ideas.

Such an intervention cannot be justified by the rhetorical and discourse analysis itself. Its justification thus leads towards the realms of political theory and political philosophy – understood not as a canonical history of texts but as a philosophical practice of inquiry into politics within the human condition. The pragmatic study of the structuring of political thought is handmaiden to the practice of philosophy. In that sense, I am interested in making a connection or communication between popular political thought and political theory and philosophy rather than describing a supposedly self-contained domain indifferent to the question of truth.[3] There is no domain of human experience indifferent to truth. I disagree that the analysis of political thought is an end in itself (morphology, social science) and claim that it is an aid to an intervention (politics). Thus, it is related to political theory and philosophy teleologically so that it is only a *relatively or momentarily* independent domain and not actually an independent one as morphology would have it.

Notes

1   The terminology here is not universally accepted and is based in my reading of classical political philosophy in the light of contemporary interpreters and issues. The main point marking the difference – political theory versus political philosophy – appears within philosophy as that between the current historical situation (as evaluated by the philosopher) and the human situation outright. This distinction explains why political theory within political science accepts historical specifications that philosophy does not. But while the terminology may seem to be influenced by the academic division of labour, the distinction itself is not. Most of the political philosophy that is known as such is political theory in the sense that it addresses issues not solely or primarily of the human condition as such but in a certain historical form.

Indeed, it is entirely possible that political philosophy in this strong sense of addressing the human condition as such is possible only as approached through a historical situation. This is the genius of the shift that Plato depicts in Socrates' attention to politics in *Republic*.

2 I cannot date this piece exactly since I am using a readily available reprint version, but the reference section at the end suggests that it was written in the 1990s. Unfortunately, Stan died in 2004.

3 It is for this reason that I continue to use the word "ideology" in the Marxist sense of incorrect ideas rather than as equivalent to political ideas outright, as it has been used by social scientists who are interested in the content of those ideas independently of their truth. In particular, I do not rule out the truth of Marx's analysis of the exchange of commodities containing presuppositions such that what is involved in the practice is not visible to the actors. But this does not and cannot mean that it is in principle *never* possible for them to see it. It means that they must struggle away from their "natural" preconceptions rooted in practice to see it. In that sense it is like Freud's unconscious. I understand my use of rhetoric and discourse theory in this sense.

References

Angus, Ian. 1997. *A Border Within: National Identity, Cultural Plurality, and Wilderness*. Montreal and Kingston: McGill-Queen's University Press.

–. 2000. *Primal Scenes of Communication*. Albany: State University of New York Press.

–. 2001a. *Emergent Publics: An Essay on Social Movements and Democracy*. Winnipeg: Arbeiter Ring.

–. 2001b. "Subsistence as a Social Right: A New Political Ideal for Socialism?" *Studies in Political Economy* 65: 117–35.

–. 2005. "Media, Expression and a New Politics: Eight Theses" *Media and Cultural Politics*, 1 (1): 89–92.

2008. *Identity and Justice*. Toronto: University of Toronto Press.

–. 2014. "*A Border Within*: 15 Years On." *International Journal of Canadian Studies* 50: 325–46.

Aristotle. 1984. *The Rhetoric and Poetics of Aristotle*, trans. W. Rhys Roberts. New York: Random House.

Battiste, Marie, and James [Sa'ke'j] Youngblood Henderson. 2000. *Protecting Indigenous Knowledge and Heritage: A Global Challenge*. Saskatoon: Purich Publishing.

Berkes, Fikret. 2012. *Sacred Ecology*. 3rd ed. New York and London: Routledge.

Bissoondath, Neil. 1994. *Selling Illusions: The Cult of Multiculturalism in Canada*. Harmondsworth, UK: Penguin.

Day, Richard J.F. 2000. *Multiculturalism and the History of Canadian Diversity*. Toronto: University of Toronto Press.

Devall, Bill, and George Sessions. 1985. *Deep Ecology: Living as if Nature Mattered*. Salt Lake City: Peregrine Books.

Freeden, Michael. 2015. "The Morphological Analysis of Ideology." In *The Oxford Handbook of Political Ideologies*, ed. M. Freeden, L.T. Sargeant, and M. Stears, 1–27. New York: Oxford University Press.

Hogan, L. 2009. "A Different Yield." In *Reclaiming Indigenous Voice and Vision*, ed. Marie Battiste. Vancouver: UBC Press.

Little Bear, Leroy. 2012. "Traditional Knowledge and Humanities: A Perspective by a Blackfoot." *Journal of Chinese Philosophy* 39 (4): 537–48.

McGaa, Ed. 2005. *Nature's Way: Native Wisdom for Living in Balance with the Earth.* New York: HarperCollins.

Morales. E. 2007. "Let's Respect Our Mother Earth." Address by President Evo Morales of Bolivia to the member representatives of the United Nations on the issue of the environment. September 24.

Naess, Arne. 1995. "The Shallow and the Deep, Long-Range Ecology Movement: A Summary." In *The Deep Ecology Movement,* ed. Alan Drengson and Yuichi Inoue, 3–9. Berkeley, CA: North Atlantic Books.

Plato. 1997a. *Phaedrus.* In *Plato: Complete Works,* ed. John M. Cooper. Indianapolis: Hackett Publishing.

–. 1997b. *Republic.* In *Plato: Complete Works,* ed. John M. Cooper. Indianapolis: Hackett Publishing.

Rowe, Stan. 2006. *Earth Alive: Essays on Ecology.* Edmonton: NeWest Press.

Taylor, Charles. 1992. *Multiculturalism and "the Politics of Recognition."* Princeton, NJ: Princeton University Press.

World Conference on Climate Change and the Rights of Mother Earth. 2010. "People's Agreement of Cochabamba." https://pwccc.wordpress.com/2010/04/24/peoples-agreement/.

Young, Iris Marion. 1996. "Communication and the Other: Beyond Deliberative Democracy." In *Democracy and Difference: Contesting the Boundaries of the Political,* ed. Seyla Benhabib, 120–36. Princeton, NJ: Princeton University Press.

Žižek, S. 1997. "Multiculturalism, or the Cultural Logic of Multinational Capitalism." *New Left Review* 225 (September-October): 28–51.

Mobilizing Political Strategy
The Global Practices of Taxpayer Groups

KYLE WILLMOTT

A debt clock looming under the shadow of a provincial legislature. A public relations campaign to publicize the mundane and extraordinary expenses of politicians. A push to publish the salaries of bureaucrats in a searchable online database. Each of these tactics seem standard-issue in the repertoire of Western populism. The information that flows out of these tactics allows for a very specific form of critique directed at the state and its "wards." This chapter pieces together a small part of the ideological infrastructure that exists to share, spread, and promote a form of liberal political reason executed by "taxpayer" political subjects.

As the essays in this volume collectively demonstrate, a central concern of analysts of politics must be how political reason travels, breaches jurisdictional and symbolic boundaries, and mutates in the morass of spaces and scales of political and institutional contexts. Here, I explore how the political knowledge produced and deployed by networks of taxpayer groups circulates in material space, and briefly explore the implications of this enormously mobile and malleable form of liberal political reason. The notion of a kind of vernacular "taxpayer" political reason is not new, but little empirical or theoretical work has been done on the notions of "taxpayers," "taxpayer subjects," or "taxpayer groups" (see Hall and O'Shea 2013; Hackell 2013; Björklund-Larsen 2017; Williamson 2017; Walsh 2018). Although several scholars have touched on some of the effects the "taxpayer" notion has produced, most scholarship has analyzed some of the conceptual categories that taxpayer groups inhabit or to which they are adjacent. I provide a clear and present example of the importance of examining how this political reason produces political subjects, and how this subjectivization is arranged, assembled, and organized in haphazard ways (Björklund-Larsen 2017). I identify taxpayer groups as central authors of this subject, but certainly not the only ones.

This chapter argues that taxpayer groups operate as key centres of the organization of political knowledge authored for a specific political subject, "the taxpayer." Specifically drawing upon the insights of governmentality literature (Foucault 2008; Miller and Rose 1990; Rose 1993) and policy mobilities literature (McCann and Ward 2012, 2013), I argue broadly that taxpayer groups should not be looked at specifically as objects in and of themselves or as producers of normative policy and political action, but should be analyzed as networks of knowledge production and subjectivization, organized around the problematic: how do you encourage people to reason politically as "taxpayers"? In order to carry out this analysis, I draw upon two vignettes from field work on knowledge circulation to show how strategies and concepts are mobilized, packaged for consumption, and brought into the realm of possibility for other ideologically aligned activists. Ultimately, these mobilities demonstrate how, where, and through what means that taxpayer reason circulates within a network.

What Is a "Taxpayer" Group?

Similar to think tanks and other advocacy groups with which they are organizationally similar, taxpayer groups are difficult to define through a traditional typology. The organizations that share this name perform a myriad of tasks, all of which differ across their broad geographic and scalar range. Taking them at their word, a taxpayer group is an organization that advocates for "taxpayers." Unfortunately, this definition only raises a basic prior question, namely, who counts as a taxpayer? In parsing the broad question of what a taxpayer group is, I am influenced by Thomas Medvetz's (2012) scholarship on think tanks and Eugene McCann and Kevin Ward's (2012) geographies of policy mobility. Medvetz (2012) approaches think tanks from a relational perspective, borrowing largely from Pierre Bourdieu. He describes two serious problems that flow from *definitionalist* approaches that attempt to delineate objects by defining their essential characteristics (e.g., which organizations can lay claim to the term "think tank"). First, he identifies the problem that not all "think tanks" will hold the exact "substantive properties" (ibid., 34). Second, he critiques definitionalism for its implicit endorsement of a specific interpretation of the terms of debate. The struggle to establish a definition enters into the debate that abounds within the social space of think tanks. In short, the definitional work that goes into claiming a concept or an association with a concept is contested – when scholars accept one of these accounts, they become conceptually devoted to that definition: staking a claim within the field might mean that the boundary work, the internecine struggle, and the travel of ideas, notions, and tactics within this field or network are ignored. Geographers McCann and Ward (2012, 327) offer a similar methodological warning, arguing that "overly prescriptive models and definitions of what is or what is not ... allow the models and typologies themselves to be reified, becoming the objects of debate rather than facilitating analyses."

The traditional conception of taxpayer groups is aligned with the notion of "the taxpayer" as an inherently neutral subject, as a collective of righteously involved citizens, and as a genuine expression of democratic mobilization against recalcitrant elites or governments. Camille Walsh (2018) has shown how taxpayer as a political identity became historically linked with racial ideas of worth and legitimate citizenship during debates around education and racial segregation in the United States. Vanessa Williamson's (2017) work has also built on the idea of the taxpayer as a symbolic identity that simultaneously produces civic pride feelings of responsibility, but also creates an imagined out-group of "non-taxpayers," which in different contexts includes people of colour (Walsh 2018), Indigenous people (Henderson 2015), and poor people (Williamson 2017).

Isaac William Martin (2013) contends that, historically speaking, certain taxpayer groups have been institutionally aligned with capitalists. Taxpayer groups such as the American Taxpayer Association and many local taxpayer leagues populate a historical register of activist groups that Martin (2013) contends work towards increased income inequality through the pursuit of public policies. Martin's work begins to show how anti-tax activism coordinated by businesses, capitalists, and their benefactors linked their demands with more populist notions of tax politics, to the point where all anti-tax politics are conceived of as populist, broad-based, and in defence of vulnerable taxpayers.

Rather than parsing whether taxpayer groups are fundamentally benevolent defenders of government accountability or are simply "astroturfing" elites, I understand taxpayer groups as a performative network of organizing political action and knowledge mobilization. They should be viewed as bundles of relations and practices that have come to populate a highly specific genre of political organization. They operate as a network of institutions, like think tanks, business/industry interest groups, and others, while simultaneously building and managing this network by facilitating the assemblage of a political subjectivity that I call the taxpayer subjectivity (Björklund-Larsen 2017). It is especially important to describe the *practices* associated with taxpayer groups in order to facilitate analysis of their *effects*.

Typically, most of these groups perform "advocacy" for "taxpayers" by meeting and pressuring parties, politicians, bureaucrats, and other state power brokers. Many groups coordinate with ideologically similar organizations, such as business lobbyists, industry advocates, and industry issue groups (Pridgen and Flesher 2013; Martin 2013). From my own field work and analysis of organizational literature and websites, I have found that many others do much of their coordinating work with the intellectual nuclei of liberalism, such as think tanks, economic institutes, and other forums for liberal economic philosophy. However, most do public political work not through the traditional or formal means of policy formulation but through public awareness campaigns, through anti-state, anti-tax/spending crusades, and through the publication and publicizing of specific forms of knowledge about the state (e.g., publishing, editorializing, or pushing for disclosure of public sector salaries), about state fiscal practices (e.g., budget "improprieties" such as deficits, misdirected funds, and so on), or about the conduct of those who control state fiscal practices (e.g., exposing expenses of bureaucrats or politicians) or who are "supported" by state expenditure (groups typically imagined as morally unworthy, such as welfare recipients or Indigenous people).

While such campaigns are strategically chosen and timed, at an aggregate level they are marked by a kind of atemporal permanence, in the sense that these practices do not have any necessary immediate relationship with the effects they might produce; campaigns of critique are always regenerated. These are relatively unique practices that involve coordination across the network, drawing on academic research, public relations and advertising, journalism, and activism, all of which work to produce knowledge and evidence that goes into these "everyday" campaigns. All of these practices are important for maintaining the network: meeting, debating, fundraising, consulting, and learning. These practices internal to the network are integral to producing political effects. The production of evidence is a constant process involving dredging, extrapolating, and circulating figures, statistics, and stories about putatively objective representations of government excess and the positive impacts of tax reductions and restrained government. Most

important of these effects is the nudging of citizens to think about government and politics with the set of evidence the campaigns and organizations
produce – and to empower *taxpayers* to act on government and politics in
a very particular way *with* this evidence.

There are dozens of taxpayer groups stretching across the globe. Most
"developed" countries have a national taxpayer group that primarily speaks
to the concerns of the aforementioned fictive taxpayer within their national
boundaries. Many US states, cities, and counties have their own taxpayer
organizations that speak to the interests of whichever rung of taxpayer
interests they claim to represent. Typically, organizations at lower orders
of government – especially municipal – are less well organized, less professional, and often disconnected from the national and international groups.
National and state/province-level organizations typically have more stable
access to funds, meaning they can sustain their activity; they also benefit
from broader geographic mandates, which widens their field of vision and
expands the fields in which they can claim a legitimate interest to operate.

Mobilities of Political Reason

The intervention of geographers in debates about what had traditionally
been called policy transfer has been marked by a fundamental methodological reconfiguration of what it means to study policy – broadly defined – and
its movement. Several of these scholars, such as McCann and Ward, have
argued for a different approach to the study of policy movement, conceived
of as policy *mobilities* rather than policy *transfer*. They offer a number of
critiques of existing policy transfer literature (cf. Benson and Jordan 2011,
2012): that it is too concerned with typologies rather than the exploration of
practices, that it is methodologically nationalist (Wimmer and Glick Schiller 2002), and that it is centred on formal state institutions (McCann 2011;
McCann and Ward 2012, 2013).

The broadly social constructivist and post-structuralist lens of the policy mobilities approach identifies "policies" as in-process *assemblages* of
knowledge, interacted with by irrational agents with imperfect information.
The research agenda that has flowed from these broad critiques builds on
a number of strands of the sociological (Urry 2000; Sheller and Urry 2006),
anthropological (Marcus 1995), and geographic (Peck and Theodore 2001)
literatures. The opposition to what Mimi Sheller and John Urry (2006, 211)
call "sedentarist" social science has spurred scholarship that has eschewed
stasis, stability, and placelessness. McCann and Ward (2013, 9) sum up the
contributions of this varied approach by describing mobility as a "complex,

power-laden process, rather than a straightforward a-to-b movement. It is one that involves a wide range of practices and sites. It is about fluidity, mobilisation and deterritorialisation, but, necessarily also about 'moorings,' stabilities and territorialisations."

This chapter is indebted to the methodological framework of policy mobilities scholars. In analyzing how political knowledge is mobilized, how it mutates, where it moves, and through which practices it is moved, the chapter looks less at substantive instances of policy knowledge frameworks – such as Business Improvement Districts (Cook and Ward 2012) – but more at how strategic knowledge circulates in a network of advocacy groups. The methodological lessons of mobilities scholars have informed how I have conceived of the object of this chapter. In accordance with that paradigm, I position policy as active, mobile, fraught assemblages, and circulations of knowledge. A similar theme is found throughout this volume, which challenges scholars to think about ideologies and concepts less as things in and of themselves and more as products of contestation, movement, and tenuous strategic affinities.

Governmentality and Strategies of Liberal Government

The contributions of both geographic and sociological mobilities literatures dovetail well with the second key analytic that undergirds this chapter, Foucauldian-inflected "governmentality studies." This "analytic of government" challenges the centrality and stability of the state as the answer to questions of the exercise of political sovereignty. For scholars working with this suite of concepts, the state is conceived of as a diffuse field of action and as an effect of power, rather than as a sovereign entity that exercises power at will. As Michel Foucault (2006, 16) suggests, thinking of the state as a universal "thing" is "much too broad, much too abstract to designate these immediate, tiny, capillary powers that are exerted on the body, behavior, actions, and time of individuals."

One of the main contributions of this conceptualization is the location of key sources of power, authority, and contestation outside the state, not just inside the state. For scholars of governmentality, the work of centring *government* outside the state means that the governing of human conduct is complex, and can be understood through Foucault's conception of power as a diffuse, strategic relation rather than a substance wielded by "big" institutions. I have used these Foucauldian analytical precepts to conceptualize how forms of political knowledge and discursive strategies are assembled through complex and multivalent processes, and what political subjectivities these discursive strategies are aimed at conducting. How do these strategies move? How do these forms of political knowledge travel? How are subjects constituted in dissimilar political spaces? How is liberal political reason such an effective and mobile "technology" (to use Foucault's term) of government?

These broad questions wed these two literatures of policy mobilities and governmentality. The literatures complement one another by sharing a focus on (1) the multiplicity of political practices that constitute the exercise of power, (2) the in-built method of paying close attention to the assembling of concepts rather than accepting them as real, and (3) a very general focus on the importance of the discursive politics of knowledge. Some prominent Foucault scholars have recently pushed back on an overextension of what they call "statephobia" present in governmentality studies (Dean and Villadsen 2016), but there is still a very productive research program to be located outside of the state.

The aforementioned body of scholarship relies on an ostensibly imprecise definition of liberalism. For scholars drawing on Foucault, this is a strategic analytical imperative rather than a weakness in operationalization. Rather than attach my research object (critique of government) to a specific strand of liberalism, such as neoliberalism, I argue, in line with Foucault scholars like Mitchell Dean (2010), Nikolas Rose (1993, 1996), and Graham Burchell (1996), that liberalism need not necessarily be approached as a coherent ideology or a positive pronunciation about what should be. This analytical approach grew out of Foucault's lectures on governmentality, whereas Gane (2008) points out that Foucault's analysis of liberalism began through the schematizing of the classical liberalism of the eighteenth century.

In this rendering, liberalism is not a conceived as a "philosophy based on the 'rule of law' and the protection of individual rights and freedom against the unnecessary encroachments of the state" (Dean 2010, 61), nor is it to be taken as a "theory, an ideology, a juridical philosophy of individual freedom, or any particular set of policies adopted by a government" (Burchell 1996, 21). Instead, I approach liberalism as a rationality of rule with a central characteristic: critique of the exercise of state power or state-centric models of sovereignty (Rose 1993; Dean 2010). Because my research focuses on this very *practice* of critique of government, I point out that it is necessary to align my own work with the strategic choice of a nebulous liberalism that other governmentality scholars have preferred to use. As I point out later in this chapter, taxpayer governmentality can be used to govern to a number of ends, and is "enacted" through a number of tactics, none of which have been inscribed with a specific variant of liberalism. Empirical specificity might change this argument.

In "Rethinking Neoliberalism," Dean (2014) argues that much of the agenda attributed to neoliberalism has been inflated beyond its means; it can read as a set of outcomes, an ideology, an economic rationality, or a host of policies. Dean advocates a much narrower analysis of the term centring on the economists and philosophers who made up the thought collective that arose out of the Mont Pelerin Society. His argument leads away from neoliberalism as adjective to neoliberalism as a description of a highly specific movement of economic thought: "we should restrict the use of the adjective "neoliberal" to a certain regime of government and not to a specific form of state itself" (ibid., 7).

Dean's argument is about the need for specificity and for a more focused analytical use of neoliberalism as an intellectual project. The organizations I look at in this chapter can be described as neoliberal in ideological disposition; the very network that makes these organizations hum is linked clearly with a host of neoliberal think tanks that advocate quite specifically for the forms of economic thought born of the Mont Pelerin Society. But I wish to stress that I am not focusing my analysis on these organizations' ideological dispositions; rather, I am empirically examining their strategies, which are much less specific and much more broadly liberal in the sense I described earlier.

At what point does the taxpayer rationality *become* neoliberal? Is it in its rhetoric? In and through policies? In the subjects it interpellates? Or is it through the outcomes it could be said to produce? In avoiding the term "neoliberal," I am avoiding inscription of an essential "form" of "the taxpayer" subject. Beyond critique of state reason, and "defining the limitation of governmental practices" (Foucault 2008, 21), there is little that unites "the taxpayer" as a subject beyond the many cases where it emerges, as I have explored in previous research (Willmott 2017; forthcoming).

I argue that taxpayer governmentality directs its subjects towards the practical governing of the political self in relation to the state. To think about politics as a taxpayer is to think about oneself in alignment with liberal notions of rational governmental political-economic conduct, which I outline below. Taxpayers govern their own political conduct in the space of liberal critique of the acceptable shape and scope of governments; thinking within this space, taxpayers become governable in accord with a liberal telos of government – that government must be limited and restrained (Lemke 2001; Miller and O'Leary 1987; Miller 2001; Foucault 2008). This form of governmentality is premised upon a depiction of the state that flows from critique of excessive governing or expansion of the purview of the state (Foucault 2008). Taxpayer governmentality does the work of liberal critique of government by harnessing a practical vernacular that allows its subjects to capture the state, read it through the logics of the market, and produce local symbolic critiques of the state's ineffectiveness, its feebleness, and, somewhat paradoxically, its ravenous will to expand, expropriate, and interfere.

Taxpayer governmentality shapes political self, allowing subjects to think as *homo economicus* in relation to questions of state conducts (Dean and Villadsen 2016). To think with a collection of evidence, and to grapple with the ethical quandaries posed by this evidence, enables a number of questions to be asked of one's own political conduct and especially of the political conduct of others. What are the limitations of government? What can be asked of "taxpayers"? Under what conditions are extraction and expenditure just? What political demands are reasonable, and who has the moral integrity to make political demands? In taxpayer reason, these questions of politics, government, and the role of the state become symbolically limited to questions of the putative fiscal capacity of the state, intricately linked with the morality of the capacity and willingness of the apolitical "taxpayer."

Nikolas Rose (1999) suggests that the creation of scales of evaluation and judgability is key to the operation of liberal political reason. This judgability, he suggests, allows scepticism to be positively applied to programs of government (ibid., 197). Of liberalism, Rose asserts a need for a calculatory citizenry, whose lives, "commerce," and politics are subject to the ethic of calculation. He introduces the concept of a "public habitat of numbers" that helps to furnish political spaces as calculatory, expert-driven, and consumed with valuation based on a specific understanding of notions of budget, efficiency, and value. When figures of and about the state and its branches are assembled, each with its symbolic weight, they become part of this habitat. These numbers and stories about numbers are drawn upon by discerning and calculating taxpayers and ultimately structure how they think and act on questions of the government's size, scope, and reach. The habitat of numbers and stories about numbers helps to constitute political subjects. Taxpayer groups, I argue, are key centres that do organizational work in furnishing this habitat. The strategies, tactics, and institutional work that is done to "equip" the habitat comes out of key moments of collaboration and convergence. A key site where this comes together is conferences.

Circulations of Taxpayer Reason

Several tactics have become commonplace among taxpayer groups; most of these tactics circulate within the network of politically aligned groups that collaborate with taxpayer groups. The network in effect furnishes taxpayer groups both in terms of strategic learning of tactics and political "moves," and also helps to furnish the "public habitat of numbers" that taxpayer groups rely on for critique (Rose 1999). At a 2014 taxpayer conference I attended, to be discussed in detail below, a bevy of outside groups were active participants who ostensibly would have "nothing to do" with taxpayer "interests" or groups. Such conferences are not just for taxpayer groups; they are the circulatory space in which taxpayer interests are actively woven together through the fusion of other interests, values, and ideas. The collaborations that occur between groups flow from the conversations that take place in this space. As Ian Cook and Kevin Ward (2012) and Cristina Temenos (2016) show in their exploration of business improvement districts and harm-reduction policies, conferences are one of the places where policy (broadly conceived as political knowledge) is made mobile and is mutated, and are often sites where policy repertoires are assembled. Temenos (2016, 125) positions conferences as spaces of "social reproduction" for political and policy movements. As "fleeting" spaces where actors come together to disseminate knowledge, discuss challenges and movement futures, and strengthen ties, conferences are spaces of convergence. Convergent space "facilitates the production, exchange and legitimation of knowledge, by convening people from varying interest groups and resources in a particular place at a particular time" (ibid., 128). Thinking about conferences as convergent spaces, Temenos argues that they "constitute the space of mobility within an advocacy movement. It allows the drawing together of people and resources to engage in knowledge production, exchange, planning and actions to address specific issues of contention" (ibid.). Clearly, these spaces do more than draw people together – they help to assemble entire repertoires of action into coherent strategies. While these spaces do not necessarily show the exact movement or successful adoption of policies or ideas, they are capable of methodologically producing the means through which policies and ideas become mobile.

In the case of taxpayer groups, the movement of political strategies occurs across national and subnational jurisdictional borders, across scales, and within political movements. I am also interested in how strategies and tactics are changed during this movement, how their focuses shift, to which contexts they are applied, and which institutions they are mobilized for or against. The work done at conferences, through educational sessions, speeches, and training, is integral to the taxpayer movement.

The conference I attended featured a number of accountability/transparency organizations dedicated to procuring or uncovering specific forms of knowledge about the conduct of governments and politicians. Many industry groups were present, including representatives from real estate, oil and gas, and business associations. Think tanks and academics had a large presence, offering analysis of how to think about the "issues" of the day. Finally, activist groups and education/leadership groups figured in the conference mostly by bringing youth to the largely older crowd. Most of the people present were involved in organizing and activism, and had professional backgrounds in business, law, policy (e.g., researchers in neoliberal think tanks), professional political advocacy (e.g., communications, political aides, employment in activist or lobbyist groups), and sometimes academia (almost uniformly economists).

The geographic distribution of these organizations was mostly but not entirely limited to the West. However, the international umbrella organization that has attempted to organize taxpayer groups on a global scale, the World Taxpayer Associations (WTA), has put significant resources into promoting the growth of taxpayer organizations in non-Western contexts. At the conference, an entire session dedicated to the operation of taxpayer organizations in "lower income countries" featured groups from Ukraine, Tanzania, and China. These groups discussed differences in strategies, and the challenges they faced operating in a space where the notion of a taxpayer as a salient political subject has comparatively little public purchase.

A series of short vignettes can shed light on how taxpayer reason circulates and how ideological strategies are readied for movement within the network of taxpayer groups. I use ethnographic observations from field work I conducted at a single conference that brought together taxpayer advocacy groups, activists, and allied political groups, business groups, and other players in the field of neoliberal and right-wing politics. Broadly construed, these groups have many divergent interests yet come together because of commonly held political affinities. The most important is the imperative notion that government must be atrophied and limited. This imperative is advanced in a number of ways, primarily through the sharing of tactics, strategies, and stories about effective political change.

Vignette One: Mashing the Beer Tax

A representative from the UK-based TaxPayers Alliance (TPA) spoke to the entire conference on its second day. Underlining the pedagogical function of this gathering, the presenter spent the allotted time extolling the TPA's campaign against a proposed tax on alcoholic beverages, which was cleverly cast as "the beer tax." The presenter explained that it was an easy strategic decision to pursue the campaign because of the tangle of symbols involved: beer, pubs, and the working class. He encouraged other taxpayer organizations to select issues to campaign on that could draw effectively on local symbols to increase "grassroots" involvement. Besides the objective of the campaign, which was ostensibly to kill a proposed tax increase in the Tory budget, there were three "secondary" goals. Conference attendees were most interested in hearing about the secondary goals because of their transferability and generalizability: raising awareness of the increasing taxes taxpayers are paying, building the brand of the taxpayer group, and growing bases of support for future campaigns. In sum, this triad of secondary goals amounted to asking how people could become more permanently engaged in critical reflection on issues important to the taxpayer group. To do this, the presenter argued that the battle to kill the tax rested on two key alliances: one with pubs, the other with media.

During his discussion of "media impact," the presenter detailed the campaign's launch through an alliance with *The Sun*, which produced and featured stories in their paper's signature populist style calling the Tory party "sipocrates" for its support of a higher alcohol tax and warning the government to "steer clear of our beer." The success of the TPA campaign, the presenter argued, could be replicated across jurisdictions and applied to different scenarios. The presentation ended with a photo of a beaming TPA executive sharing a pint with then chancellor of the exchequer George Osborne, who held up one of the beer mats. Not wishing to offend "the taxpayers," the Tory government had reversed itself. The boastful presentation pushed for replication of the organization's success in other contexts, and remained ideologically fervent, never straying from the broadly held ethos of the conference, namely, the arresting of government. Of its audience, the fellow advocates of liberal political reason, the presentation pedagogically asked: Which campaigns of critique are worth pursuing? How do you best arouse the interests of everyday people? How can taxpayer groups and other liberal groups work with media and issue-adjacent organizations to build both temporary and more consistent coalitions?

This vignette helps illustrate the discursive work done by taxpayer groups in directing and shaping subjectivities. At the centre of the presentation was the question of how a campaign could be successful, but beneath this, the presentation tacitly asked how people could be shaped *to be interested,* or how political affinity could be fostered. The taxpayer subject as I have described it is not a natural disposition – it requires constant work, revisitation, enlargement, contraction, and new tactics. The strategic nature of governmentality means that, while members of taxpayer groups and their allies might be more interested in lowering taxes for businesses or ending regulations, it is necessary to *cultivate* a taxpayer ethos. Who is addressed in campaigns, and how they are addressed, shows that these groups understand the importance of a judicious solicitation of taxpayer outrage. The political residue from this campaign yielded two results: (1) positive identification with the TPA as an organization, especially on the part of those imagined to be "working class" everyday voters; and (2) the political effects of a campaign that might invite citizens to think sceptically about government and taxation, and to reason with the sort of evidence that the TPA produced throughout the campaign.

Vignette Two: Taxpayers in the Developing World
As I have noted, the geographic distribution of taxpayer organizations is weighted heavily towards the West. As mentioned earlier, the World Taxpayer Associations attempted to foster the growth of taxpayer organizations in non-Western countries. The bi-annual gathering of taxpayer associations is one of the key resources for these fragile organizations in learning, networking, and adapting strategies. At the conference I attended, an entire session was dedicated to the operation of taxpayer organizations in lower-income countries, and featured groups from Ukraine, Ghana, and China. For these groups, the primary challenge lies in promoting government limitation and the supremacy of the market in states where household income is far lower than in states where taxpayer movements have flourished. The conference program listed the per capita GDP in the participating countries in order to outline the cascading disadvantage that each group faced.

After panel members spoke about their own countries, eager audience members peppered the panel with questions about the politics of their organizations, totalitarian government, and market challenges. With the help of a translator, a representative spoke proudly about his organization, and was interrupted by an audience member who exuberantly testified that their organization was "extremely entrepreneurial and very impressive." Flattery, deference, and ingratiation might be described as a networking strategy for welcoming less-established groups into the fold. Despite what might appear to an outsider as unctuousness, the speakers were not treated as tokens or novelty acts; there was real learning to be done. After their panel ended, the representatives circulated throughout the conference floor. They had become magnets for advice, compliments, and exchange of information. More experienced activists were genuinely interested in providing counsel, asking questions, and making suggestions about strategies for growth, dealing with the media, and communicating with the organizations' apparent constituents – taxpayers. These moments of connection were about building strong networks of action, collaboration, and critique, or, more fundamentally, learning the ins and outs of translating strategy from one place to another. As one delegate eagerly told the WTA president at the conclusion of their panel, "We used your book!" – a reference to the WTA's field guide to starting a taxpayer association.

These texts, in combination with face-to-face interactions at conferences, show this pedagogical function in action: how to replicate ideological success in permanent campaigns of government critique. The groups that have joined have invested heavily in the discursive work of building the moral and political character of the taxpayer. Assembling this ethical subject is not the only work done at the World Taxpayer Conference. As this vignette shows, the work of mobilization should not be overlooked: how are discursive resources, strategies, and organizational policies – the building blocks of subjectivity – taken up in this convergent space?

What is being mobilized is not the taxpayer metaphor itself but the discursive and material tools that are used to solidify and strengthen this subject. These methods are mobilized from contexts where the taxpayer is already a durable political subject and introduced as a specific discursive tool in the repertoire of political groups, business advocates, and others that have an explicit goal of restraining government. Translating the tactics that bore the politically productive taxpayer subject into entirely new political contexts – whether in China, Ghana, or elsewhere – is a process of trial and error, adaptation, and learning. While the goal may be to replicate the tactics, policy mobilities scholars have shown that in the travels and transmission of policy knowledge the tactics, ideas, and goals will never be replicated exactly (McCann 2011), but will be changed by their movement from implementation in Australia, the United Kingdom, or Canada to the convergent conference space, shaped further by the contingency of advice given and listened to, and by how sharing takes place.

Conclusion

Drawing upon the methodological insights of policy mobility and governmentality studies scholars, this chapter shows how the knowledge and strategies of taxpayer groups help to form taxpayer subjects. I have argued that
taxpayer groups are key centres of organization of knowledge used by and
reasoned with by taxpayer subjects. The work done to assemble this knowledge is multifaceted and multiscalar, and crosses ideological spaces. I locate
subject formation processes outside of what might be considered traditional
power structures. Conferences are important sites of knowledge production
and mobility (Cook and Ward 2012; Temenos 2016), where seminars on tactics, question-and-answer sessions with "policy entrepreneurs," or a debate
on overall organizational strategy are held. For taxpayer groups, these conferences address a key issue of strategy: how to successfully contribute to
the "public habitat" of numbers and stories about numbers, and how to successfully execute campaigns of critique.

As many contributors to this volume have demonstrated, scholars need
to pay close attention to the multidimensional travel of ideologies across
various vectors, such as scale, space, and jurisdiction. Various chapters
focus on multiple fronts in analyzing this: the formation of subjects (Chapter 7), the everyday practices that buttress ideology (Chapter 9), or the discursive formations that help mobilize political possibility (Chapter 5). My
contribution has been to weave together an account of how subjectivity and
political rationality and strategy are assembled and mobilized in a very specific convergent social space.

References

Benson, David, and Andrew Jordan. 2011. "What Have We Learned from Policy
    Transfer Research? Dolowitz and Marsh Revisited." *Political Studies Review* 9 (3):
    366–78.
–. 2012. "Policy Transfer Research: Still Evolving, Not Yet Through." *Political Studies
    Review* 10 (3): 333–38.
Björklund-Larsen, Lotta. 2017. *Shaping Taxpayers: Values in Action at the Swedish
    Tax Agency*. New York: Berghahn.
Burchell, Graham. 1996. "Liberal Government and Techniques of the Self." In *Fou-
    cault and Political Reason: Liberalism, Neo-liberalism, and Rationalities of Gov-
    ernment*, ed. Andrew Barry, Thomas Osborne, and Nikolas Rose, 19–36. Chicago:
    University of Chicago Press.
Cook, Ian, and Kevin Ward. 2012. "Conferences, Informational Infrastructures, and
    Mobile Policies: The Process of Getting Sweden 'BID Ready.'" *European Urban
    and Regional Studies* 19 (2): 137–52.
Dean, Mitchell. 2010. *Governmentality: Power and Rule in Modern Society*. London:
    Sage.

–. 2014. "Rethinking Neoliberalism." *Journal of Sociology* 50 (2): 150–63.

Dean, Mitchell, and Kaspar Villadsen. 2016. *Statephobia and Civil Society*. Stanford, CA: Stanford University Press.

Foucault, Michel. 2008. *The Birth of Biopolitics: Lectures at the Collège de France 1978–1979*. New York: Palgrave Macmillan.

Gane, Mike. 2008. "Foucault on Governmentality and Liberalism." *Theory, Culture and Society* 25 (7–8): 353–63.

Hackell, Melissa. 2013. "Taxpayer Citizenship and Neoliberal Hegemony in New Zealand." *Journal of Political Ideologies* 18 (2): 129–49.

Henderson, Jennifer. 2015. "Residential Schools and Opinion-Making in the Era of Traumatized Subjects and Taxpayer-Citizens." *Journal of Canadian Studies* 49 (1): 5–43.

Hall, Stuart, and Alan O'Shea. 2013. "Common-Sense Neoliberalism." *Soundings: A Journal of Politics and Culture* 55 (1): 8–24.

Lemke, Thomas. 2001. "'The Birth of Bio-Politics': Michel Foucault's Lecture at the Collège de France on Neo-Liberal Governmentality." *Economy and Society* 30 (2): 190–207.

Marcus, George. 1995. "Ethnography in/of the World System: The Emergence of Multi-Sited Ethnography." *Annual Review of Anthropology* 24: 95–117.

Martin, Isaac W. 2013. *Rich People's Movements*. New York: Oxford University Press.

McCann, Eugene. 2011. "Urban Policy Mobilities and Global Circuits of Knowledge: Toward a Research Agenda." *Annals of the Association of American Geographers* 101 (1): 107–30.

McCann, Eugene, and Kevin Ward. 2012. "Policy Assemblages, Mobilities and Mutations: Toward a Multidisciplinary Conversation." *Political Studies* 10 (3): 325–32.

–. 2013. "A Multi-Disciplinary Approach to Policy Transfer Research: Geographies, Assemblages, Mobilities and Mutations." *Policy Studies* 34 (1): 2–18.

Medvetz, Thomas. 2012. *Think Tanks in America*. Chicago: University of Chicago Press.

Miller, Peter. 2001. "Governing by Numbers: Why Calculative Practices Matter." *Social Research* 68 (2): 379–96.

Miller, Peter, and Ted O'Leary. 1987. "Accounting and the Construction of the Governable Person." *Accounting, Organizations and Society* 12 (3): 235–65.

Miller, Peter, and Nikolas Rose. 1990. "Governing Economic Life." *Economy and Society* 19 (1): 1–31.

Peck, Jamie, and Nik Theodore. 2001. "Exporting Workfare/Importing Welfare-to-Work: Exploring the Politics of Third Way Policy Transfer." *Political Geography* 20 (4): 427–60.

Pridgen, Annette, and Dale Flesher. 2013. "Improving Accounting and Accountability in Local Governments: The Case of the Tennessee Taxpayers Association." *Accounting History* 18 (4): 507–28.

Rose, Nikolas. 1993. "Government, Authority and Expertise in Advanced Liberalism." *Economy and Society* 22 (3): 283–99.

–. 1996. "Governing 'Advanced' Liberal Democracies". In *Foucault and Political Reason: Liberalism, Neo-liberalism, and Rationalities of Government*, ed. Andrew Barry, Thomas Osborne, and Nikolas Rose, 37–64. Chicago: University of Chicago Press.

–. 1999. *Powers of Freedom: Reframing Political Thought*. Cambridge: Cambridge University Press.

Sheller, Mimi, and John Urry. 2006. "The New Mobilities Paradigm." *Environment and Planning A* 38 (2): 207–26.

Temenos, Cristina. 2016. "Mobilizing Drug Policy Activism: Conferences, Convergence Spaces and Ephemeral Fixtures in Social Movement Mobilization." *Space and Polity* 20 (1): 124–41.

Urry, John. 2000. "Mobile Sociology." *British Journal of Sociology* 51 (1): 185–203.

Willmott, Kyle. 2017. "Taxpayer Governmentality: Governing Government in Metro Vancouver's Transit Tax Debate." *Economy and Society* 46 (2): 255–74.

–. Forthcoming. "From Self-Government to Government of the Self: Fiscal Subjectivity, Indigenous Governance and the Politics of Transparency." *Critical Social Policy*.

Wimmer, Andreas, and Nina Glick Schiller. 2002. "Methodological Nationalism and Beyond: Nation-State Building, Migration and the Social Sciences." *Global Networks* 2 (4): 301–34.

Walsh, Camille. 2018. *Racial Taxation: Schools, Segregation and Taxpayer Citizenship, 1869–1973*. Chapel Hill, NC: University of North Carolina Press.

Williamson, Vanessa. 2017. *Read My Lips: Why Americans Are Proud to Pay Taxes*. Princeton: Princeton University Press.

7

Telling Their Stories
Ideology and the Subject
of Prairie Agriculture

KATHERINE STRAND AND DARIN BARNEY

It is well established that the Prairie provinces of western Canada have historically been the site of considerable ideological ferment and intensity. This
is confirmed by the diverse, disruptive, and innovative political movements,
parties, and institutions that have arisen there since the early decades of the
twentieth century, as well as those that have made their way into the twenty-
first (Melnyk 1992). Often vigorously democratic in spirit (or at least in
rhetoric), these various instances of Prairie politics have taken many forms
and have adopted multiple, often competing ideological positions and programs (Laycock 1990, 2002). A long tradition of excellent scholarly work has
shown that any characterization of the Prairies (or, even worse, "the West")
as a homogeneous ideological space could only be *itself* ideological (Wiseman 2001). It is also true that what might be termed "agricultural subjectivity" remains a crucial point of ideological formation and contestation in the
region, and perhaps even beyond it. Just as a particular kind of agricultural
political subject was central to the possibilities of the cooperative, agrarian,
democratic socialism that was so consequential in the Prairies during the
twentieth century, a different kind of agricultural subject has been equally
central to the emergence of neoliberalism across significant portions of this
same geography in the twenty-first (Epp 2008; Müller 2008).

Our concern in this chapter is to inquire into how such subjects are reproduced ideologically. Political scientists, even those attuned to the category
of "political culture," tend to focus upon the rhetorical artifacts of political

leaders, parties, and governments to discern the contours of ideological reproduction (Wesley 2011). By contrast, in this chapter we will compare the ideological operation of two examples of extra-partisan cultural production that have each sought to hail distinct political subjects in different periods of Prairie political history. The first is *Paper Wheat,* a 1977 musical depicting the period of agricultural settlement in Canada leading to the establishment of the wheat pools and the cooperative movement in the early twentieth century. It was produced by Saskatoon's 25th Street Theatre Company and played to packed audiences in small towns throughout the Prairies in the mid-1970s; it was later recirculated as an influential documentary produced by the National Film Board. The second is *License to Farm,* a 2016 documentary produced by the industry organization SaskCanola, depicting the challenges facing "modern" Prairie farmers in the age of urban environmentalism, and advocating for genetically modified crops and chemical farming in Canada. At the time of this writing, the documentary has been viewed online by over 120,000 people, and likely several thousands more have seen it in organized public and private screenings across the Prairies. These will be compared both as markers of highly distinctive ideological formations in Prairie history and as means for circulating ideological claims and mediating political subjects.

On Ideology

Political subjects are people who are prepared to act in and into the settings in which they find themselves. It is customary for accounts of politics to emphasize action and its qualities: to be a political subject is to act in a range of identifiably political ways, such as voting, joining a party, running for office, or organizing an interest group. By contrast, we turn our attention to the element of political subjectivity that corresponds to preparation. Political subjects do not just act. They are *prepared* to act. Political subjects are prepared to act by the material conditions in which they find themselves, by their histories and relationships, by their experiences, and by what they have come to know and believe about themselves, about the world they inhabit, and about others. In many cases, this preparation takes the form of stories: stories people tell, and stories they hear, about themselves and others.

Ideology prepares people to act under highly overdetermined conditions, comprising one element of the complex process by which people become political subjects. Here, ideology does not name a set of true convictions codified in a political program to which one might wholly subscribe and simply follow. Nor does it denote an entirely false, illusory, or artificial account of social life that prevents people from understanding and acting upon the real conditions of their existence. In this chapter, we treat ideology as the ongoing, productive work of *being prepared to act*, the work entailed in becoming a political subject. In the cases examined here, the work of ideology arises in the form of stories told about and for the agricultural political subjects of the Canadian Prairies, narratives that call them to see and recognize themselves and thereby prepare them to act as those subjects. In this respect, the account of ideology presented in this chapter corresponds to Louis Althusser's idea of interpellation, wherein we become subjects by recognizing ourselves in the addresses directed towards us.

In Althusser's classic formulation, a policeman calls out, "'Hey, you there!'" and, in turning around, the person to whom this hail is made becomes a subject. "Why?" Althusser asks. "Because he has recognized that the hail was 'really' addressed to him, and that 'it was really him who was hailed' (and not someone else)" (Althusser 2001, 118). Althusser famously describes ideology as "the imaginary relationship of individuals to their real conditions of existence," but immediately clarifies that this does not mean it should be relegated to the status of mere illusion. As he puts it, ideological constructions "need only be 'interpreted' to discover the reality of the world behind their imaginary representation of that world" (Althusser 2001, 110). What is important for our purposes is that ideology is real, ordinary, and voluntary. It is not an exceptional moment of deception enacted by one upon another against the latter's will, but an ongoing subjective process in which subjects participate in producing themselves by turning around when they are called, because they recognize themselves in that call. In ideological moments, we are simultaneously *being prepared* by external conditions and actors and *preparing ourselves* to act in relation to them. As Althusser (2001, 118) observes, "you and I are always already subjects, and as such constantly practice the rituals of ideological recognition."

In this respect, ideology names a crucial process in the social reproduction of the arrangements of material production. In this chapter, we will compare how agricultural producers in the Prairies have been hailed in the stories told by *Paper Wheat* and *License to Farm*, both of which ask farmers and their families to recognize those stories as their own. Both are concrete instances of the "rituals of ideological recognition" that work to socially reproduce a particular mode of agricultural production, by hailing political subjects who are prepared to act under the specific conditions in which they emerge. *Paper Wheat* hailed and sought to prepare political subjects for the cooperative mode of agricultural production that persisted into the 1970s (even as it was beginning to show signs of strain). *License to Farm* hails and seeks to prepare political subjects for the competitive, biotechnological mode of agribusiness presently emergent in the Canadian Prairies. Prairie farmers are notoriously complex political subjects, embodying at once the independence of individual proprietors and the solidarity of neighbours acting together under adverse conditions (Müller 2008). As such, they have been, and remain, open to being hailed in both of these ways. As we hope to show in our treatment of these two artifacts, it is precisely under these highly contingent circumstances that ideology does its work.

Setting the Stage

Paper Wheat premiered on March 18, 1977, at the Memorial Hall in Sintaluta, Saskatchewan. The location was intentional. In 1902, a group of farmers from Sintaluta led by Edward A. Partridge successfully brought charges under the Manitoba Grain Act against the Canadian Pacific Railway for manipulating the allocation of rail cars. Three years later, Partridge – who is portrayed in the play – travelled to Manitoba to witness first-hand the speculative dealings of the Winnipeg Grain Exchange. Upon his return, he and his neighbours formed the Grain Growers' Grain Company, western Canada's first cooperative grain producers' organization, in 1906. Two years later, in 1908, the inaugural edition of the *Grain Grower's Guide,* a crucial early voice of the Prairie cooperative movement, was published at Sintaluta (MacPherson 1999, 1766).[1]

In the spring and fall of 1977, the musical was remounted for a tour of thirty-three Saskatchewan towns (with a five-day run in Toronto), where it played to packed houses, followed by a national tour of forty-six cities in 1979 (Twenty-Fifth Street Theatre 1982, 37, 97). In 1979, the National Film Board released an adapted documentary film version of the play, directed by Albert Kish as part of the NFB's Challenge for Change (CFC) program (Meir 2010). The film was rebroadcast several times by CBC Television, making *Paper Wheat* "one of the most widely-seen CFC films" (Waugh, Winton, and Baker 2017). An adapted version of the play was also produced in-studio as a "Drama Special" and broadcast by the CBC in 1980.

In 1982, Western Producer Prairie Books published *Paper Wheat: The Book,* which includes a history of the cooperative movement in Saskatchewan, an account of the play's production, itinerary, and distribution, production stills, recollections of its players, a script, and a musical score. In his essay in the book, Don Kerr (1982, 17) sums up the play's remarkable multimedia life cycle as follows:

Paper Wheat was a phenomenal Canadian theatrical success, as successful as almost any play in the country's history. It toured over eighty Canadian communities, played over 200 performances, and was seen by 65,000 people. It was televised by the CBC and its second tour was filmed by the National Film Board. Almost every review of *Paper Wheat* was enthusiastic and almost every audience even more enthusiastic.

Retrospectively, the political orientation of the play seems unambiguous, but in many ways it was also accidental. The players of the 25th Street Theatre had begun to experiment with collective, collaboratively authored productions, and at the end of the 1976 season, the company announced its intention to produce a play about the retail cooperatives familiar in Saskatoon. Kerr (1982, 19) recounts that "the company that went out to create *The Co-op Show* was largely innocent of Saskatchewan history. They didn't know the Wheat Pool from Cargill or even that the Wheat Pool was a cooperative. They didn't know the story was going to be a farmers' story or who the hero might be, or the villain." It was only after the company was exposed to some old pool organizers that its attention turned towards the history of the grain growers' cooperatives and *Paper Wheat* found its politics. Importantly, it found it in the stories, personal histories, and recollections of farmers and townspeople in Saskatchewan whom the players visited in developing successive versions of the script. As suggested by the publicity material supporting the national tour, "audiences in Saskatchewan were the same people from whom they gathered material and who were the subject and substance of the play ... people watching recognized themselves and their neighbors" (quoted in Kaye 2003, 24). The minimal financial support the production received from the institutions of the cooperative movement came only after it had already premiered. Thus, as Kerr (1982, 23) put it, "the play was not a kept play."

The ideological core of *Paper Wheat* lies in its celebration of the formation of the Saskatchewan Wheat Pool in 1924, which is presented as a heroic achievement of cooperation across difference, built upon a common experience of the adversity of prairie settlement (Act 1) and resistance to the abuses of the railway companies and private grain trade (Act 2). As Alan Filewod (2000, 82) put it, the play "appeals to a prairie and specifically Saskatchewan sentiment and celebrates the tradition of cooperative socialism." In neither respect can the play be characterized as indexical, comprehensive, or complete in its depiction of the histories it addresses. For example, the play performs a complete erasure of the exterminationist history that cleared the land for the settler-colonial grain economy of the Prairies: "In treating the pioneers as simple heroes, *Paper Wheat* avoids questions about expropriation of land and the ecological consequences of monocropping. Sintaluta is a Lakota name (Red Tail, as in red-tailed hawk), but the play completely ignored the history of Lakota and other Native people in the area" (Kaye 2003, 235; see Daschuck 2013). A critical review of the first production appearing in the left-wing magazine *Next Year Country* pointed to another silence: "Nowhere in the play is there mention of the sort of businesses the Co-ops and the Wheat Pool have become, or a glimmer of understanding of why this should be ... [it] rings false to anyone who has ever had to work for or dealt with a present day Co-op, credit union or the Wheat Pool" (quoted in Filewod 2000, 98).[2]

Subsequent versions of the play introduced a note of complexity, with concluding scenes reflecting on the changing character of the Wheat Pool in the context of the growth of agribusiness in the 1970s. As one character, Sis, observes, "Ma, co-ops today are a multi-million dollar operation; they're no different from any other big business. Well, look at how they treat their employees" (Twenty-Fifth Street Theatre 1982, 37, 97). Nonetheless, the overall theme of celebrating the cooperative ideal and its champions remained intact, as the solution offered to the problem of what the cooperatives had become was a return to what the cooperatives had been. As Kerr (1982, 28) puts it in his essay accompanying the ultimate version of the script: "*Paper Wheat* is a highly selective view of agrarian history. One of its major functions indeed is to distill from history a simple and intense myth by which people today can still live: a myth of cooperation, of people able to alter the world." The ideology of the play consists in this partiality, and operates by rendering its partial account into a narrative form in which audiences – both in the Prairies and elsewhere – might recognize something of themselves and so be prepared to act as the subjects they become by virtue of that recognition.

Similarly, the ideological character of *License to Farm*, a thirty-minute documentary film, derives from a "highly selective view" of the condition of contemporary agriculture in the Prairies, presented as a story about farming and the imperative for farmers to act in response to the challenges they face. In this case, the primary challenge to farmers' interests is presented as public misconceptions surrounding genetically modified organisms (GMOs), the environmental effects of chemical inputs used in cultivating GMO crops, and the power of the companies that develop and sell these products. Interestingly, in this case, the imperative to act is expressed specifically in terms of the need for farmers to tell their own stories, to counteract the misconceptions promoted by a variety of external actors whose opinions threaten the livelihoods of farming families. The film and its accompanying materials are aimed at preparing farmers to act in just this way.

As with *Paper Wheat*, the ideological content of *License to Farm* is marked by the conditions of its production and circulation. The film was financed by a $150,000 investment by the Saskatchewan Canola Development Commission (SaskCanola), representing three-quarters of the project budget, with an additional $50,000 contributed by the governments of Saskatchewan and Canada under the Growing Forward 2 agricultural funding framework.[3] It premiered in January 2016 at the Western Canadian Crop Production Show – an annual gathering billed as "western Canada's premier grain industry showcase" – and, as noted above, has since received over 120,000 views online (Grueter 2016).

Whether its origins and financing make *License to Farm* a "kept film" is open to interpretation. Canola is an edible oilseed developed from rapeseed in Canada in the 1970s, using conventional breeding techniques. Grown primarily in south-central Saskatchewan, Alberta, and Manitoba, it is one of the most important crops in Canadian agriculture. A survey of farmers' seeding intentions for 2017 indicated that projected acreage devoted to canola (22.4 million) would trail that projected for wheat (23.2 million) by only a narrow margin (Statistics Canada 2017). The Canola Council of Canada estimates that canola generates one-quarter of all farm revenues and contributes $26.7 billion to the Canadian economy annually, making it the country's "most valuable crop."

Ninety percent of the canola grown in Canada is exported, largely as oil or meal processed at one of fourteen crushing and refining plants operated in Canada by a short roster of the world's leading transnational agribusiness firms – Bunge, Viterra, Louis Dreyfus, Archer Daniels Midland, and James Richardson (Canola Council of Canada 2017a). As noted above, canola was originally developed conventionally, but today "about 80 per cent of the canola grown in Canada has been modified using biotechnology to make it tolerant to some herbicides" (Canola Council of Canada 2017b).[4] In particular, the bulk of canola grown in Canada has been genetically modified to make it resistant to glyphosate, the active ingredient in Monsanto's popular Roundup series of herbicides, or the glufosinate-ammonium used in Bayer's LibertyLink product.[5]

It is in this light that the material stakes of *License to Farm*'s hail to farmers, to tell "their" story about the safety of the food they grow, begin to emerge. Persistent concerns in domestic and global consumer markets over

the health and environmental risks of GMO foods and the market dominance of transnational biotechnology firms threaten not only the existing
canola industry in Canada (including the companies that sell herbicides and
the seeds modified to resist them) but also the prospects for introducing
genetic modification into other crops and categories of agricultural production, such as wheat, and the broader field of biotechnology more generally
(Peekhaus 2013; Kinchy 2012). A failure to secure consumer confidence –
or, alternatively, to establish *lack* of confidence as unfounded – could result
in undeveloped product lines, lost markets, and greater levels of regulatory
constraint, none of which would be welcomed by agribusiness.

The story of GMO agriculture is therefore the terrain of an ongoing
struggle over the meaning of farming, in which industry groups such as
SaskCanola and the governments that support them have a vested interest
(Eaton 2013).[6] In a context where the credibility of industrial voices in public
debates is routinely questioned, the affective and strategic value of farmers
telling their own stories about the food they are growing is potentially great.

License to Farm summons farmers to this cause and, like *Paper Wheat*,
it does so by inviting them to recognize themselves in its narrative, and by
enlisting their participation in a process we had a chance to witness first-
hand. We first became aware of the film in March 2015 while one of us
(Katherine Strand) was pursuing ethnographic field work in Swift Current,
Saskatchewan. While visiting with a local farmer, she learned that a filmmaker, Garry Berteig, was touring the region and asking for interviews with
agricultural producers and researchers. Strand received a call from Berteig,
who described his project as a documentary about farm families in the Prairies. He asked for quotes about the "success" of farming in the region as
the result of advances in research on synthetic fertilizers, herbicides, and
genetically modified seeds. Strand asked for more information about the
film, including funding sources, which Berteig declined to answer, so she
decided not to participate.

Several months later, Strand attended a potluck dinner hosted by the
same farmer, a regular event that included fifteen people representing
farms across the spectrum in terms of size and type of operation. The host
explained that the filmmaker planned to attend that evening. Berteig introduced himself to the group and described his project as a "film to dispel
myths about factory farming." At one point, a well-known organic farmer
from the region approached Berteig, who recognized him as the former
president of the National Farmers Union and an outspoken critic of international agribusinesses. Berteig told the organic farmer that he "simply

wanted to show the world that life in rural communities isn't in danger of fading away," as it is often portrayed in the media. The farmer responded by explaining how this very gathering represented the incredible shift in rural life that had occurred in the last fifty years. Most of his neighbours sold or rented their land because they found it impossible to keep up with the rising costs of machinery and chemical inputs. Berteig abruptly ended the conversation and left shortly thereafter.

None of the footage from the potluck appears in the thirty-minute film. Over the course of the film, an unidentified narrator guides the viewer through five chapters in which he describes the twenty-first century farm as both a vast and complex technological enterprise and continuous with the tradition of the family farm. He explains that concerned consumers represent the greatest risk to modern farmers as their unscientific and confused fears pressure the Canadian government to increase on-farm regulations. He highlights genetically modified seeds, pesticides, and factory farming as three main areas of concern for consumers, and explains how their fear of unsafe food is driving an "anti-farm movement." The anti-farm movement organizes activists who pressure the government to ban GMO seeds such as Roundup-ready canola, regulate pesticide use, and give urban consumers the false idea that all family farms have become corporate factories. In each chapter, the narrator highlights these "myths," then uses clips from interviews with farmers, researchers, and experts in public relations to dispel the concerns and encourage other farmers to educate the public by "telling their stories."

The film includes interviews with seven individuals with the designation "farmer" under their names. Five of the seven farmers are current or former members of canola industry producer groups and another, Cherilyn Nagel, works in public relations for Farm and Food Care Saskatchewan.[7] Through this organization, Nagel has hosted workshops for farmers around the province to help them "tell their story" using facts about their industry found in the publication *The Real Dirt on Farming*, which is available for purchase on the organization's website (www.farmfoodcare.org/canada). The film also relies on interview clips from representatives of SaskCanola, Agrimetrix Research and Training (a company specializing in sprayer technology), Saskatchewan Polytechnic, and Ag-West Bio Inc. (Saskatchewan's bioscience industry association). Although the film was financially supported by the government of Saskatchewan and Agriculture Canada, representatives of these governments do not appear in it. The film includes the testimony of Mark Lynas, an environmental activist based in Oxford, England, and

Dr. Joe Schwarcz, the director of McGill University's Office for Science and Society, based in Montreal. A master of science student, Ian Epp, is the only University of Saskatchewan affiliate to appear in the film. In total, *License to Farm* uses interviews with eighteen individuals, including two "concerned consumers" who represent the unscientific fears of "urban foodies." Between interview clips, the film displays footage of agricultural landscapes, on-farm practices, anti-farm protesters, unspecified laboratory and field testing sites, and one of Cherilyn Nagel's training sessions with farmers. It closes with a capitalized exhortation before the final credits: "DON'T LET YOUR SILENCE TAKE AWAY YOUR LICENSE TO FARM."

One Subject or Another

Paper Wheat and *License to Farm* cover remarkably similar ground in their efforts to hail agricultural political subjects who are otherwise remarkably different. Both begin on the farm, with farmers and their families confronting the natural adversaries that have perennially made it difficult for them to eke out a living from the land and the "natural" adversities it presents: soil that is reluctant to yield, weather that defies control, weeds and pests that refuse to give up. In *Paper Wheat*, the solution to these problems is mutual aid. In the signature scene of Act I (Twenty-Fifth Street Theatre 1982, 46–48), the Ukrainian farmer Vasil Havryshyn visits his English neighbour William Postlethwaite, convincing him to accept use of his plow in exchange for help in digging a new well. Thus the seeds of cooperation are sown. In *License to Farm*, the solution to the problems of fertility, weather, and pestilence is "cutting edge technology," including "breakthroughs in genetics, communications and chemistry" that enable farmers to "grow our food more quickly, with less energy, less environmental impact and in greater abundance than ever before" (0:30–0:45). It bears mentioning that there is no indication that any of these technologies are borrowed from or shared with the neighbours: they are all purchased by individual farmers from the corporations that develop and sell them. Here, too, we are presented with the germinal form of the political subjectivity that will be summoned more directly as the story unfolds.

In both *Paper Wheat* and *License to Farm*, farmers are portrayed as vulnerable to external forces that come from beyond the farm gate to threaten their livelihoods. For the farmers in *Paper Wheat*, this threatening force is represented by the Winnipeg Grain Exchange, made up largely of five companies that control the price of grain at local elevators. In the scene "Who Are the Scales Working for Today?" Irish farmer Sean Phelan brings a load of grain into town to sell at the local elevator, where the agent tries to cajole him into disclosing whether recent rains might have introduced unwanted moisture into his grain (Twenty-Fifth Street Theatre 1982, 53–54). From the moment Sean leaves his farm gate, he is entering a space that is beyond his control and hostile to his interests. Moisture is not the problem. The problem is that he has no choice but to deliver his crop to the local elevator, where he is exposed to the abusive practices of railway and grain companies whose controlling interests are, both spatially and economically, distant from his own.

In *License to Farm*, the malevolent force is not the handful of transnational corporations that control the technologies of genetic modification, dominate the sale of chemical inputs, and control access to grain handling, transportation, and marketing. Instead, it is the growing legion of uninformed consumers and irrational activists whose political influence threatens to undermine markets for farmers' products and to pressure governments into increased regulatory intervention in the agricultural sector. As the narrator explains: "Public fears about food safety are putting pressure on government and decision-makers to restrict the approval of GM Foods, like the oil from the canola grown here, and to ban the use of certain pesticides. Canada's food certification process is already one of the strictest in the world. But will it become so restrictive that farmers will lose their choice about how they manage their crops?" (1:49–2:18).

In both narratives, the insecurity of farmers' livelihoods extends from vulnerability to natural forces inside the farm gate to exposure to political forces beyond it. For the farmers in *Paper Wheat*, these forces are the private grain trade and the railway companies. For the farmers in *License to Farm*, it is the organized movement – largely urban and vaguely foreign – in opposition to GMOs and chemical agriculture. When the president of Agrimetrix describes these political actors as the "anti-farm movement" (3:25), the message is clear: opposition to companies like Monsanto and Syngenta is a direct threat to farmers themselves. Against the backdrop of a montage of scenes from random anti-GMO and food-safety demonstrations in cities around the world, a voice-over declares, "Canadian farmers have never before faced a challenge of this magnitude" (1:49–2:25).

There are, of course, many ways to farm, including viable options at the scale of commodity grain production (Stevenson 2015). As framed by *License to Farm*, the threat posed by environmentalists, food security activists, and critics of companies such as Monsanto is that they will deprive farmers of the right to choose to grow genetically modified crops using chemical inputs. The film thus appeals directly to the value of independence typically attributed to farmers and their families. The issue of freedom of choice is also prominent in *Paper Wheat*. When Sean Phelan arrives at the local private elevator to find that his grain has been graded and weighed differently from the previous week, he has no choice but to accept it because his options are limited by the oligopolistic organization of the grain industry (Twenty-Fifth Street Theatre 1982, 55). As the cast sings in "The Grain Exchange Rag": "There's five companies trading and betting / Hiking and charging, and gorging and getting / Wheat's the thing; money's the game / But win or lose, it's all the same" (ibid.).

This experience of constrained choice prompts action by the farmers, the success of which relies heavily on state intervention in the form of regulation of the abusive practices of the grain and railroad companies and the provision of statutory support for producer-managed alternatives. By contrast, in *License to Farm*, it is not the "five companies" who control the intellectual property in GMOs and dominate the retail inputs and grain-handling sectors, or the contractual obligations through which they bind their customers, that threaten farmers' freedom of choice. Instead, the threat is that governments might respond to public concerns over the environment and food safety by increasing regulatory intervention in the biotechnology and agribusiness sectors.

As PR consultant Megan Madden warns: "Farmers are going to see increased legislations [sic] that aren't coming from a place of agronomy, they're not coming from a place of agriculture. They're going to be coming from politics and farmers like my dad will be forced to change how they grow food" (4:03–4:15). Cherilyn Nagel adds: "Europe would be a perfect example. They don't have the option to grow genetically-modified seeds" (4:16–4:21). Here, regulatory oversight of biotechnology and agribusiness firms, practices, and products are presented as a violation of individual famers' right to choose to grow GMOs and use chemical inputs, as a threat to their licence to farm as they please. While the integrity of the regulatory apparatus is invoked at other points in the film as guaranteeing the safety of biotechnologically produced food, the prevailing message is that farmers must rise to protect their freedom of choice by advocating for regulatory forbearance in relation to an industrial complex designed to limit their options in other ways.

The problem of information looms large in both *License to Farm* and *Paper Wheat*. In the latter, the fulcrum of the narrative is price, which is information about the value of a commodity. Price, and its manipulation, is the material expression of farmers' abusive relationship with the grain and railway companies. A major element in the play's dramatic arc is the farmers' pursuit of information about how, where, and by whom prices are set, as lack of access to this information leaves them vulnerable to the depredations of those who have it. The opening of Act 2 finds Ed Partridge waiting for a train at the railway station in Sintaluta. "One thing we'd love to know," he says, "is just how that Grain Exchange works. We figure the best way to find out is to send someone there ... We'd also like to know why prices fluctuate so much, and who is responsible. Well, frankly, we don't know. But, as sure as I'm sitting on this hard railway bench, I'm going to find out" (Twenty-Fifth Street Theatre 1982, 55). Upon his return, Partridge shares the information he has gathered about price setting in the grain industry: "There are twenty-odd companies that deal in grain on the exchange. Five of these companies are so big that they have a monopoly on marketing. They determine how high and how low prices will be. I believe they are in league to undermine the farmer and exploit us in every way possible" (ibid., 58).

In *License to Farm*, the problem is not the small number of highly integrated agricultural biotechnology firms that control information about their products via intellectual property regimes, or the price of inputs and technologies whose costs contribute to farmers' continuous and escalating debt (Reuters 2016). Instead, the problem is that the general public is being intentionally misled about the safety of GMOs and the reality of contemporary farming. At one point, agribusiness executive Tom Wolfe says: "There is money in the anti-farm movement. Someone is making money off it. They're making money off it. They're selling an alternative, and farmers are *paying the price*" (3:24–3:31). In this formulation, price – the most important piece of information in a farmer's operation – is mobilized rhetorically in a way that drains it of its meaning in the context of actual farming, and directs attention away from, rather than towards, the source of the prices that farmers actually pay.

To address misunderstandings about food safety, the film uses the image of farmers who care deeply about their soil and the food they grow, bolstered by testimony from experts whose relationship to the science of GMOs and agronomy is mostly oblique but who nevertheless speak with authority about the scientific consensus concerning the safety and environmental benefits of these products, and cast opposition to GMOs as misleading, harmful, and anti-scientific (3:34–3:52). To correct public misperceptions concerning the nature of contemporary farming, the film adopts a contradictory posture. On the one hand, today's farm is presented as a sophisticated, technologically intensive, and abundantly productive operation, in contrast to the romantic ideal of pastoral agriculture to which anti-GMO activists would condemn contemporary farmers. On the other hand, responding to concerns about corporate agriculture, later segments of the film assert that these large-scale operations nevertheless remain "family farms." The modern farm is presented as simultaneously the site of past family traditions and a forward-looking, technological future. In this light, the claims of those concerned about the role of GMOs in intensifying corporate dominance in agriculture are presented as wholly regressive and unfounded.

Both *Paper Wheat* and *License to Farm* culminate in accounts of farmers acting in response to the challenges they diagnose. In *Paper Wheat*, the problem of price manipulation by an oligopolistic grain industry requires a strategy of collective action that takes the material form of alternative, farmer-owned and operated institutions for grain handling and marketing such that farmers might participate in the grain economy as price-makers rather than price-takers. Tellingly, the notion occurs first to a pair of farm women who have just received notice of a meeting to organize an association of territorial grain growers. Anna's husband is reluctant to join but, as she tells her friend Elizabeth, she forces him to "go and talk ... Find out why we're getting such bad prices." She describes how she has also told him to avoid the elevator company altogether by ordering his own rail cars from the CPR to load and ship his grain directly.[8] When Elizabeth replies that her husband doesn't produce enough grain to fill a car on his own, Anna responds with a big idea: "Well, why don't we get together. Put all our grain together and ship it away. We'd get better prices than we're getting now" (Twenty-Fifth Street Theatre 1982, 53).

During his report to the Territorial Grain Growers Association of Sintaluta about his trip to the grain exchange, Ed Partridge says he did "a little arithmetic" on the train that added up to "five million bushels of ... bargaining power." This prompts him to make a proposal: "Why don't we form a company, why don't we form a grain company in which all the shareholders are farmers – those that grow the grain. Why don't we buy a seat on the Winnipeg Grain Exchange ... and why don't we market our own grain? ... I move that here and now, at this meeting, we accept in principle the idea of a cooperative grain marketing company, in which all the profit goes right back to the farmer" (Twenty-Fifth Street Theatre 1982, 58–59). The motion carries. Three decades later, at a gathering to celebrate the opening of a cooperative coal shed during the depths of the Depression, Louise Lucas reflects on the story of the Wheat Pool and implores, "Let's not stop here.

Let's include all the things we need for daily life in a program of cooperative buying ... Let's have more cooperative enterprises, such as a farm implement manufacturers' co-op. And why not co-operative health care, and our own money co-ops?" (ibid., 70).[9] In response to the material problem of price, and the ability of private corporations to manipulate it in their own interests, the farmers depicted in *Paper Wheat* are prepared to step beyond the farm gate to enact a decidedly material collective response.

Likewise, the action recommended by *License to Farm* corresponds to its diagnosis of the challenge facing farmers in their current circumstances. This challenge is not the material organization of the status quo of industrial agriculture in the Prairies, which would call for collective action to structurally alter the present situation – indeed, the imperative implied by *License to Farm* is to continue and even intensify the existing order of things. Instead, the challenge facing farmers is a discursive one: the potential that public opinion about GMOs and chemical agriculture might be swayed against the interests of the global biotechnology industry with whom farmers are called by the film to identify. The danger is that a general public convinced by misinformation that GMOs are unsafe or environmentally harmful, or that biotechnology companies are too powerful and abusive, might be reluctant to consume GMO foods and could lead governments to withhold product approvals or to impose additional regulatory burdens on the industry. The problem of public opinion calls for a discursive response, a strategy in which farmers have an important role to play.

In a context where dissemination of scientific information does not automatically translate into public knowledge, and where the credibility of industry-driven public relations is low, the discursive value of farmers narrating their personal experience is potentially great, especially given popular perceptions of hardworking, honest, trustworthy farmers. Thus, the film calls upon farmers to "rise to the occasion and start telling their own stories and proactively sharing information about their farms, about their production practices, about their values" (3:52–4:03). Especially important is that farmers learn "how [they] can talk to the public about food safety," specifically in relation to "three areas of public concern: genetically-modified foods, agriculture's use of chemicals and the idea that the small farm of yesteryear is gone and that food production has been taken over by mega-corporations." To do this, farmers must learn how to "speak directly to the public about their farming practices, explain why they use certain technologies and re-assure the public that their food is safe" (5:17–5:51). As Janice Tranberg, executive director of SaskCanola observes, "they need to stand up. They need to get out there and tell their stories ... if you don't tell the story, someone else is going to" (25:30–25:44).

The question is to what extent the story farmers are being summoned to tell in *License to Farm* is really their own or, instead, the story that biotechnology companies and large-scale agribusiness need farmers to tell on their behalf. As depicted in *Paper Wheat*, the material project of cooperative organization required farmers to assemble and communicate with each other, in meetings where an alternative infrastructure could be built and collectively enacted. In an interview at the premiere of *License to Farm*, the film's director, Alexei Berteig, promoted a very different dynamic. "We have this shift in the culture of agricultural communities," he said, "from farmers talking to each other to farmers really becoming interested in speaking to the public" (Guenther 2016). When farmers talk to each other, they know what to say and they say it in their own words. Speaking to the public requires a different vocabulary, and this is exactly what *License to Farm* and its related apparatus seeks to provide. According to Berteig, "the hope of this film is that farmers will look at the arguments that are made in this film and take inspiration from them and maybe have a little more language about something to explain next time they receive opposition from neighbours, or from cousins or from family members that are questioning them and their farming practices" (ibid.). In this sense, *License to Farm* is not just a film, it is also a script.

Conclusion: Hey, You There!

In some respects, the agricultural political subjects hailed by *Paper Wheat* and *License to Farm* are quite similar. Both arise from experiences grounded in farmers' ongoing struggles to eke out a productive livelihood from a resistant landscape whose conditions are mostly beyond their control. In both works, farmers are portrayed as independent producers performing the good work of growing food but subject to larger economic systems, market logics, and political forces to which they must respond and adapt in order to prosper. Both involve action beyond the farm gate and engagement with a broader world of actors and powerful institutions whose interests are at odds with farmers' own. In both cases, these subjects are as often women as they are men. And they are subjects who are untroubled by the history of violence against Indigenous peoples and species that cleared (and clears) the way for their existence. It is because they refer to real material conditions and concrete experience that both *Paper Wheat* and *License to Farm* have the potential to interpellate Prairie farmers as political subjects.

However, as vectors of interpellation, the play and the film also hail agricultural political subjects that are marked by their differences. *Paper Wheat* looks to a past of collective action that, at the time, was passing – or being designed – out of existence. *License to Farm* evokes a technologically enabled future of competitive striving that is still unfolding. The farmers of *Paper Wheat* have corporate enemies, while those of *License to Farm* have only corporate friends. *Paper Wheat* hails the subject of cooperation, who works collectively into the future with other producers to build material infrastructures that can support their freedom, equality, and well-being in the face of industrial configurations that bear in the opposite direction. *License to Farm* hails the subject of competition, who adapts to prevailing market, industrial, and technological conditions and is prepared to defend the status quo against those who might question it. One of these works is a threat to the organization of industrial agriculture along capitalist lines, the other is not.

Ideological operations are not innocent. As we have shown, they seek to interpellate particular subjects to suit particular interests and, in the process, they both reveal and conceal various elements of the material relations to which they refer. There is always a gap between subjective recognition and the objective conditions that any given ideological hail mediates. On this basis, we could ask which of the two, *Paper Wheat* or *License to Farm*, prompts subjective recognition of the "real conditions" of Prairie farmers' existence and which prompts misrecognition. We certainly have views about this, but our more limited critical aim in this chapter has been to show that each of these artifacts operates ideologically by preparing subjects to act politically in distinctive ways. The task has not been to determine which work tells the "true" story but instead to explore how each hails a different political subject of Prairie agriculture. The critical question prompted by our analysis is whether subjects recognize themselves in these hails, turn around, and go about the everyday activity of preparing themselves to be those sorts of subjects.

In this respect, it is an empirical question, and difficult to know, whether *Paper Wheat* or *License to Farm* has been more successful. In the mid-1970s, dynamics were just beginning that ended in the privatization of the wheat pools, the dismantling of collective grain marketing, the dismantling of the country elevator and railway branch line systems, and the increasing consolidation of both farms and global agribusiness. It would be difficult to say that many responded other than nostalgically in the 1970s to the hail of *Paper Wheat*. By the same token, at a time when the struggle over GMOs and industrial agribusiness is just getting started, the fate of *License to Farm* and the subjects it tries to recruit remains uncertain. It is rare that a subject ever responds to the hail of ideology by turning around completely. Being prepared to act is not a state; it is an uneven process that is always underway. Sometimes those who are hailed turn around. Sometimes they turn away.

Notes

1 The *Grain Grower's Guide* (1908–28) notably provided a platform for women's issues and was an important vehicle of the early women's movement in Canada (see Freeman 2011, 67–92). Similarly, *The Western Producer,* founded in 1923 as *The Progressive* and renamed in 1924, promoted cooperation among western farmers. It was purchased in the 1930s by the Saskatchewan Wheat Pool and remained an important advocate of cooperation until sold to a private newspaper company in 2002.

2 By contrast, *No. 1 Hard,* a play sponsored by the militant National Farmers Union that was performed in 1978, presented the achievement of the wheat pools without sentimentality as part of, rather than apart from, the overall capitalist and class structure of the grain industry (Filewod 2000, 85–89).

3 Growing Forward 2 was an initiative of the Harper government supporting "innovation, competitiveness and market development" in the agribusiness and agri-food sectors. Its mandate spanned the years 2013–18. See Agriculture and Agri-Food Canada 2018.

4 This is a conservative estimate provided by the industry council. The Canadian Biotechnology Action Network (2015) estimates that 95 percent of canola grown in Canada is genetically modified.

5 In September 2016, Monsanto and Bayer announced a merger deal valued at US$66 billion. Similar mergers are planned between Dow and DuPont, and between Syngenta and ChemChina (Harwell 2016).

6 In 2015, Premier Brad Wall of Saskatchewan sent a letter urging the three main federal parties to signal their support for "fact-based" policy in the development of GMOs in Canada (CBC News 2015). In 2011, the Conservative government of Stephen Harper (joined by Michael Ignatieff's Liberals) defeated Bill C-474, a Private Member's Bill that would have placed additional regulatory constraints on the introduction of new GMO crops in Canada.

7 The film includes clips from farmer interviews with Stan Jeeves (former president of the Saskatchewan Canola Growers Association), Doyle Wiebe (chair of the SaskCanola board of directors), Val Wiebe (Doyle Wiebe's wife), Brett Halstead (former president of the Canadian Canola Growers Association), Dale Leftwich (former chair of the Saskatchewan Canola Development Commission), and Terry Youzwa (former board chair of SaskCanola).

Farm and Food Care Saskatchewan (farmfoodcaresk.org) is the provincial division of Farm and Food Care Canada. The organization's 2015 Donor Investment Report (http://www.farmfoodcare.org) lists the Alberta Canola Producers Commission, the Canadian Canola Growers Association, and SaskCanola as "Champion" donors of $100,000 or more.

8 On the history of producer cars, see Barney 2011, 15–18.
9 Louise Lucas was known as the "Mother of the Co-operative Commonwealth Federation (CCF)" and was one of the earliest leaders of the Saskatchewan farmers' movement (see Wright 1965).

References

Agriculture and Agri-Food Canada. 2018. "Growing Forward 2." http://www.agr. gc.ca/eng/about-us/key-departmental-initiatives/growing-forward-2/.

Althusser, Louis. 2001. *Lenin and Philosophy and Other Essays*. New York: Monthly Review Press.

Barney, Darin. 2011. "To Hear the Whistle Blow: Technology and Politics on the Battle River Branchline." *TOPIA: Canadian Journal of Cultural Studies* 25: 5–28.

Canadian Biotechnology Action Network. 2015. *Where in the World Are GM Crops and Foods?* Ottawa: Canadian Biotechnology Action Network. http://www.cban.ca.

Canola Council of Canada. 2017a. "Industry Overview." http://www.canolacouncil. org/markets-stats/.

–. 2017b. "Canola: The Myths Debunked." http://www.canolacouncil.org/oil-and-meal/ canola-oil/canola-the-myths-debunked/.

CBC News. 2015. "Premier Brad Wall Asks Federal Leaders for Position on GMOs." CBC News Saskatchewan, August 18. http://www.cbc.ca/news/canada/ saskatchewan.

Daschuck, James. 2013. *Clearing the Plains: Disease, Politics of Starvation, and the Loss of Aboriginal Life*. Regina: University of Regina Press.

Eaton, Emily. 2013. *Growing Resistance: Canadian Farmers and the Politics of Genetically Modified Wheat*. Winnipeg: University of Manitoba Press.

Epp, Roger. 2008. *We Are All Treaty People: Prairie Essays*. Edmonton: University of Alberta Press.

Filewod, Alan. 2000. *Collective Encounters: Documentary Theatre in English Canada*. Toronto: University of Toronto Press.

Freeman, Barbara M. 2011. *Beyond Bylines: Media Workers and Women's Rights in Canada*. Waterloo, ON: Wilfrid Laurier University Press.

Grueter, Ellen. 2016. "License to Farm." *Agriculture More Than Ever*, June 21. http:// www.agriculturemorethanever.ca.

Guenther, Lisa. 2016. "Director of *License to Farm* Shares Thoughts on Agriculture." *Grainews*, January 22. http://www.grainews.ca.

Harwell, Drew. 2016. "Bayer and Monsanto to Merge in Mega-Deal That Could Reshape World's Food Supply." *Washington Post*, September 14.

Kaye, Frances W. 2003. *Hiding the Audience: Viewing Arts and Arts Institutions on the Prairies*. Edmonton: University of Alberta Press.

Kerr, Don. 1982. "*Paper Wheat*: Epic Theatre in Saskatchewan." In *Paper Wheat: The Book*, ed. Twenty-Fifth Street Theatre, 17–30. Saskatoon: Western Producer Prairie Books.

Kinchy, Abby. 2012. *Seeds, Science and Struggle: The Global Politics of Transgenic Crops*. Cambridge, MA: MIT Press.

Laycock, David. 1990. *Populism and Democratic Thought in the Canadian Prairies, 1910–1945*. Toronto: University of Toronto Press.

—. 2002. *The New Right and Democracy in Canada: Understanding Reform and the Canadian Alliance*. Don Mills, ON: Oxford University Press.

MacPherson, Ian. 1999. "Partridge, Edward Alexander." In *The Canadian Encyclopedia*, 2000 edition. Toronto: McClelland and Stewart.

Meir, Christopher. 2010. *"Paper Wheat*: Alternative Theatre Meets Alternative Filmmaking." In *Challenge for Change: Activist Documentary and the National Film Board of Canada*, ed. Thomas Waugh, Ezra Winton, and Michael Baker, 295–302. Montreal and Kingston: McGill-Queen's University Press.

Melnyk, George, ed. 1992. *Riel to Reform: A History of Protest in Western Canada*. Saskatoon: Fifth House Publishers.

Müller, Birgit. 2008. "Still Feeding the World? The Political Ecology of Canadian Prairie Farmers." *Anthropologica* 50: 389–407.

Peekhaus, Wilhelm. 2013. *Resistance Is Fertile: Canadian Struggles on the Biocommons*. Vancouver: UBC Press.

Reuters. 2016. "Canadian Farmers' Debt Seen Hitting Fresh Record High: Lender." September 6. https://www.reuters.com/article/canada-farming-debt-idUSL1N1BE19F.

Statistics Canada. 2017. "Principal Field Crop Areas, March 2017." *The Daily*, March 21. http://www.statcan.gc.ca.

Stevenson, Lorraine. 2015. "Federal Government Pledges $1.2 Million to Help Expand Organic Farming." *Manitoba Co-operator*, June 16. http://www.manitobacooperator.ca.

Twenty-Fifth Street Theatre. 1982. *Paper Wheat: The Book*. Saskatoon: Western Producer Prairie Books.

Waugh, Thomas, Ezra Winton, and Michael Baker. 2017. "Playlists: Challenge for Change." National Film Board of Canada, http://www.nfb.ca/playlists/michael-brendan-thomas-waugh-ezra-winton/challenge-for-change/.

Wesley, Jared J. 2011. *Code Politics: Campaigns and Cultures on the Canadian Prairies*. Vancouver: UBC Press.

Wiseman, Nelson. 2001. "The Pattern of Prairie Politics." In *Party Politics in Canada*, 8th ed., ed. Hugh G. Thorburn and Alan Whitehorn, 351–68. Toronto: Prentice Hall.

Wright, J.J.C. 1965. *The Louise Lucas Story*. Montreal: Harvest House.

8

Laborlore and the Ideology of the British Columbia Labour Bureaucracy, 1900–2015

MARK LEIER

The formal ideologies of workers and their organizations have long been studied by historians using sources such as government documents, political platforms, legal cases, conventions, minutes, newspapers, and biographies. Competing ideologies, within and across specific occupations and class positions, have been carefully parsed, with the Tories, Whigs, Republicans, Democrats, Liberals, and Conservatives of traditional political history replaced with labourists, social democrats, communists, a bewildering array of Trotskyist grouplets, syndicalists, and anarchists. Thus A. Ross McCormack could categorize the labour and left movements in western Canada as reformers, rebels, and revolutionaries, capturing in turn labourism, the syndicalism of the Industrial Workers of the World (IWW), and the politics of the Socialist Party of Canada that ranged from social democracy to democratic socialism and back (McCormack 1991).

There are, however, informal ideologies of workers that are not expressed in official pronouncements and platforms. In *The Making of the English Working Class*, published in 1963, British historian E.P. Thompson suggested ways to explore these less structured ideologies. Thompson wrote explicitly to challenge both the liberal structural-functionalist school and the orthodox Communist Party school he had been immersed in. In doing so, he outlined a broader way of considering ideology that resembles Michael Freeden's call to analyze political concepts "through locating them within the patterns in which they actually appear. Such patterns are most

conveniently known as ideologies, those systems of political thinking, loose
or rigid, deliberate or unintended, through which individuals and groups
construct an understanding of the political world they, or those who preoc-
cupy their thoughts, inhabit, and then act on that understanding" (Freeden
1988, 3). Thompson ([1963] 1980, 8–9) used different conventions and language but approached ideology in a similar way:

> Class happens when some men, as a result of common experiences (inher-
> ited or shared), feel and articulate the identity of their interests as between
> themselves and as against other men whose interests are different from
> (and usually opposed to) theirs. The class experience is largely determined
> by the productive relations into which men are born – or enter involuntar-
> ily. Class-consciousness is the way in which these experiences are handled
> in cultural terms: embodied in traditions, value-systems, ideas, and institu-
> tional form. If the experience appears as determined, class-consciousness
> does not. We can see a *logic* in the responses of similar occupational groups
> undergoing similar experiences, but we cannot predict any *law*. Conscious-
> ness of class arises in the same way in different times and places, but never
> in just the same way.[1]

Thompson explored the experiences, stories, poems, and broadsheets
produced and shared by workers to show, contrary to the structural-
functionalists, that they identified as a class, and one that was in conscious
opposition to the class of employers. Informal, imprecise, even contradictory in ways not appreciated by Communist Party ideologists, this working
class culture – or informal ideology – reflected working class experience
and bound workers together.

The American folklorist Archie Green coined the term "laborlore" to
describe the "broad range of culturally expressive practices within trade
unions, among them clothing styles, songs, shop-floor stories and jokes, post-
ers, work rituals, and strike chants." This was later expanded to include "the
work traditions and cultural practices of all workers." In Green's view, studying laborlore could help create a more inclusive history and pedagogy built
from the bottom up, rooted in class and class conflict in the service of a broad
democratic politics (Burns 2011, 106–7; Green 1993, 1996, 2001, 2006).[2]

For example, in 2014, the Canadian government commemorated the
centenary of the completion of the Grand Trunk Pacific Railway (GTP)
through proclamations and the minting of special coins. Chartered in 1903
and completed in 1914, the GTP received massive subsidies from the federal

government, and its two principal owners, William Mackenzie and Donald Mann (the British Columbia community of Port Mann and the Port Mann Bridge are named after the latter), were knighted for their work in 1911. Members of the Industrial Workers of the World, or Wobblies, had their own story to tell about the working conditions of the great transcontinental project. When the union organized the construction workers, or navvies, in a strike that stretched across seven hundred miles of railway construction from Edmonton to Prince Rupert in 1912, its newspaper, the *Industrial Worker*, published this joke on July 12:

UNDERTAKER: I've advertised for an assistant. Have you any experience at funerals?
APPLICANT: I should say so! I was doctor in a railway construction camp for three years!

This story supports Green's contention that laborlore can help create an ideology that is transgressive and that reflects class tensions. The power of this informal ideology is no less formative and influential for being taught outside the official writings, classes, minutes, and meetings of the labour movement and left parties. It is, however, an ideology that needs to be examined critically, especially as a new generation of activists seeks to reshape the labour movement.

While Thompson wrote as an activist who saw class as an experience with the potential to unite workers, and Freeden wrote as an analyst without a class-based political project, nothing in their work suggests that ideology prevents or papers over splits and fractions in a group, or the sharing of ideologies across class lines. Indeed, much labour and left history describes a working class divided by occupation, gender, race, and ethnicity, and with ideologies that transcend class boundaries. Organizations, in the case of workers, especially unions, may be divided in another way: by a split between the leadership and the rank and file (Leier 1995).

To the degree the labour leadership forms a group with distinct interests, it uses ideology to articulate and defend those interests. However, since unions are ostensibly democratic organizations, the ideology of leadership is rarely set out formally and explicitly. Instead, it is more often expressed informally, through stories, tales, "common sense," and the like. Thus, while the history and ideologies of British Columbia's labour and left movements have been much studied, we need to examine different sources in order to understand the informal ideology of the labour leadership (Hak 2013; Isitt 2011; McCormack 1991; Robin 1968).

Other examples from the period of the GTP strike reveal that laborlore may also reveal these cracks and fissures in the labour movement. The GTP strike was only one in a year of strikes and labour unrest in British Columbia. The IWW struck another railway line, the Canadian Northern, and mobilized workers in a free speech fight to protest the banning of soapboxing and union organizing in Vancouver. In September, coal miners in the United Mine Workers of America (UMWA) began a strike that would last two years. The first picket lines went up at the Canadian Collieries mines owned by Mackenzie and Mann. Capital and the state responded to the strikes and demonstrations with the deployment of the militia, mass arrests, lengthy prison sentences, and refusals to negotiate (Leier 1990; Stonebanks 2004; Hinde 2003).

In the context of these battles, the *BC Federationist*, the newspaper of the overarching provincial labour body, the BC Federation of Labour, published a short history of labour in the province. In it, George Bartley wrote about a strike of fifty Italian muckers – pick and shovel workers – that he claimed took place in 1888, just two years after the city of Vanouver was incorporated. Hired to dig the trenches for the large pipes that would bring water from the Capilano watershed to Vancouver, the muckers demanded a wage increase. The employer refused, and although they were not organized in a union, the men went on strike. When it became clear after two days that the strike could not be won, they voted to return to work at the same wage rate. The night before they returned to work, however, each cut an inch off the blade of their shovel. If they could not increase their pay, they would move less earth each day to make their work commensurate with their pay (Bartley 1912).

It is a fine story of ingenuity and even success in the face of great odds. However, although Bartley told the story as history, it is fiction, similar to contemporary "urban legends" collected by folklorists (Brunvand 1981, 1984, 2000; Donovan 2003). This is not to say that there is no value in such stories. They function as modern myth and speak to our fears, anxieties, hopes, and concerns. Often, they serve as morality tales and cautionary stories.

One clue that a story is an urban legend is that it is collected over a wide area and period, and is told as a unique and true tale by people who did not observe it and cannot authenticate it. By this logic, we know that Bartley's story is not factually true. The shovel-shortening story has been told and collected in many regions and over many periods. Archie Green, for example, collected twelve versions, not including the Vancouver one, that range from 1875 to the 1940s. One appeared in a 1913 book by the British American unionist and socialist John Spargo as a British story told about Chinese coolies prior to 1896. The French anarchist Emile Pouget published a variant in 1910, alleging that the shovel cutting occurred in Indiana in 1908. There are versions from the American South and even another version from British Columbia, in the logging industry in 1920. That the story is widespread is grounds for presuming that it is lore, not fact. Furthermore, in all the variants, the storyteller is never a participant or a direct observer of the incident; its provenance is always from the equivalent "a friend of a friend." This is true of Bartley's tale as well: there are no contemporary accounts of the strike in the newspapers of the day, and Bartley arrived in Vancouver in 1889, too late to observe the strike himself (Green 1993, 327–41; Leier 1995).

This does not mean that the story has no lessons for us. It is a parable of resourcefulness and creativity in the face of harsh conditions, and holds up the tactics of direct action and sabotage as alternatives to strikes in the face of the employer's intransigence. It gives agency to workers who were marginalized by their ethnicity, their class, and their occupation. In the context of the complex and bitter labour struggles in British Columbia in this period, it is a story of a simpler approach to class conflict, of solidarity that arose quickly and without factors, and of struggles that could be waged and won without the complicated dance of negotiations and contracts and the prolonged hardship of the lengthy strike.

But the story is also a tale of exclusion. The workers in most variants, including Bartley's, are so-called unskilled workers, so-called because skill is often socially constructed rather than objectively measurable. They were not members of craft or trade unions that represented specific crafts and trades, such as carpenters, printers, cigarmakers, and boilermakers. These unions restricted admission to the craft to reduce competition between workers and thus keep wages high. Employers, for their part, sought to "de-skill" work by introducing new technology that did not require much training or arcane knowledge. Changes in the work process meant that the trade unionist's monopoly of skill would be made irrelevant and he could be replaced with unskilled, cheaper labour. As Karl Marx ([1867] 1990, 778) noted in *Capital*, "a greater number of inferior labour-powers is set in motion by the displacement of more skilled labour-powers." In this period, "unskilled" labour was often done by women and recent male immigrants. Labelling work as "skilled" often demarcated not actual skill and training so much as gender, race, ethnicity, and citizenship as unions fought to protect their wages (Burr 1999; Tillotson 1991).

Thus, it is significant that the workers in the shovel story are usually non-Anglo immigrants, typically Italian, Chinese, and Eastern European, some of the workers actively excluded from the craft union movement. The story emphasizes their marginalization: they could expect no solidarity from the mainstream labour movement and had no political rights or social connections to press their claims. Indeed, in 1903, when baggage handlers, navvies, and freight handlers in British Columbia joined the new United Brotherhood of Railway Employees, the railway unions of engineers, firemen, and brakemen refused to honour the picket lines. Likewise, when the IWW organized navvies on the Grand Trunk and Canadian Northern lines in 1912, it garnered very little support from the craft unions in the province. The shovel-cutting story was a way to reinforce that rigid separation between "legitimate," "respectable" Anglo male trade unionists and the rough, marginalized, disenfranchised, "ethnic" "unskilled" workers. It buttressed the formal position and ideology of the labour movement with laborlore (Gatour 2007; Tuck 1983; Leier 1990).

It is therefore telling that George Bartley wrote the Vancouver version of the shovel story. A printer and member of the International Typographical Union, and later a proprietor of his own shop, Bartley was a founding member of the Vancouver Trades and Labour Council (VTLC) in 1889, a federation of craft unions. He knew first-hand how employers used machinery to replace labour, for in 1894, "work for printers was curtailed by fifty per cent, hand work being replaced by machinery ... [the] *World* [newspaper] cut down from six to five columns, eight pages, employing two operators instead of four" (cited in Campbell 1946). In 1900, Bartley became the editor of the *Independent,* the newspaper of the VTLC. In its first issue, alongside stories of solidarity – an American Federation of Labor organizer is in town, Vancouver needs a labour hall, the carpenters are meeting – there is a warning about the "Mongol invasion" of British Columbia and the threat it posed to workers – meaning, of course, "skilled" male, white, Anglo workers (*Independent* 1900).

The shovel story is also a cautionary tale about laborlore as a source. What gets kept is a matter of who keeps it. In the case of laborlore, it is often kept and transmitted by the George Bartleys, by union leaders, union officials, and labour bureaucrats, and they are not simple custodians or archivists. They have specific interests as leaders and an informal ideology that articulates these interests.

Thus C. Wright Mills was right – and wrong – when he noted that "labor leaders do not live by ideology" (Mills [1948] 2001, 190). They may not live by formal ideologies such as liberalism, socialism, or social democracy, but they do live by an ideology of pragmatism. By this I mean an ideology that insists that the primary purpose of the union is to negotiate contracts within the rules set by capital and the state, and that the rank and file must be managed by reasonable, pragmatic leaders.

This became much more apparent by the 1940s, after the passage of the Wagner Act, or the National Labor Relations Act, in the United States in 1935 and, in Canada, Privy Council Order 1003 (PC 1003) of 1944, and subsequent federal and provincial legislation. In each country, legislation gave workers and unions new rights and protections. These included the right to be the bargaining agent for workers once a majority had joined the union, the insistence that collective bargaining take place and be undertaken in good faith, and protection from being fired or otherwise discriminated against for belonging to a union.

These were important, but as many historians and activists have noted, they came at a price. Securing the collective agreement became the principal goal of the labour movement. What could be bargained for was limited and management's rights were enshrined in the collective agreement. Wildcat strikes were banned. The effect of this has been to make the union, or, more accurately, the union leadership, responsible for policing the union membership, to ensure that it does not stray outside the lines carefully drawn by legislation and policy (Mills [1948] 2001; Lynd 2014; Fudge and Tucker 2001). Union leaders do not represent their members so much as direct them. They direct them with a careful eye to stay within the boundaries the state has drawn and enforces. When in 1967 the president of the United Fishermen and Allied Workers Union (UFAWU), Homer Stevens, was ordered by the courts to end a strike, he replied that he could not: as the president, he did what his members told him to do, not the other way around. For his commitment to democracy, Stevens served a year in prison. This principled stand has rarely been taken by other labour leaders (Stevens and Knight 1992).

Instead, the labour bureaucrat claims legitimate authority, the right to make decisions on behalf of others, based on the pragmatic argument that they know what is best, that they can make the best deal possible. This pragmatism often transcends left and right ideologies and leaders on both sides share a commitment to bureaucracy, that is, rule by the officeholders (Leier 1995). Thus a great deal of laborlore is about the need for order, for top-down unionism, for less rank-and-file democracy.

Modern laborlore gives us numerous examples of this. For many years, the largest and most influential union in British Columbia was the International Woodworkers of America (IWA). The IWA was an industrial union, formed in 1937 as part of the Congress of Industrial Organizations. Like most CIO unions, the IWA had a strong communist cadre of organizers and officials, including its founding president, Harold Pritchett. Born in Birmingham, England, Pritchett and his family had moved to British Columbia by 1912. His Communist Party membership prevented him from entering the United States, so he resigned the IWA presidency, becoming instead president of the IWA's BC District. The IWA had a reputation for militancy and success in organizing loggers and millworkers, bringing them up to a decent standard of living where other unions had failed (Lembcke and Tattam 1983; Neufeld and Parnaby 2000; Loomis 2015).

The union leadership has its own store of laborlore too. Sometime in the 1960s, one story goes, the IWA sent a young, inexperienced organizer into a mill town somewhere in British Columbia to organize the millworkers into the union. It was a tough company town, and no one was prepared to listen to the organizer. After several days, he called the union headquarters. "I'm not getting anywhere!" he complained. "Every day, I go to the mill gates at the beginning and the end of every shift. I have a stack of pamphlets and union cards and newspapers, and nobody will even talk to me!" The grizzled union official gave him some advice. "Don't try to organize at the mill," he said. "Go to the bar and talk to the fellas after work. When they've got a couple of drinks in them, they'll be more willing to talk." Three days later, the green organizer called back, bursting with excitement. "You were right!" he said. "At first, it was the same thing: nobody would talk to me! Finally, out of desperation, I stood up and shouted, 'I'll buy a beer for everybody who signs a union card!' And I signed up 300 men last night!" After a long pause, the old vet replied, "That's sure good news, all right. But there's only 200 guys who work in that mill!"[3]

The second story is set in the early 1970s, when the IWA and the labour movement in British Columbia was at its peak, as measured by the number of union members, the number of strikes, particularly wildcat strikes, and the election of the social democratic New Democratic Party in 1972. The IWA workers shut down a logging camp with an illegal wildcat strike, or a "wobble." When the union and the company investigated, they found that the strike was launched in protest over the camp food, historically a crucial issue in the industry. Further investigation revealed, however, that the wildcatting workers acknowledged that the camp had vanilla ice cream and strawberry ice cream, but no chocolate ice cream. The union members formally demanded that chocolate ice cream be duly delivered as a condition of ending their wobble. The union officers and company begged, threatened, and pleaded with them to return to work, promising chocolate ice cream as soon as possible, but the men stood firm, united, and strong. The story ends with the chocolate ice cream being helicoptered in at huge expense.

It never happened. All the hallmarks of the urban legend are there: the time and place of the event shift with each telling, and none of the tellers was a participant or observer or could positively identify someone who was. But the story does tell us some important things about the IWA in British Columbia in the 1970s. It speaks to the huge improvement in camp conditions the IWA had forced on reluctant employers, and to the union's giving voice to workers who were long considered "timber beasts," neither deserving nor appreciative of the trappings of civilization. It demonstrates the strength of the labour movement before the great collapse of the 1980s, the sheer exuberance of workers who could unite and fight, and resistance in the face of alienation.

But this story also speaks to the power of the rank and file to run amok. It is a cautionary tale about workers who get too feisty, workers who refuse to be reasonable, who take matters into their own hands and must be brought back into line. In their refusal to return to work even when the ice cream has been promised, the workers flouted one of the basic principles of the industrial relations regime of the Wagner Act and PC 1003 – work now and grieve later. Collective agreements contain dispute resolution mechanisms that are designed precisely to keep production going while paid company and union officials deal with the problem.

The rank and file are largely irrelevant to the negotiation process that insists production must continue. If rank and file members take matters into their own hands, as they did in this story, the union officials and the company together pressure them to return to work. In this story, democratic power, militancy, and solidarity are problems, not assets, to the union, and one of its lessons is that workers' demands should be reasonable. After all, two kinds of ice cream should be sufficient for anyone. But the trivial demand in this story is a way to head off discussions about what would be reasonable for the rank and file to insist upon during bargaining. It is also a way to sidestep the fact that when the industrial relations regime does not allow unions to consider fundamental questions of control over the work process, alienation, and exploitation, strikes that appear to be over inconsequential matters may in fact be over much more important questions that union officials never ask.

The way laborlore is often controlled and deployed by union officials – bureaucrats – was illustrated at the memorial service for one of the IWA's most colourful leaders, Jack Munro. Munro was the president of the BC District of the IWA from 1973 until 1992, when he retired. A millwright – ironically, he never worked as a millhand or faller – Munro joined the IWA and was hired as a business agent in 1962 at the age of thirty-one. He led a seven-and-a-half month strike of interior loggers in 1967, and made his way up the union hierarchy. He led further strikes that are inconceivable to activists today. One in 1986 lasted nearly five months and may have cost the provincial economy $2.5 billion.

For years, the IWA was the largest and most powerful union in the province, and Jack Munro was its face and voice. He was responsible for the creation of a fair bit of laborlore himself, some of which was recounted by Rod Mickleburgh in an obituary for Munro in the *Globe and Mail*. Knocking on doors in an organizing drive in Newfoundland, Munro had a shotgun pushed in his face by one anti-unionist. Asked later if he was scared, Munro replied, "Scared? You couldn't have knocked a hatpin up my ass with a sledgehammer!" At a meeting with Prince Philip, Munro started talking about affordable housing for workers. When the prince replied, "Canadians are always complaining about something," Munro characteristically replied, "Well, that's bullshit!" and continued to harangue the prince until he was steered away (Mickleburgh, 2013).

Munro led several strikes, bargained fiercely for his members, and used the power of the IWA to help weaker unions. In 1977, for example, SORWUC – the Service, Office, and Retail Workers Union of Canada, an independent, feminist, socialist union – had organized the workers, most of them women, at Bimini's, a pub in the trendy Kitsilano area of Vancouver. Pubs were new in the province, and unlike the large hotel beer parlours, were not unionized. The owner of Bimini's fought the union ferociously, and the workers finally went on strike. It was a nasty one: in another piece of laborlore, community members who volunteered to walk the picket line in support of the union were warned to bring hats. When asked why, experienced picketers pointed out that the pub was on the second floor of the building and the owner gave free beer to any patron who would urinate on the people walking the picket line.[4]

In the middle of the strike, Local 40 of the Hotel, Restaurant, Culinary Workers and Bartenders' Union applied to the Labour Relations Board to become the union for the scabs working behind the picket line. While some union leaders dithered – Local 40 claimed that it, not SORWUC, had jurisdiction over the pub workers – Jack Munro announced that "the lowest form of humanity that exists is a scab, and how any respectable trade union can go and even talk to them, never mind sign them, is a complete disgrace ... They are acting as traitors to the trade union movement." That is how it was reported in the papers; the laborlore version is that Munro announced that if "Local 40 doesn't take those goddamned scabs out of there, the IWA will take them out." And within a week Local 40 was out (Smith 2014).

He was less progressive on other matters. When environmentalists sought to protect forests from logging and preserve habitats for species such as the spotted owl, Munro was, according to a Vancouver newspaper, quoted in the *New York Times* as saying, "I tell my guys if they see a spotted owl to shoot it" (Ward 2013). In 1983, British Columbia's Social Credit government introduced an austerity budget and twenty-six bills to cut social services, restrict trade union rights, and shut down government regulatory bodies. Unions took to the streets in protest in what became known as Operation Solidarity and joined with social justice groups to form the Solidarity Coalition. As protests grew and talk of a general strike heated up, one of the pressing questions was what the IWA would do. This single union would make the difference; while the austerity bills largely targeted public sector workers, these workers were not strategically placed to put real pressure on the government. Only the IWA could. Munro's response was to retreat. He put it succinctly in his memoirs, saying he was not going to take his members out on strike to support the Rural Lesbians Society. He was not alone: other union leaders were determined to stop the rank and file protest while they could still contain it. Munro was chosen to meet with the provincial premier to sign a peace treaty (Munro and O'Hara 1990; Palmer 1987).

Munro was heavily criticized for this, perhaps most notably by Tom Wayman, a poet about work and dissent. In a poem titled "The Face of Jack Munro," Wayman celebrated the rank and file militancy of Operation Solidarity. "The world was full of love," Wayman (1986, 111–23) wrote, but

> In our midst, though,
> was error
> greater than the leeches:
> a cancer
> few could see ...
> a man called Jack Munro ...
> he entered the Kelowna house
> of the man who headed
> this government of death.
> And the two men shook hands ...

and now we saw the cancer,
saw how deep the cancer had spread
among us,
and were told Jack Munro's orders
were non-debatable by us,
were told voting by us on this issue
was irrelevant
and we did not know what to do
and we were lost ...
Jack Munro sold out this province
house by house,
district by district,
kilometre by kilometre.

This is not how Munro is remembered by other union leaders, however. At his memorial service in Vancouver on January 4, 2014, trade union officials who had worked with him for years told stories. Two in particular demonstrate the way laborlore is crafted to shape an ideology of pragmatism in the labour movement. The first was told by Angie Schira, long-time executive officer of the BC Federation of Labour, where Munro was long a vice president. Munro was a ferocious anti-communist. As C. Wright Mills observed, by the 1940s most trade union leaders were anti-communist, and more generally anti-leftists. Sometimes this stemmed from a genuine ideological disagreement, though as Mills put it, formal "ideology is not a strong point of American [or Canadian] labor leaders." More often, and certainly in Munro's case, these leaders opposed the left in their unions because it offered a challenge to their leadership. Thus "the labor leader fights Communists as he would any other rival faction within his union." Since the left aimed at the labour bureaucrat's weak points by calling for more democracy in the union and for better contracts, it presented a more significant threat than opponents on the right and so was fought with greater tenacity and less principle. Finally, union leaders such as Munro fought the left in their unions because "Communists are bad for public relations ... in particular with the businessmen with whom the labor leader negotiates, the workers whom he organizes, and the federal government upon which he may be dependent" (Mills [1948] 2001).

Schira spoke approvingly of the way Munro shut down leftists at conventions:

One of the things I remember about Jack was how he ran conventions. I remember at one of them, one of the "comrades" got up at one of the microphones in the hall and pulled out his manifesto, which he started to read. Jack let it go on for a while, then cut in to say, "Look, brother, we have a lot of people waiting at the other microphones to speak, so I'm going to have to ask you to hurry it up." The comrade got rattled, and said, "I, I've lost my place." "I can help you out, brother," said Jack. "I recognize the speaker at microphone number 5!"[5] (Mickleburgh 2014)

The crowd, made up largely of older union officials, responded enthusiastically and positively to Schira's story. The characterization of Munro's critic as a "comrade" and his notes as a "manifesto" is clearly a way to label him as a communist and thus, in the mind of Schira and the appreciative audience, fair game for ridicule and abuse of the rules of order. The effect of this was to dismiss criticism from the left that challenged the assumptions that Munro made about the role of the union and the leadership, and the public humiliation helped Munro ensure his position in the union.

The second story was told by Ken Georgetti, long-time head of the BC Federation of Labour and the Canadian Labour Congress, the counterpart to the US AFL-CIO. Georgetti called Munro his mentor and said that the thing he admired most about him was that Munro always knew the exact moment to settle a strike or a labour dispute (personal recollection, author, Vancouver, January 4, 2014). There is, of course, no way to test Georgetti's assertion that Munro knew when to settle and thus win all that could be won at the bargaining table. "It was the best we could do at the time" may be used to justify any decision, and it is difficult to refute after the contract has been signed. It is particularly the refrain of those whose claim to authority, to the right to make decisions on behalf of others, is their alleged expertise.

For elected labour leaders, being right, or appearing to be right, is the key to holding their jobs. And these are good jobs: white collar, managerial, much better paid than the jobs in the steel mill Georgetti came from or the sawmill Munro came from. In the 1960s, the head of the AFL-CIO, George Meany, boasted he had never walked a picket line in his life. At a time when the average US income was $6,000 a year, Meany was, as laborlore had it, the only plumber in America who made $60,000 a year without ever making a house call.

These positions bring access and honours: both Munro and Georgetti regularly met with business and political leaders, received the Order of Canada, and were made members of foundations and boards and, in the case of Georgetti, of a large real estate development company controlled by union leaders (Offley 2004). Knowing just when to settle, or more accurately, determining when to settle and then how to sell the deal to the membership, is a critical skill for the union leader that transcends left and right ideologies. It is part of the union leader's ideology of pragmatism, of what is possible, viewed through the lens of self-interest and contrasted with the larger principles often assumed to be part of the trade union movement, such as the need for militancy, more radical perspectives, and rank and file control.

This was expressed with humour by Tom Cameron-Fawkes, who worked for several unions in British Columbia and Alberta, including the IWA and the United Food and Commercial Workers, from the 1970s until 2007. Cameron-Fawkes remarked (personal communication, Burnaby, 2003):

> The trouble with you academics is you think the first principle of the labour movement is "solidarity forever." Well, it isn't. Our first principle is "don't fuck with me." Our second principle is, "if you fuck with my membership, you're fucking with me." And our third principle is, "we never forget." Sure, "solidarity" is on the list, but it's way down there.

As if to confirm his observation, Ken Georgetti, head of the CLC, and Jim Sinclair, head of the BC Federation of Labour, spoke briefly at Cameron-Fawkes's memorial service in 2011, then left the hall just as the crowd rose to sing "Solidarity Forever." When challenged to stay by the singer leading the crowd, the two replied that they had a plane to catch (personal observation by author, May 18, 2011).

Critical examination of the labour bureaucracy is of particular importance today, and too important to be restricted to an examination of laborlore, for the provenance of laborlore today is largely in the hands of the labour bureaucracy, a bureaucracy created by legislation, formal regulation, the courts, and the industrial relations regime crafted since the Second World War. The effect of this industrial relations regime has been to isolate and insulate leaders from the rank and file, to create a trade union culture that is very much top-down, a culture in which larger political questions are discouraged and marginalized. Laborlore is crafted and passed down in the service of this labour bureaucracy to create a particular kind of "common sense" that reinforces ideas of leadership and of abiding by rules laid down by others.

Thus, George Bartley could tell the story of the Italian muckers and their shovels to argue that direct action was futile and that solidarity was a matter of ethnicity and occupation. Thus, Jack Munro could be celebrated for his exclusion of the left and for his uncritical pragmatism. Better to blame the loss of jobs and the decline of the IWA – now no longer an independent union – on the spotted owl than on technological change, for no union and certainly no union leader has ever been able to win that battle. That, however, is an admission no union leader is likely to make.

This labour leadership has been unable to confront the challenges of neoliberalism, however. As a result, new activists are asking important questions about union democracy, militancy, and capitalism (Fraser 2015; Aronowitz 2014; Camfield 2011; Workman 2009; Lynd 2015; Ness 2014). Indeed, Ken Georgetti, the longest-serving head of the CLC, was ousted at a fiercely contested convention in 2014, the first time a sitting president of the congress had lost an election. Later that same year, Jim Sinclair, head of the BC Federation of Labour, declined to seek another term when it was made clear he could not win an election at the convention. In short, activists are asking the labour leadership the question Florence Reece asked of workers during a 1931 strike of coal miners in Harlan County, Kentucky, in her song "Which Side Are You On?"[6]

The answer to that question is not always easy to come by. Labour bureaucrats have long crafted and imposed an informal ideology that serves their particular interests. This ideology is all the more powerful because it masquerades as common sense and because it is informal. As Baudelaire put it, "the loveliest trick of the Devil is to persuade you that he does not exist!"

But the conservative, anti-democratic ideologies of the labour bureaucrats are revealed when we examine the patterns, the systems of loose, even unintended political thinking, that Michael Freeden draws our attention to. Just as E.P. Thompson's examination of working class culture and Archie Green's laborlore revealed democratic, oppositional currents in the labour movement, so can their methods help us understand how the ideology of the labour bureaucracy was shaped by, and in turn shaped, the labour movement even as today's activists seek to transcend it.

Notes

1 Thompson's gendered language is a relic of the time in which he researched and wrote *The Making of the English Working Class*. It is clear from the book and Thompson's discussions of the issue that he used "men" here in the old sense of "people" and did not mean to exclude women.
2 Contemporary Canadian usage is to spell "labour" with a "u." This has not been a consistent usage. In 1910, Vancouver's labour hall was opened on 411 Dunsmuir street, and named the "Labor Temple." The original wording, carved in stone above the main entrance, may be seen there today. I have chosen, for simplicity, to use "laborlore" instead of "labourlore."

3 This story and the following one were told to me on several occasions by various IWA officials between 1997, when I began teaching labour history to IWA members, and 2004, when the IWA merged into the Steelworkers. See Chapter 9 for the uses of personal experience in understanding working class ideology.
4 I was told this when I appeared for picket duty, and heard it repeated several times to other newcomers.
5 I attended the service and my recollection is similar to Mickleburgh's.
6 Ironically, the song is set to the tune of an old English ballad titled "Jack Munro."

References

Aronowitz, Stanley. 2014. *The Death and Life of American Labor: Toward a New Workers' Movement*. New York: Verso Books.

Bartley, George. 1912. "Twenty-Five Years of Labor in Vancouver." *BC Federationist*. December 27, p. 2.

Brunvand, Jan Harold. 1981. *The Vanishing Hitchhiker: American Urban Legends and Their Meanings*. New York: W.W. Norton.

−. 1984. *The Choking Doberman and Other "New" Urban Legends*. New York: W.W. Norton.

−. 2000. *The Truth Never Stands in the Way of a Good Story*. Urbana: University of Illinois Press.

Burns, Sean. 2011. *Archie Green: The Making of a Working-Class Hero*. Urbana: University of Illinois Press.

Burr, Christina. 1999. *Spreading the Light: Work and Labour Reform in Nineteenth Century Toronto*. Toronto: University of Toronto Press.

Camfield, David. 2011. *Canadian Labour in Crisis: Reinventing the Workers' Movement*. Halifax: Fernwood Publishing.

Campbell, Burt R. 1946. "From Hand-Set Type to Linotype." *British Columbia Historical Quarterly* 10 (4): 253–72.

Donovan, Pamela. 2003. *No Way of Knowing: Crime, Urban Legends and the Internet*. New York: Routledge.

Fraser, Steve. 2015. *The Age of Acquiescence: The Life and Death of American Resistance to Organized Wealth and Power*. New York: Little, Brown.

Freeden, Michael. 1998. *Ideologies and Political Theory: A Conceptual Approach*. Toronto: Oxford University Press.

Fudge, Judy, and Eric Tucker. 2001. *Labour before the Law: The Regulation of Workers' Collective Action in Canada, 1900–1948*. Toronto: Oxford University Press.

Gatour, David. 2007. *Guarding the Gates: The Canadian Labour Movement and Immigration, 1872–1934*. Vancouver: UBC Press.

Green, Archie. 1993. *Wobblies, Pile Butts, and Other Heroes*. Urbana: University of Illinois Press.

−. 1996. *Calf's Head and Union Tale: Labor Yarns at Work and Play*. Urbana: University of Illinois Press.

−. 2001. *Torching the Fink Books and Other Essays on Vernacular Culture*. Chapel Hill: University of North Carolina Press.

−. 2006. *Harry Lundeberg's Stetson and Other Nautical Treasures*. Crockett, CA: Carquinez Press.

Hak, Gordon. 2013. *The Left in British Columbia: A History of Struggle*. Vancouver: Ronsdale Press.

Hinde, John. 2003. *When Coal Was King: Ladysmith and the Coal-Mining Industry of Vancouver Island*. Vancouver: UBC Press.

Independent. 1900. "Some Mongol Statistics." March 31.

Isitt, Benjamin. 2011. *Militant Minority: British Columbia Workers and the Rise of a New Left, 1948–1972*. Toronto: University of Toronto Press.

Leier, Mark. 1990. *Where the Fraser River Flows: The Industrial Workers of the World in British Columbia*. Vancouver: New Star.

–. 1995. *Red Flags and Red Tape: The Making of a Labour Bureaucracy*. Toronto: University of Toronto Press.

Lembcke, Jerry, and William Tattam. 1983. *One Union in Wood: A Political History of the International Woodworkers of America*. Vancouver: Harbour Publishing.

Loomis, Eric. 2015. *Empire of Wood: Labor Unions and the Pacific Northwest Forests*. Cambridge: Cambridge University Press.

Lynd, Staughton. 2014. *Doing History from the Bottom Up: On E.P. Thompson, Howard Zinn, and Rebuilding the Labor Movement from Below*. Chicago: Haymarket Books.

–. 2015. *Solidarity Unionism: Rebuilding the Labor Movement from Below*. Oakland, CA: PM Press.

Marx, Karl. (1867) 1990. *Capital: A Critique of Political Economy*. Volume I. London: Penguin Books.

McCormack, A. Ross. (1977) 1991. *Reformers, Rebels, and Revolutionaries: The Western Canadian Radical Movement, 1899–1919*. Toronto: University of Toronto Press.

Mickleburgh, Rod. 2013. "Union Leader Jack Munro Was Labour King of B.C. Forests." *Globe and Mail*. December 13. https://www.theglobeandmail.com/news/british-columbia/union-leader-jack-munro-was-labour-king-of-bc-forests/article15968925/.

–. 2014. "A Last Farewell for Big Jack Munro." Mickleblog, https://mickleblog.wordpress.com/2014/01/06/a-last-farewell-for-big-jack-munro/.

Mills, C. Wright. (1948) 2001. *The New Men of Power: America's Labor Leaders*. Urbana: University of Illinois Press.

Munro, Jack, and Jane O'Hara. 1990. *Union Jack: Labour Leader Jack Munro*. Vancouver: Douglas and McIntyre.

Ness, Immanuel, ed. 2014. *New Forms of Worker Organization: The Syndicalist and Autonomist Restoration of Class-Struggle Unionism*. Oakland, CA: PM Press.

Neufeld, Andrew, and Andrew Parnaby. 2000. *The IWA in Canada: The Life and Times of an Industrial Union*. Vancouver: IWA Canada/New Star Books.

Offley, Will. 2004. "Unionism as Business: Are the Union Leaders Becoming Bosses?" *New Socialist*. May 14. http://newsocialist.org/old_mag/magazine/47/article11.html.

Palmer, Bryan D. 1987. *Solidarity: The Rise and Fall of an Opposition in British Columbia*. Vancouver: New Star Books.

Robin, Martin. 1968. *Radical Politics and Canadian Labour, 1880–1930*. Kingston, ON: Industrial Relations Centre, Queen's University.

Smith, Julia. 2014. "An 'Entirely Different' Kind of Union: The Service, Office, and Retail Workers' Union of Canada (SORWUC), 1972–1986." *Labour/le travail* 73: 23–65.

Stevens, Homer, and Rolf Knight. 1992. *Homer Stevens: A Life in Fishing*. Vancouver: Harbour Publishing.

Stonebanks, Roger. 2004. *Fighting for Dignity: The Ginger Goodwin Story*. St. John's: Canadian Committee on Labour History.

Thompson, E.P. (1963) 1980. *The Making of the English Working Class*. London: Pelican Books.

Tillotson, Shirley. 1991. "'We May All Soon Be First-Class Men': Gender and Skill in Canada's Early Twentieth Century Urban Telegraph Industry." *Labour/le travail* 27: 97–125.

Tuck, J. Hugh. 1983. "The United Brotherhood of Railway Employees in Western Canada, 1898–1905." *Labour/le travail* 11: 63–88.

Ward, Doug. 2013. "BC Forest Labour Icon Jack Munro Dies at Age 82." *Vancouver Sun*, November 14.

Workman, Thom. 2009. *If You're in My Way, I'm Walking: The Assault on Working People since 1970*. Halifax: Fernwood Publishing.

A Reconnaissance of Everyday Working Class Ideology in British Columbia

DENNIS PILON

Where does ideology come from and what sustains it on an ongoing basis? A glance at various academic debates might lead one to single out elite theorists, political leaders, or full-time political activists. The role of average people in the process, by contrast, is either ignored or assumed to exist somehow, though the "what" and "how" questions are seldom explored. This seems curious because we can point to many oppositional movements, both past and present, that have relied on extensive and sometimes clandestine support from average people: guerrilla movements, resistance to occupying powers, mass parties, and so on. Public support for such politically charged actions is influenced by broadly accepted ideas about the world and how it works, ideas that fit the frame of what we might call ideology.

Here I am specifically interested in what I am calling "working class ideology," to distinguish it from the more familiar understandings of ideology on the left (e.g., socialism, communism, or anarchism) as well as different versions of populism, both left and right. Working class ideology is distinctive in that its origins do not lie in a seminal book or tract, or emerge from a specific political actor or event. Instead, it is the product of working class experience, comprising a host of observations and lessons about how the world works and the place of working people within it, that then in turn inform how working people should respond both socially and politically. While not always a logically rigorous doctrine, this collection of ideas does form a coherent world view that can be understood as ideological.

Studying working class ideology poses a host of methodological problems, particularly the absence of the kind of documentary records that
would permit a detailed exploration of the development of such views, their
use, and their impact. Put bluntly, working people either did not produce
or tended to have to throw away most of the stuff that might be useful here:
diaries, letters, evidence of participation in public events or political organizations, and so on. We are left with the challenge of reconnaissance: how
to go back and rediscover what was often never put on paper (McKay 2000).
Some have argued that the project itself – to recover what working class
people thought and why – is doomed because, as they argue, the "subaltern
cannot speak." Basically, they suggest, attempts to give voice to subaltern
views will just recode such experience back into dominant understandings
of the world (Spivak 1993; Trowler 2014). While this has certainly occurred
and poses some challenges, such critiques are too sweeping and dismissive
of what might possibly be discovered through a self-reflexive and critical
engagement with working people, the experiences of their lives, and the
broader historical trajectory of events (for a concrete exploration of these
challenges, see Pilon 2015a).

To address these methodological challenges, I plan to use a form of
auto-ethnography to jumpstart this research. Auto-ethnography involves
researchers' use of their own experience to inform the analysis of social
phenomena. In this case, having spent a great deal of time with my maternal grandparents, Vera and Tom, I can testify to the existence of a working
class ideology through my experience of them via what they conveyed to me
about their lives and their thinking. This will require combining what they
said with a critical assessment of their life trajectories, the way their experiences and choices appeared to reflect their exposure to and involvement
with the broader social struggles occurring around them. It will also require
bringing their personal experiences into dialogue with what we know about
working people and social change from existing academic work. Through
such a process, their particular experiences can tell us a lot about how a
working class ideology was shaped, sustained, and acted on more concretely.

Theory and Method

Our first question must be, what is ideology? How does it differ from just
ideas? How does my proposed working class ideology differ from characterizations of working class culture? This then leads to our second question: how should we study it? Terry Eagleton (1991, 1–2) famously set out at
least sixteen different – sometimes overlapping, sometimes contradictory –

definitions of ideology. Clearly, for intellectuals and academics, ideology is an "essentially contested concept" (Gallie 1956). Nevertheless, if we set aside characterizations of ideology as deliberately misleading views or false consciousness, many approaches to understanding ideology suggest that it is a systematic set of ideas that then act as a world view or prism through which to understand that world, interpret specific events, and inform what actions should or can be taken.

Eagleton himself formulated a number of useful conditions to distinguish ideology from ideas, values, preferences, or cultural tastes. He claimed that an ideology involves a "general material process of production of ideas, beliefs and values in social life," one where the meanings of ideology are informed by a "social determination of thought" (as opposed to simply idealism). Furthermore, he suggested that an ideology "turns on ideas and beliefs (whether true or false) which symbolize the conditions and life-experiences of a specific, socially significant group or class." At the same time, such an ideology "attends to the *promotion* and *legitimation* of the interests of such social groups in the face of opposing interests." Finally, ideologies are utilized to sustain or challenge "a whole political form of life." As Eagleton (1991, 28–29) neatly sums it up: "Ideology [is] a discursive field in which self-promoting social powers conflict and collide over questions central to the reproduction of social power as a whole." Ideologies, then, can be both the product of life experiences and the means by which self-conscious actors seek to reshape the world and their place in it.

Eagleton's approach fits well with the working class ideology set out above but differs markedly from more traditional discussions of ideology, particularly discussions about the source of ideological thinking and conflict. In conventional accounts, ideological thinking is often tracked back to canonical thinkers like Edmund Burke for conservatives, John Locke for liberals, Karl Marx for socialists, and so on (Graham 1986; Vincent 2010). The assumption here is that ideological thoughts are created by great men, then disseminated somehow to various elites who act on them, influencing the broader public through their actions. Over time, and particularly in light of declining public engagement in politics over the past three decades, such narratives have led to a general acceptance among public intellectuals and some academics that while elites may be ideological, their followers, as a rule, are not (Fiorina 2006). Indeed, some have suggested that ideology in the hands of average people is like a loaded gun in the hands of a child, contributing to a dangerous, blind populism (for an influential formulation of this, see Lipset 1959). A considerable behavioural literature emerged in the postwar period in the United States lending credence to such views, arguing that average people were not ideological in their political choices. In fact, they barely knew anything about politics; their political action or inaction was influenced either by cultural factors (voting as their parents did) or by considerations of short-term self-interest (Converse 1964; Downs 1957).

Such views have been challenged in a host of ways. First, behavioural work has been criticized for its rather narrow understanding of what constitutes ideology and the limitations inherent in the survey method in grappling with complex social ideas (Robertson 1993; Gibbons 2006; Pilon 2015a). Second, the idea that survey researchers can simply ask people about their ideology assumes that ideology operates only at a self-conscious level. One view says that whether self-consciously or not, all people necessarily operate with an overarching world view, influenced by ideological understandings of how the world works and what motivates people. In modern capitalist societies, dominant conservative and liberal ideologies operate in a non–self-conscious way on most people, while a minority has explicitly worked to develop an ideology in reaction to their experience. My example of Tom and Vera's working class ideology would be an example of the latter approach. Behavioural approaches fail to capture the ideological influence on the first group and have proven weak in understanding its impact on the second.

To fill the gaps in quantitative approaches, researchers have taken up a number of more intimate approaches to investigating what people think, primarily by drawing on ethnographic techniques. Traditional ethnography saw researchers live among different communities as a way of becoming acquainted with their world view and social interactions. Ethnographic work in class-riven societies has demonstrated the reality of working class culture and a kind of working class ideology (e.g., Willis 1977; Nayak 2006). Pierre Bourdieu developed a sophisticated ethnographic method particularly attuned to class and class experience, combining concepts of habitus (the cultural environment), field (the specific setting), and social capital (the degree of social power) to explain the development of both self-conscious and other ideological thinking (Bourdieu 1984, 1999).

Historical studies of the working class have explored ideological thinking through an examination of cultural practices, noting the many ways that culture has been reshaped to take up new challenges, that is, how ideas shaped in the past help inform responses in the present (e.g., Thompson [1963] 1980). But how do we pursue this in more modern settings? Much past research has focused on obvious and readily accessible sources, such as unions, left parties, and middle-class activists (Montgomery 1988; Sassoon 1997). It is harder to get at what working class people more generally thought about politics and society. And yet what if the strength of left ideology historically was anchored in and given sustenance by a broad working class ideology? We know that working class parties in the twentieth century could not count on elite or media support in their electoral campaigns. Yet millions of working people across Western countries voted for them. It was precisely the link between left parties, their distinct representation of what was political, and its resonance with concrete working class experience that enabled them to succeed in the face of almost unified elite opposition (Eley 2002). It may then be crucial to understand how such a relationship worked if we are to respond effectively to the challenges of the present.

The twentieth-century left's broad historical strokes involve struggle, revolution, reform, and retreat, with the fuel of its success largely resting on the millions of average working people – most with little formal education or economic privilege – who supported its agenda. How can we recover the thinking that went into that working class support, assess why and how it could be sustained over decades, and appreciate what informed its development and reproduction? Historians have tracked the broad sweep of such developments, but their focus has tended to be on elite actors (Eley 2002; Moschonas 2002). Exceptions include Canadian historian Craig Heron and American social scientist Michael Yates, both of whom used their own family history to demonstrate the varied impacts of class on their consciousness, though in each case the experiences did not lead to any unproblematic "working class" ideology (Heron 2009; Yates 2009). Another is the tradition of oral history, which has captured working people directly speaking about their lives and how they have understood them (Terkel 1974; Sangster 2013). The method I am taking up – auto-ethnography – is similar to oral history in many ways, except that an auto-ethnographic researcher knows her subjects much better and is usually inextricably connected to their story and its telling. In auto-ethnography, researchers are also the subjects and are bound to the story they are telling by their personal involvement in it.

Auto-ethnography can add a rich dimension to research, combining deep personal testimony with a rigorous engagement with the relevant academic literatures on the topic (Ellis, Adams, and Bochner 2011; Denshire 2014; Forber-Pratt 2015). For instance, a great deal of social analysis moves vertically, from events to individuals understood as demographic categories. Thus, we can measure statistics about class location or gender as examples against specific events (like an election) to gauge the relationship between the two. By contrast, an ethnography allows the researcher to move out horizontally, exploring the range and depth of an individual's responses to events. But it is impossible to go back in time ethnographically, in a traditional way. This is where an auto-ethnography allows researchers to revisit the past either through their own relationship with it or via testimony from other informants. It has the potential to provide insight that is literally unavailable with any other methods.

For instance, what does this kind of storytelling add to our understanding of working class support for left parties and working class political involvement? Its value is in connecting how life experience may inform judgments to better answer the "why" questions, to get at the *meaning* that actors attribute to their actions. It should be underlined that such testimony, whether personal or indirect, cannot be taken just at face value. We must always juxtapose such stories with a critical assessment of why people made the choices they did. As Dorothy Smith (2006, 3) has noted, people know their own experience, but not necessarily the broader social forces or events that have shaped the world they are making their choices in. Exploring working class ideology does not require us to agree with anyone's assessments of the political world or their choices about how to respond to it; the point is to understand how they came to their understanding and what factors contributed to its reproduction or change.

Working Class Ideology and British Columbia

Scholars have routinely characterized British Columbia as a class-polarized polity (Pilon 2015b). On the left, the literature paints the province as more militant, Marxist, and class-oriented than the rest of the country. Labour historians have explored the waves of radicalism that have influenced the province's union movement (Phillips 1967; Leier 1990; Isitt 2007), while political analysts have highlighted the strong class focus of early socialist and labour politicians as well as the provincial Co-operative Commonwealth Foundation (CCF)/New Democratic Party (NDP) (Isitt 2009, 2011; Naylor 2013). Prominent BC socialists resisted incorporation into the CCF in the early 1930s, repudiated the reformist Winnipeg Declaration in 1956, and were uneasy about the CCF's reinvention as the NDP in 1961, all because they deemed such initiatives as insufficiently socialist. Scholars have either applauded (Isitt 2011) or condemned (Young 1969) such orientations, but few disputed the general assessment.

Where they do disagree is about the roots of the behaviour. One group blames the political leaders, arguing that their extremism and inability to control their party members kept the left from power for most of the twenti-eth century (Young 1969). Another group goes further, suggesting that there really was no ideological radicalism below the level of the leadership itself. In this view, the BC public was never ideological or class-conscious as much as small "l" liberal in an unself-conscious way (Barman 1996; McDonald 2013). Such views have been hotly countered by others who claim that working class culture did exist in the province and that elements of it were strongly leftist (e.g., Palmer 1987; Leier 1990; Naylor 2013). But their evi-dence still tends to reflect the actions of organizers and activists rather than more average working people. What we need is testimony from working class British Columbians themselves about their political ideas and how those influenced their behaviour. As noted above, however, documentary evidence about such twentieth-century actors is largely missing. Indeed, in British Columbia, even the papers of well-known working class leaders are often missing or were destroyed (e.g., Bill Pritchard, Effie Jones).

This is where auto-ethnography comes in. My working class maternal grandparents, Vera and Tom, came to British Columbia in the 1920s and sustained a commitment to left politics throughout their lives. They were not political activists or leaders, but they worked a range of working class jobs and demonstrated their support for the left by donating money to left causes, voting in elections, maintaining memberships in political parties, and sometimes participating in events organized by the left. They were "average" working class people, not "un-average" working class activists and leaders of left organizations. The latter comprised a fairly small group of people who mostly knew each other and worked together on numerous occasions. "Average" working people in the hundreds of thousands barely knew anyone outside their own circle of workmates, family, and acquain-tances. And yet, I would argue, they were loosely bound together by a shared working class ideology.

In what follows, I use techniques from auto-ethnography to draw out insights about working class ideology from the lives of Vera and Tom as I experienced them over the course of a number of decades, through family visits, from living with them for a number of years, and through my ongoing relationship with them thereafter. In showcasing Vera and Tom, I am not suggesting that they can stand in for all twentieth-century left supporters in British Columbia. Nor am I arguing that all working people possessed a developed and consistent sense of a working class ideology (Boyd 2016). However, Tom and Vera's experience does tell us something about how some working people understood and responded to what was going on in the province during their lifetimes, so considering this experience may help us to see something we've been missing as well as spur us to further inquiry into other people like them. Of course, Tom and Vera's "experience" is, in this telling, unavoidably my experience of them, translated, interpreted, and indeed shaped by my own historical and personal development.

We shall now track the particular way in which their consciousness of class arose in British Columbia over the course of the twentieth century.

Vera and Tom's Working Class Ideology

> *"Working people have got to stick together."*
> *– Vera*
> *"The working man is his own worst enemy."*
> *– Tom*

Tom and Vera were married in 1946. Vera was thirty-nine, Tom thirty-four. Both had been previously married and had children from their previous relationships. Together they had two more children. As one of their children's children, I came to know Tom and Vera in the 1970s, when their home in East Vancouver was the hub of our extended family. Holidays, long weekends, or just any time my parents wanted to drop in were spent with uncles, aunts, cousins, or just my grandparents.

In 1982, I left home to move in with Vera and Tom for my final year of high school, and stayed until the end of my two-year broadcasting program over three years later. Living with them enabled me to see how they saw the world, over meals, watching the nightly news, debating political events, doing chores, and so on. What I saw was a couple engaged with what was going on in the world around them, exuding a clear sense of political commitment. But they were not elite members or activists of a political party or union. They were just working class people who had lived a long life, seen a great many things, experienced hope and failure, and learned from their experiences. These experiences shaped how they saw the world, how they understood what caused what, and informed their responses to what they read and heard and saw.

After I left their home in 1985, I visited with them regularly over the next two decades. As my grandfather was dying in 1996, my grandmother and I spent most evenings together for several months, reviewing the details of her life. I developed a coherent picture of their lives before they met each other, and of how they interacted with and were shaped by the events of the day. Just as my grandfather was dying I was starting to understand how I could use my university study of left and labour history, social theory, and class analysis to ask him informed questions about his experience, but I didn't get very far before he passed away. However, I spent a great deal of time exploring such themes with my grandmother over the following decade and a half. Such exposure to these two people is like a kind of ethnography, without a forward-organized methodology. I am left with a project of reconnaissance, recovering what insights I can from what I recall, in dialogue with social science research on topics related to their lived experience.

The two quotes that open this section are emblematic of Tom and Vera and their unique perspectives on their experiences. Vera was an optimist who drew from her experience as a farm girl on the Canadian Prairies key lessons about the possibility of collective action and cooperative behaviour. Tom was less positive, his views powerfully shaped by the challenges involved in forging a union movement in the 1930s and 1940s that could bind workers together to face down the power of the bosses and the state. Vera was more confident, using her experience and accomplishments on the farm as the basis for developing new skills and taking on new challenges. Tom's masculine bluster of the mid-twentieth-century man masked a host of insecurities related to his youth as a runaway, lack of education, and absence of many trade-worthy skills.

Vera was born in Southampton in 1907. Her father was a street railwayman who helped organize the union of tram drivers. Her mother "worked in service" in London, travelling to and from "the city" to maintain her courtship. Vera's parents saved money for a decade to buy a house before getting married, but decided in their mid-thirties to sell up and move to Canada to become farmers in 1913. The family settled on a farm outside the village of Eastleigh, not far from Moose Jaw, Saskatchewan. A large album of photos documents their time on the farm over the next decade with pictures of horses, farm equipment, the local one-room schoolhouse, and community picnics. Vera's description of farm life highlighted the self-sufficiency of farming communities, a quality crucially reliant on a measure of collective interdependence among local families. They made their own clothes, built their own homes, and shared equipment with their neighbours. They also made their own fun with local fairs and picnics and card and music nights, and whiled away the long winter nights by making their own candy.

The photos capture the events of the day and her parents' involvement in them. In one photo, dated June 1919, a large group of people are attending a picnic with a small plane in the background. It was not uncommon for flyers to land in fields after spotting picnics to offer locals the novelty of a ride for a price. But Vera recalled that the big topic at the picnic was the ongoing Winnipeg General Strike. In her recollection, farming families were very interested in politics. Later, Vera's father would attend meetings of the farmer-based Progressive Party and support it in the 1921 election. The problems facing farmers in Canada in the 1920s hit Vera's family directly – in 1923 they lost their farm. They decided to relocate to Vancouver, where other relatives from the "old country" had settled.

In Vancouver, Vera's family set up a family business in a succession of large houses in the downtown neighbourhood of the city, offering rooms to let and meals to men who worked at the sawmills on False Creek. Once a prestigious community with many large houses, the West End became more working class as the better off moved to new suburbs created on the city's west side. Vera described their tenants in very positive terms. "You met a lot of interesting people," she said, and countless photos from the period feature her posing with residents that she could still name in the 1990s. Vera and her mother cooked meals, cleaned, and did laundry for the men, with her father acting as gardener and general handyman. Vera attended local dances, listened to residents play on an old piano, and filled evenings with card games in the days before radio.

The 1920s were an interesting time for a farm girl to relocate to what was quickly becoming the country's third-largest city. Vera had a boyfriend on the prairie and would probably have married him had she stayed. Upon arriving in the city, after a few exchanges of letters, she decided she didn't want to marry him any more. "There was just too much going on," she suggested wryly. The emerging urban spaces in Canada offered newly enfranchised women a chance to defy some traditional gender stereotypes, specifically to remain in the workforce longer and delay marriage. I asked Vera why she married so late in life. "I didn't see the point in getting married when there were so many things I could do," she responded. Over the next two decades, she worked in a host of jobs, many repurposing skills she had picked up on the farm, like making clothes. Initially, she worked in restaurants while helping her parents with the rooming houses. Eventually, she turned to dressmaking, opening a shop with a friend whose parents provided the money to rent a space, with Vera designing and making the clothes and the friend managing the finances. In the late 1920s, she was even able to buy a house, with financial help from girlfriends she took in as roommates. The Great Depression altered this trajectory. Her friend's parents pushed her out of the dressmaking business and she lost the house when her roommates left to live with their relatives as they lost their jobs in the service sector. In the 1930s, she was back with her parents in the rooming houses and working in clothing cleaning factories, specializing in ironing different parts of men's clothing.

The Great Depression solidified a lot of life lessons for Vera. Given her experience on the farm, the socialist argument that workers were the ones who knew how to do things and bosses were not needed rang true. She had grown up surrounded by people who knew how to do all the things required to reproduce humanity: grow food, operate and fix machinery, make clothing, and so on. She also knew that it was not the workers' fault that they lacked work or opportunities. Like many others in the 1920s, her family had lost their farm, despite a decade of back-breaking work. The men crowding the cities in the early 1930s were like the sawmill workers she had known in the rooming houses. In her view, the problem wasn't with the workers but with a system that rewarded the wealthy at the expense of everyone else. In the 1930 federal election, the first she could participate in, Vera voted for the local Communist Party candidate because, she said, "they were the only party for the working man." She also attended rallies and parades for the unemployed in this period, joined the CCF shortly after it was formed in 1932, and maintained her membership in the party for the rest of her life.

In the 1930s, Vera married and gave birth to her only son, but the marriage didn't last. She had discovered shortly after giving birth that her husband had another family in a different suburb of Vancouver, a not uncommon occurrence in an era of itinerant working men. She left him and moved back in with her parents in the late 1930s. During the war, Vera raised enough money with her parents to purchase a small house in east Vancouver. At the war's end she met Tom at a dance and they married after a brief courtship.

Tom was born in Liverpool, England, in 1912. His father had been in the army and was by all accounts a bitter and unpleasant man. Little is known about Tom's mother. Whereas Vera had been an only child, Tom had a much older brother (who died in the First World War) and much younger sister. Tom ran away from home at fourteen and lived "rough" for a time, eventually falling under the guardianship of an organization that specialized in relocating runaway children from the United Kingdom to farms in Canada. In 2006, I visited the Canadian Museum of Immigration in Halifax and saw a facsimile of docking papers detailing Tom's arrival in Montreal in 1929, just before the border was closed to immigrants in response to the stock market crash. He arrived with almost no money and was sent to a farm in Peterborough, Ontario to help pay off the cost of his passage. He returned to Montreal but quickly had a falling out with relatives there and left to "ride the rails" across Canada in the early 1930s.

What Tom did in the 1930s is difficult to document. Various relatives claim he participated in the "On to Ottawa" trek in 1935 and the Vancouver Post Office sit-in strike of 1938, and we have pictures of him at British Columbia's work camps for the unemployed (one photo is inscribed to "Doc Tom" because he was designated the first aid attendant). It was also alleged that he was involved in various efforts to organize unions, and he often spoke positively of the Wobblies, a militant union that focused on direct action. Tom's first marriage also occurred in the mid-1930s, producing a daughter and a son, but his wife died just before the start of the Second World War. The portrait of Tom's commitment to the left and unionism showcased some troubling gendered dimensions at the same time. It was alleged that Tom was keen to join the fight in Spain with the Republican forces against the Fascists, but before his train could leave Vancouver with the Mackenzie Papineau Brigade, his mother-in-law intervened to insist he fulfill his family responsibilities. Tellingly, his dying wife made Tom promise that their children would be cared for by her parents rather than by him alone. During the war, Tom was rejected for armed service for health reasons and joined the British Merchant Marine, having one ship blown out from under him while in harbour. After the war, he trained as a lumber inspector and travelled across British Columbia in the course of his work before being assigned to the Vancouver region.

Tom's political views were shaped by his experience of deprivation as a runaway child, an itinerant worker, an unemployed man in the 1930s, and a supporter of and participant in organizing unions. He was confident about the power of collective action on the part of workers if they could stick together. He had no illusions about the benevolence of bosses or the wealthy – they would do what they could to enrich themselves at any cost. "Don't ever fool yourself" was Tom's classic catchphrase just before setting out his views about the meanness of the powerful and the difficulties involved in challenging their power. He expressed frustration with workers taken in by the false promises of the bosses and those he viewed as their political lackeys, a sentiment captured in his oft-stated judgment that "the working class is its own worst enemy."

Tom also had strong views about the kind of individual commitment required to make collective action work. He would often observe, usually in reaction to news about some strike, that "you don't get a union man with the closed shop." I recall being horrified by what I thought this implied, as my own high school dropout father had painstakingly set out the common sense game theory behind the closed shop and why it was needed to maintain union strength. But Tom's point has only become more salient over time: workers that don't fight for a union may not really understand what they have or why it should be defended. While Tom would admit that the automatic dues check-off system made practical sense in the postwar era, he never quite made his peace with the idea of coexisting in the union with workers whose sacrifices did not match his own and that of others in the 1930s.

After their marriage in 1946, Tom and Vera's family initially lived in her small house with her parents. They moved briefly to Chilliwack in the mid-1950s after Vera's father died, and then back to east Vancouver in the early 1960s, where they remained until 1985. Patching together the fabric of their day-to-day lives as a married couple proved more difficult research-wise than living their previous lives. It is clear that family life was not all bliss. Tom had never really had a stable home or relationships. He was a difficult man to be around and had a serious drinking problem. He had a knack for turning everything into an argument and often appeared to be arguing even with people who were agreeing with him. Vera provided the stability he craved and enforced the discipline he needed in order to function effectively. She could usually deflect and soften his argumentative nature, she put a stop to his drinking, and she handled the family finances and bills (Tom would give her his unopened pay packet and she would give him back an allowance). His life improved immeasurably under her influence.

Despite their differences, Tom and Vera shared a broadly similar ideological outlook, rooted in a "common sense" class analysis of power. It was "common" in the sense that it was derived from experience rather than what Tom referred to as "book learning." Of course, other workers may have had and did draw different conclusions from similar experiences. Simply put, as Tom and Vera understood it, the rich used their superior economic power to keep and enhance that power, by controlling what went on in the workplace, by keeping wages and benefits low, and by influencing governments to pass laws that favoured them, and to use the force of the state against their opponents. By contrast, working people had only themselves to draw support from, either by forming unions to directly challenge employers or by supporting a political party dedicated to putting working people in charge. Vera and Tom would not cross picket lines or knowingly buy products produced by scab labour. The paid their membership dues to the CCF/NDP every year and at election time donated more to help the party's campaign. They placed a large CCF/NDP sign on their lawn during every election.

In the time that I lived with them from 1982 to 1985, I was part of many conversations and witness to many actions that showcased their working class ideology, whether in reaction to the daily radio and TV newscasts, newspaper stories, or particular events and elections. Tom and Vera always had the radio news on during breakfast, would read the paper throughout the day, and would eat their small meal at night on "tea trays" in front of the evening television newscast. Interestingly, they did not listen to or watch the CBC, whose highbrow, middle-class demeanour was off-putting to them. Instead, they listened to the right-wing private news radio station CKNW, and watched the popular (and no less right-wing) BCTV evening newscast. This led to a rather participatory approach to news watching, as my grandfather regularly interacted (often at the top of his voice) with politicians and political actors that received coverage; my grandmother, less so. Election coverage was always dissected for evidence of bias against the left.

Sometimes we disagreed about how the left was responding to different events. During the Solidarity opposition to the Social Credit government's "restraint" budget following the 1983 provincial election, I expressed my outrage when International Woodworkers of America leader Jack Munro made a deal with Social Credit Premier Bill Bennett that effectively extinguished the campaign, just as things were building towards a provincial general strike. My grandfather defended Munro's action: "They would have crushed them if he didn't make a deal," he claimed. I disagreed at the time but now better understand his response, given the state actions he witnessed first-hand in the 1930s and 1940s.

Vera and Tom's working class ideology was also manifested in their responses to larger world events; they often empathized with struggles elsewhere in terms that made sense from their own experience. While not uncritical of the Soviet Union, they were prepared to see aspects of its revolution and role in world affairs in a positive light. They spoke positively of Fidel Castro and Cuba and were pleased by the initial success of the Nicaraguan revolution in the early 1980s. Here and in other cases, their judgment was influenced by the belief that improving the conditions of average people was motivating these left-identified movements and events. By contrast, they were very critical of the United States and its role in world affairs, seeing American interventions as self-serving interference in aid of the rich and powerful at home and abroad. This was not some blind anti-Americanism – in fact, they had great sympathy for working people in the United States, who they thought were denied much political choice given the absence of a real left party. But, again, their own experience was crucial in informing their judgments. For instance, watching American popular culture exposed them to a national discourse where the United States won every war single-handedly. Yet Vera and Tom knew this wasn't true; they knew that the United States entered both world wars late and that their contribution, while important, was part of a broader effort among allies.

During a visit with me in Toronto in 1996, my grandmother asked: "Now I see you've got a lot of books by this fellow Marx, dear. Is he 'our' kind of socialist?" Such a simple and innocent question effectively illustrates a number of things about working class ideology. First, it doesn't bear any necessary relationship to the traditional written canon of the left: Marx, the Fabians, Lenin, and the like. Working people like my grandparents responded to a broad social dialogue about politics, one where "socialism" was given meaning through their own experience. This also means that attempts to convert working people into proto-liberals by demonstrating they haven't read the classics is superficial. Second, Vera and Tom were not merely socialists, but a "kind" of socialist who did not blithely accept that cheering for your team at election time was enough. One must also attempt to influence what kind of team was on the field. Tom and Vera regularly complained that the electoral left was not doing enough to engage working people, speak to their problems, and take appropriate sides against the bosses, US influence, and other tainted players.

Tom passed away in 1996. Vera lived to just past her 103rd birthday in 2010. The last time I spoke with her, she was full of criticism for Stephen Harper but not sure whether Jack Layton had the right stuff to defeat him, not convinced he was "our kind of socialist." At her service, I brought out my guitar and sang "Solidarity Forever" while my relatives looked on, most bewildered by the spectacle. As they had gone on with their lives, they had lost touch with where Vera and Tom had come from. Academically, as my grandparents' generation has passed into history, historians and political scientists now tell their broad story through ideological lenses of their own. BC historian Jean Barman tells us that working people in 1920s British Columbia just wanted to get ahead, raise a family, buy a home, and so on (Barman 1996). That may have been true of some. Another BC historian, Bob McDonald, would have us believe that working class people who voted for the left in interwar British Columbia were really just reform liberals, not socialists at all (McDonald 2013). Who is left to dispute such characterizations?

My insights here derive from a mixture of evidence: some oral history, a kind of auto-ethnography, with insights from institutional ethnography and critical theory (for a defence of such a mixed-method approach, see Taber 2010). I don't have recordings of or detailed notes about my grandparents talking about their lives, which limits this study as an example of oral history. These are just my recollections of things they said and did. And what appears here is mostly focused on my reconstruction of their lives, rather than being an account I personally witnessed or participated in, which means that the auto-ethnography is really about me and my experiences of my grandparents, which may be partial and influenced by my experiences and historical development.

Nevertheless, I do think I have captured something real, something important, something that might have gone unnoticed but for this effort. My knowledge of the history of the Canadian and comparative left has enabled me to put my grandparents' experience in a broader perspective, to draw out collective insights from their individual experiences. During their lives, they participated in a broad social reality, the creation and maintenance of a distinct working class ideology. They were not liberals in the sense that political theorists and historians would have us believe. They saw themselves primarily as part of a group with interests in common, not as individuals. They had a sense of class politics, namely, that society was organized in an antagonistic way where the rich won because everyone else lost. Finally, and explicitly, they disavowed liberalism as a false characterization of how politics and the state worked – neither was neutral. To think so, in their view, was dangerously naïve. Instead, they expressly self-identified as socialists who sought political power so that the working class could make the rules, rules that would work for them.

Conclusion

Most working class experience is lost to us but I hope I have demonstrated that it has more meaning than has been typically attributed to it. While the discussion here has focused on Vera and Tom, the point is to use them as illustrations of the existence of a broader set of collective values and ideas. Part of what made working class experience so powerful, what converted individual circumstance into potential political action, was the recognition by working people that such personal experiences were not unique: they were systemically produced, the product of relations of power. Out of such recognition, average working people developed their own practical working class ideology, a set of ideas and prescriptions shaped by their experience that they in turn used to interpret and attempt to change the world. Exploring this more deeply may hold the key to understanding the strength and resiliency of the twentieth-century left and what might be required to rejuvenate the left today.

References

Barman, Jean. 1996. *The West beyond the West: A History of British Columbia.* Toronto: University of Toronto Press.

Bourdieu, Pierre. 1984. *Distinction: A Social Critique of the Judgment of Taste.* Cambridge, MA: Harvard University Press.

–. 1999. *The Weight of the World: Social Suffering in Contemporary Society.* Stanford, CA: Stanford University Press.

Boyd, Jade. 2016. "Performing 'East Van': Spatial Identifications and Class Anxieties." *Journal of Contemporary Ethnography* 45 (2): 198–226.

Converse, Philip E. 1964. "The Nature of Belief Systems in Mass Publics." In *Ideology and Discontent,* ed. David Apter, 206–61. New York: Free Press of Glencoe.

Denshire, Sally. 2014. "On Auto-Ethnography." *Current Sociology Review* 62 (6): 831–50.

Downs, Anthony. 1957. *An Economic Theory of Democracy.* New York: Harper.

Eagleton, Terry. 1991. *Ideology: An Introduction.* London: Verso.

Eley, Geoff. 2002. *Forging Democracy: This History of Left in Europe, 1850–2000.* Oxford: Oxford University Press.

Ellis, Carolyn, Tony E. Adams, and Arthur P. Bochner. 2011. "Auto-Ethnography: An Overview." *Historical Social Research* 36 (4): 273–90.

Fiorina, Morris P., with Samuel J. Abrams and Jeremy C. Pope. 2006. *Culture War? The Myth of a Polarized America.* 2nd ed. New York: Pearson Longman.

Forber-Pratt, Anjali J. 2015. "'You're Going to Do What?' Challenges of Auto-Ethnography in the Academy." *Qualitative Inquiry* 21 (9): 821–35.

Gallie, W.B. 1956. "Essentially Contested Concepts." *Proceedings of the Aristotelian Society* (New Series) 56: 167–98.

Gibbons, Michael T. 2006. "Hermeneutics, Political Inquiry, and Practical Reason: An Evolving Challenge to Political Science." *American Political Science Review* 100 (4): 563–71.

Graham, Gordon. 1986. *Politics in Its Place: A Study of Six Ideologies.* Oxford: Oxford University Press.

Heron, Craig. 2009. "Harold, Marg, and the Boys: The Relevance of Class in Canadian History." *Journal of the Canadian Historical Association* 20 (1): 1–56.

Isitt, Benjamin. 2007. "Searching for Workers' Solidarity: The One Big Union and the Victoria General Strike of 1919." *Labour/Le travail* 60 (Fall): 9–42.

–. 2009. "Elusive Unity: The Canadian Labour Party in British Columbia, 1924–28." *BC Studies* 163 (Autumn 2009), 33–64

–. 2011. *Militant Minority: British Columbia Workers and the Rise of a New Left, 1948–1972.* Toronto: University of Toronto Press.

Leier, Mark. 1990. *Where the Fraser River Flows: The Industrial Workers of the World in British Columbia.* Vancouver: New Star.

Lipset, Seymour Martin. 1959. "Democracy and Working-Class Authoritarianism." *American Sociological Review* 24 (4): 482–501.

McDonald, R.A. 2013. "'Telford Time' and the Populist Origins of the CCF in British Columbia." *Labour/Le Travail* 71 (Spring): 87–100.

McKay, Ian. 2000. "The Liberal Order Framework: A Prospectus for a Reconnaissance of Canadian History." *Canadian Historical Review* 81–84 (December): 617–45.

Montgomery, David. 1987. *The Fall of the House of Labor: The Workplace, the State, and American Labor Activism, 1865–1925.* Cambridge: Cambridge University Press.

Moschonas, Gerassimos. 2002. *In the Name of Social Democracy: The Great Transformation, 1945 to the Present.* London: Verso.

Nayak, Anoop. 2006. "Displaced Masculinities: Chavs, Youth and Class in the Post-Industrial City." *Sociology* 40 (5): 813–31.

Naylor, James. 2013. "The British Columbia CCF's Working-Class Moment: Socialism Not Populism." *Labour/Le travail* 71 (Spring): 101–21.

Palmer, Bryan D. 1987. *Solidarity: The Rise and Fall of an Opposition in British Columbia.* Vancouver: New Star Books.

Phillips, Paul. 1967. *No Power Greater: A Century of Labour in British Columbia.* Vancouver: BC Federation of Labour.

Pilon, Dennis. 2015a. "Researching Voter Turnout and the Electoral Subaltern: Utilizing 'Class' as Identity." *Studies in Political Economy* 96 (Autumn): 69–91.

–. 2015b. "British Columbia: Right-Wing Coalition Politics and Neoliberalism." In *Transforming Provincial Politics: The Political Economy of Canada's Provinces and Territories in the Neoliberal Era,* ed. Brian Evans and Charles Smith, 284–312. Toronto: University of Toronto Press.

Robertson, David Brian. 1993. "The Return to History and the New Institutionalism in American Political Science." *Social Science History* 17 (1): 1–36.

Sangster, Joan. 2013. "Oral History and Working Class History: A Rewarding Alliance." *Oral History Forum d'histoire orale* 33: 1–15.

Sassoon, Donald. 1997. *One Hundred Years of Socialism.* New York: New Press.

Smith, Dorothy, ed. 2006. *Institutional Ethnography as Practice.* Oxford: Rowan and Littlefield.

Spivak, Gayatri Chakravorty. 1993. "Can the Subaltern Speak?" In *Colonial Discourse and Postcolonial Theory: A Reader,* ed. Patrick Williams and Laura Chrisman, 66–111. New York: Columbia University Press.

Taber, Nancy. 2010. "Institutional Ethnography, Auto-Ethnography, and Narrative: An Argument for Incorporating Multiple Methodologies." *Qualitative Research* 10 (1): 5–25.

Terkel, Studs. 1974. *Working: People Talk about What They Do All Day and How They Feel about What They Do.* New York: Pantheon/Random House.

Trowler, Vicki. 2014. "May the Subaltern Speak? Researching the Invisible 'Other' in Higher Education." *European Journal of Higher Education* 4 (1): 42–54.

Vincent, Andrew. 2010. *Modern Political Ideologies.* 3rd ed. Chichester, UK: Wiley-Blackwell.

Willis, Paul. 1977. *Learning to Labor: How Working Class Kids Get Working Class Jobs.* New York: Columbia University Press.

Yates, Michael D. 2009. *In and Out of the Working Class.* Winnipeg: Arbeiter Ring.

Young, Walter. 1969. *The Anatomy of a Party: The CCF.* Toronto: University of Toronto Press.

Conclusion

DAVID LAYCOCK

Shared Themes, Perspectives, and Concerns

The chapters in this volume cover a wide range of empirical, historical, and contemporary cases, utilizing discipline-specific and interdisciplinary theories and methods. Across this range, we see not just a rich diversity of ideological experience and expression but also a striking set of shared features in the analysis of this experience and expression.

As noted in the Introduction, readers will notice a broad "morphological sensibility" across the chapters despite their diverse approaches to analysis of ideology in organizational discourse, institutionally produced texts, and all levels and types of macro-, meso-, and micro-level political speech. Contributors were not asked to work with a specific set of analytical tools. Nonetheless, all of the chapters here treat ideological expressions, discourses, actions, and convictions as dynamic elements of political life whose meaning arises from and needs to be decoded in relation to their structural relationships to other experiences, ideas, and concepts.

The contributors also shared an appreciation of the importance of case studies for fine-grained analysis of ideological concepts, themes, purposes, and functions in political imaginaries and identities. They showed that the study of ideology can range over a variety of sites and practices located at the macro-, meso-, and micro levels of social and political experience outlined in the Introduction to this book. Remaining at the level of macro-ideological expression and/or "high politics" was shown not to be conducive to the kinds

of more nuanced appreciation of ideologies made possible by cross-disciplinary innovation such as is displayed in Chapters 1, 2, 4, 5, 7, and 9.

Incorporating non-canonical and "non-professional" as well as vernacular data into textual analysis of ideological practices was also important to
other contributors. Our experience in this regard supports Freeden's contention (2013, 4) that "the political dimensions of human thought-practices,
like their cultural and psychological dimensions, interpenetrate all forms of
discourse, from the specialized to the common, from the professional to the
vernacular, from the institutionalized to the informal, though their significance and impact will vary from instance to instance."

The additional difficulties involved in obtaining and decoding this wider
range of relevant research material are substantial, especially when we have
to make sense – that is, to uncover the underlying conceptual decontestations and larger political intentions – of strategically presented rhetorical constructions in political speech. But as the contributors can all attest,
incorporating a more inclusive range of political discourses into our research
often brings analysts into contact with non-academics who convey valuable insights about the complexity of politics' ideological dimensions. The
applied political and social theory involved in the study of ideologies inevitably involves engagement in the messier and preconception-unsettling
worlds of meso- and micro-level ideological expression and experience.

Contributors have clearly decided that the rewards of such engagement
easily outweigh the inconveniences of venturing beyond the proverbial
ivory tower. And, as Darin Barney pointed out at a lively and productive
2016 workshop, "Ideologies and Conceptual Travel," at Simon Fraser University,[1] broadening our understanding of what counts as relevant political
expressions of ideology beyond the realm of "high politics" is a necessary
condition of facilitating a meaningfully interdisciplinary study of ideology.
This means that to the extent that political scientists lead such a project of
study, they must move beyond many conventional political science conceptualizations of ideology, which are too often restricted to the world of partisan competition and governance, and reduced to psychologically driven
attitudes and values.

Many of the chapters in this book reveal what Maiken Umbach called
the unintended collateral conceptual baggage that accompanies the excava-
tion and recycling of ideological repertoires.[2] This is particularly evident in
Chapters 1, 3, 5, 6, 7, 8, and 9. The first two deal primarily with the effects of
such recycling, modification, and repurposing in high-profile competitive
politics and governance, while the latter five show how politically significant
ideological repertoires inflect and interweave with cultural, economic, and

personal domains to create a complex, multidimensional context in which ideology shapes social life. Several of these chapters emphasize the role that social movements play in relaxing constraints on such innovative ideological recycling and repurposing, while others emphasize political entrepreneurs' contribution to this conceptual travel and transformation.

One of the great pleasures for those attending the 2016 workshop was hearing theoretical perspectives and analytical approaches from outside our respective academic silos. We discovered that our distinctive theoretical languages often disguised levels of basic analytical compatibility for the study of ideologies. For example, the communications theory with which Katherine Reilly frames her analysis of the Harper government's reorientation towards international development in Chapter 2 is quite compatible with David Laycock and Steven Weldon's efforts to offer a morphological account of the same government's attempt to reframe and repurpose multiculturalism (Chapter 3). To take another example, Ian Angus's account of how rhetoric and discourse theory could help us appreciate social movement politics (Chapter 5), does not share a political purpose with Ivan Jankovic's challenge to Louis Hartz's analysis of the ideological character of early American politics (Chapter 1). Nonetheless, each can see the merits of the other's analysis, and each has found a way to square his approach with the main analytical thrust of Freeden's morphological approach to the study of ideology.

In the workshop's concluding session, historian Howard Brick displayed his talent in translating across the semi-private theoretical languages of the different disciplines. He observed that most of the presentations had been concerned with uncovering basic unstated assumptions held by political, cultural, and economic actors, as well as "public intellectuals," about the working of the world. And he noted that we had all trained our sights on assumptions that were put into practice and contributed to the operations of ideology by being constitutively related to various contending political imaginaries.

Workshop participants also displayed enthusiasm for moving beyond multiple disciplinary analytical perspectives towards a productively interdisciplinary approach to the study of ideologies. In the final section of this Conclusion, I will comment on a project intended to pursue this objective.

Analytical Disagreements and Bridge Building

We learned a good deal from one another at the 2016 workshop, and discussion of presentations was unfailingly collegial and supportive. Yet it would be bizarre to experience theoretical unanimity in a workshop that intentionally sought diversity across and within disciplinary boundaries. Acknowledging some dimensions of this diversity can identify potential avenues for exploring the challenges of analyzing ideologies.

One basic line of division among the contributors to this volume concerns whether one can meaningfully undertake analysis of ideologies without at the same time attempting to advance a political position or perspective. Ian Angus takes the most explicit position in this regard. He suggests that while one can temporarily suspend political concerns in analyzing complex ideological statements and activities, the motivation for conducting such analysis is hard to fathom except as a desire to intervene in political life and debate. As he puts it in Chapter 5, "analysis of the *structuring* of political thought aims to allow an intervention that does not succumb to the existing structuring but purports to alter it." In simpler terms, this position holds that doing political analysis of ideas/ideologies necessarily entails acceptance of a normative obligation to critique the existing order. Freeden claims that one can detach analysis from normative position taking through political engagement; Angus, following the Frankfurt School, denies that such detachment is possible, and suggests that not responding to the obligation to critique reveals normative acceptance of the existing order.

Although other chapters do not engage this issue so directly, Chapters 6 to 9 convey their broad acceptance of the inherently political purpose of the study of ideologies. In one way or another, with Mark Leier making the most forceful statement (Chapter 8), these contributors all accept that ideology can't be understood except with reference to class and group interests, and that emphasizing such connections of interests to ideas is inherently critical in nature. In Chapters 1 to 4, the remaining contributors accept that their political commitments and orientations shape their choice of topics, analytical methods, and broader theoretical approaches in their studies of particular ideologies. However, few if any in this group would argue that their analyses' purposes and contributions cannot be thought of as distinct from their possible status as political interventions. None of their analyses, in other words, are guided by Marx's famous dictum that "philosophers heretofore have only interpreted the world in various ways; the point is to change it" (Marx 1845).

However, as Angus points out in Chapter 5, division on this issue need not put analysts on irreconcilable sides of an unbridgeable theoretical division. Common or at least highly compatible analytical tools may be appreciated and adopted despite analysts' divergent political commitments. One could push this further to contend that such appreciation and application of analytical tools can occur even when explicitly irreconcilable political interventions accompany analysis of ideologies. We can think ourselves politically engaged while presenting an analysis of ideology, or not, and either way contribute to an analysis of the ideological dimensions of contemporary political or social life that can be appreciated by others who do not share our ideological commitments or motivations.

This last claim is not meant to erase key methodological and normative-epistemological disagreements in the study of ideologies, but is intended to remove gratuitous interpretive and analytical barriers. The 2016 workshop and, for that matter, most professional social scientific gatherings provide multiple examples of learning and cross-fertilization across not just theoretical but also deeply felt political orientations. Drinking the same Kool-Aid with the same intellectual partisans may be satisfying in the moment, but it is often less rewarding or productive than we might wish.

Another line of division that surfaced both at the workshop and in this volume involves a related issue: how should we understand the relationship between normative analysis and morphological or related analysis of ideological concepts? As Mat Humphrey pointed out at the workshop's concluding session, pursuing the project of interdisciplinary and cross-theoretical analysis of ideologies requires that we open up discussion of how various morphological and other analytical approaches to the study of ideology can be combined with normative analysis. He briefly noted four possible strategies: (1) we follow G.A. Cohen's injunction to just "jump in" (Cohen 2011); (2) we bring the study of political thought back into social science, using Freeden's (2013) or a variety of other methods; (3) we follow a hybrid model of the first two, in which returning political theory to social science sets the agenda for jumping in; and (4) our jump into a particular case study or theoretical challenge sets the agenda for use of political theory that has made its peace with social science methods of analysis rather than attempting to guide conceptual analysis from a perch of ideal or normative theory.

The clearer we are individually about how we understand our own combinations in this regard, and how this might combine with simultaneously open or implicit political engagement in such analyses, the easier it will be for others to appreciate the value (and limits) of our work, and to recognize opportunities for theoretical innovation and cross-fertilization. We can clarify some of the key issues at stake in navigating the potential minefield of normatively motivated analysis of ideologies by distinguishing the role of normativity at different levels of analysis and points along the research trail.

First, virtually all theoretically self-conscious social scientists acknowledge that researchers' values shape their choice of research topics and methods. However, none of this comes in prepackaged, predictable fashion. For example, though social scientists on the left have been suspicious of the ontological assumptions underlying methodological individualism, it is still possible for avowed socialists – perhaps even Marx (Elster 1985) – to employ it for analytical purposes, just as the left's widespread critique of rational choice theory can be finessed to conduct radical socio-economic critique (Roemer 1986).

Second, ideological orientations grounded on normative values typically shape use of research methods, in ways that are sometimes explicitly but usually only implicitly acknowledged by social scientists. Nothing in the positions taken by Angus or Freeden on whether a normative obligation accompanies analysis of ideologies, however, requires them to disagree with either of these statements regarding the normative content of social analysis and theory construction. Nor would any contributors to this volume take issue with either statement.

It is only when we get to the next level of analysis, concerning normative obligations to explicitly critique the existing order that might be entailed in the enterprise of social or political analysis, that a clear disagreement arises and divides not just our contributors but social scientists and humanists generally. It might be true that most academic analyses of ideology are not just normatively and "politically" motivated but combined with serious social and political critique. And most contributors to this volume have accepted that this normative obligation to critique is entailed by the work of ideology analysis. However, we have also seen that such a critique is by no means a necessary element in an effective and systematic conceptual analysis of any given ideology (Freeden 2013, ch. 2). In other words, other contributors defend the value of analysis that does not take this final normative step of "system critique," so long as the analysis of ideology engages the relevant social phenomena – including ideologically-specific understandings of key normative concepts – in good faith and with regard to defensible standards of empirical research.

Finally, another broad division cuts across the chapters in this volume, though it is more appropriate to think in terms of their placements along a continuum. At one end, one would find analyses devoted exclusively to functional explanation: how does the ideology in question support some particular social objective or state of affairs, whether or not this is the conscious intention of its supporters? Marx's approach to ideology is perhaps the best known among primarily functionalist explanations and treatments of ideology, while the many variants of structural-functionalism in social science and philosophy, from Sigmund Freud to Talcott Parsons to David

Easton to Michel Foucault and Slavoj Žižek, range reasonably close to this pole of the continuum. The other pole is also an ideal type, and is characterized by an exclusively logical and relational conceptual focus on the content of the ideology, as opposed to either its historical context or its political and social effects. Insofar as analysis of relations between concepts is almost impossible to present without at least some reference to historical events, previously established institutions, ongoing cultural traditions or organizational experience, adherents of the "pure conceptual" pole of this continuum are harder to identify. For our purposes, however, Gallie's (1956) work on "essentially contested concepts" may serve as an example, as his key arguments have to do with the logical features of irremediably distinct conceptualizations of key concepts in political and social discourse.

If we imagine a ten-point scale, on which 1 is the position allocated to an exclusively functional explanatory account, and 10 is the exclusively conceptual account, we can easily see that none of the chapters in this volume score either 1 or 10. Most of them cluster closer to the middle of the scale, with Chapters 2, 6, 7, 8, and 9 leaning more in the functional explanatory direction and Chapters 1, 3, 4, and 5 focusing more on morphological or conceptual analysis.

However, as noted in the Introduction, most analysts – in this volume and elsewhere – draw, at least to some extent, on explanatory or analytical tools from the other half of the continuum sketched above. They do so because it is difficult to detach accounts of the impact of ideologies from analyses of their conceptual, symbolic, or other meaning-granting elements. It is also frustrating to remain at the level of conceptual analysis exclusively when it is so tempting to deploy such analysis within explanations of how social and political forces interact to generate broader social impacts. We want to understand how ideas fit together as instruments of socially created meaning, but we also wish to understand how, in conjunction with economic, social, and cultural forces, and political and other institutions, they produce or inhibit change. So even though contributors can be found at often different points along the explanatory/analytical continuum, they also draw on broad orientations to understanding ideology that, while not providing their primary analytical tools, are nonetheless helpful for some aspects of their overall analysis.

Developing a Network for Analysis of Ideologies

This volume is intended to have value both on its own and as a stepping stone in the development of a network of scholars who wish to learn from and contribute to an interdisciplinary exploration of political ideologies. The network was initiated in a small workshop held at the University of Virginia in December 2013, hosted by Alon Confina, then a member of the Department of History at the University of Virginia. This workshop was organized by Mat Humphrey, Maiken Umbach, and Michael Freeden, at that time all co-directors of the Centre for the Study of Political Ideologies at the University of Nottingham. Subsequent interactions between the three colleagues from Nottingham and me led to the 2016 workshop at Simon Fraser University.

Planning is now underway for more multidisciplinary workshops. One was held at the University of Nottingham in the summer of 2018, and another is planned for the University of Michigan at Ann Arbor in the near future. These aim to build on the Simon Fraser University workshop with numerous participants from the United Kingdom, Europe, North America, and perhaps Asia. At these meetings we will advance our research network's agenda of developing more nuanced and analytically effective tools for understanding ideological innovation and change.

For the founding members of this network, this study involves analysis of substantive political ideas and sentiments, as well as the processes by which these are conceived, asserted, modified, and discarded. Ideologies have typically been studied in isolation or in relation to one political rival. This research network focuses on understanding how political entrepreneurs, social movement actors, and contemporary media draw on global discursive repertoires when staking out their distinctive ideological claims or shaping their ideological filters. We assume that ideological appeals draw on pre-existing stocks of cultural, social, and political ideas and representations. We ask how common conceptual elements – an imagination of freedom, order, community, equality, or nature, for example – are activated, rearticulated, and recombined to different political ends. We consider how these ubiquitous concepts are framed and "naturalized," or translated into political "common sense," in different political orders, and how they are combined with historically or geographically specific concerns.

The members of this network strongly believe that compelling answers to such questions cannot come exclusively from one discipline, so we invite contributions from a range of social science and humanities scholars. Current core members of the network believe that an interdisciplinary analytical toolkit that draws particularly on recent developments in political theory will enable us to assess the importance of historically inflected ideas, representational tropes, and thought habits in the modern world. With such tools, the hope is that scholars can probe more deeply into the processes of innovative ideological activity across time and space.

Although this volume focuses on North American experiences with political ideologies, it has been influenced by contributions originating in the European, British, and Asian experiences as well. We hope that the multidisciplinary reach and hints of interdisciplinary insight in this collection attract new participants to this research network's study of political ideologies.[3]

Notes

1 "Ideologies and Conceptual Travel," a workshop held at the Burnaby, BC, campus of Simon Fraser University, July 4–5, 2016.
2 Ibid.
3 If you wish to become involved, please contact Mat Humphrey or Maiken Umbach at the University of Nottingham or David Laycock at Simon Fraser University.

References

Cohen, G.A. 2011. "How to Do Political Philosophy." In *On the Currency of Egalitarian Justice, and Other Essays in Political Philosophy*, ed. G.A. Cohen, 225–35. Princeton, NJ: Princeton University Press.

Elster, Jon. 1985. *Making Sense of Marx*. New York: Cambridge University Press.

Freeden, Michael. 2013. *The Political Theory of Political Thinking*. Oxford: Oxford University Press.

Gallie, W.B. 1956. "Essentially Contested Concepts." *Proceedings of the Aristotelian Society* (New Series) 56: 167–98.

Marx, Karl. 1845. "Theses on Feuerbach." Marx/Engels Internet Archive, https://www.marxists.org/archive/marx/works/1845/theses/theses.htm.

Roemer, John, ed. 1986. *Analytical Marxism*. New York: Cambridge University Press.

Contributors

Ian Angus is Professor Emeritus from Simon Fraser University, where he taught in the Department of Humanities. His most recent book was *The Undiscovered Country: Essays in Canadian Intellectual Culture* (Athabasca University Press, 2013). His book *Love the Questions: University Education and Enlightenment* (Arbeiter Ring, 2009) appeared in Spanish translation from Wolkowicz Editores (Buenos Aires) in fall 2018. He is currently working on a manuscript on Edmund Husserl and Karl Marx.

Darin Barney is the Grierson Chair in Communication Studies at McGill University. He is the author and editor of several scholarly works, including *The Participatory Condition in the Digital Age* (University of Minnesota Press, 2016). Barney's current research focuses on materialist approaches to media and communication, infrastructure, and radical politics.

Laurent Dobuzinskis teaches political science at Simon Fraser University. His current research interests encompass a range of issues in the history of ideas and the philosophy of economics, more specifically the importance of the concepts of reciprocity and "enlightened self-interest" in debates centred on the theory and practice of economic justice and institutional design.

Ivan Jankovic is an assistant professor of economics at University of Mary, North Dakota. His research concentrates on the history of economic and political thought, economics, and American politics. His research has been published in the *American Journal of Economics and Sociology, American Political Thought,* and *Journal des Economistes et des Etudes Humaines,* among others. His book *American Counter-Revolution in Favor of Liberty: How Americans Resisted Modern State 1769–1850* was published by Palgrave Macmillan in 2019.

David Laycock is a professor of political science at Simon Fraser University. He has authored *Populism and Democratic Thought in the Canadian Prairies, 1910–45* (University of Toronto Press, 1990) and *The New Right and Democracy in Canada* (Oxford University Press, 2001); edited *Representation and Democratic Theory* (UBC Press, 2004); and co-edited, with Lynda Erickson, *Reviving Social Democracy: The Near Death and Surprising Rise of the Federal NDP* (UBC Press, 2014).

Mark Leier is a historian at Simon Fraser University. His books include *Rebel Life: The Life and Times of Robert Raglan Gosden, Revolutionary, Mystic, Labour Spy* (New Star Books, 2013), *Bakunin: The Creative Passion* (Seven Stories Press, 2006), *Red Flags and Red Tape: The Making of a Labour Bureaucracy* (University of Toronto Press, 1995) and *Where the Fraser River Flows: The Industrial Workers of the World in British Columbia* (New Star Books, 1990).

Dennis Pilon is a product of working class British Columbia but presently teaches politics at York University in Toronto. His research focuses on historical and contemporary struggles over democracy in Western countries, with particular attention to the role of working class movements and political parties. His books include *Wrestling with Democracy: Voting Systems as Politics in the Twentieth Century West* (University of Toronto Press, 2013) and *The Politics of Voting: Reforming Canada's Electoral System* (Emond, 2007).

Katherine Reilly is an associate professor in the School of Communication at Simon Fraser University. Her work focuses on the relationship between knowledge, information, data, international development, and social change. She is co-editor of *Open Development: Networked Innovations in International Development* (MIT Press, 2014), and a special edition of the *Journal of Developing Societies* on the sharing economy in developing countries.

Katherine Strand is a PhD candidate in the Department of Anthropology at McGill University. Her ethnographic research within dryland farming communities began in the High Plains of the United States and now extends into the Prairie provinces of Canada. Her work focuses on the historical development of concepts within agriculture that continue to shape farming practices. She currently lives and works with her partner on an organic grain and bison farm within the Palliser's Triangle of Saskatchewan.

Steven Weldon is an associate professor of political science at Simon Fraser University. His research focuses on political representation, extremism, and elections in advanced democracies, and has been published in, among others, the *American Journal of Political Science, British Journal of Political Science, European Journal of Political Research,* and *Party Politics.*

Kyle Willmott is a PhD candidate in sociology at Simon Fraser University with broad interests in political sociology, economic sociology, Indigenous-settler relations, and the politics of policy knowledge. He researches how fiscal and economic knowledge and ideas about taxation reconfigure political subjectivity and transform the relationship between citizens, states, and First Nations. His work has been published in *Economy and Society.*

Index

Adams, Samuel, 30
affirmative action: CPC and, 75; for immigrants, 68
AFL-CIO, 181
AgResults program, 47, 53
agribusiness: and canola, 155; and food production, 163; government regulatory intervention in, 160; increasing consolidation of, 165; and *License to Farm*, 152, 156–57, 166; *Paper Wheat* and, 154. *See also* farming/farmers
agricultural political subjects/subjectivity: and cooperative socialism, 149; and ideological formation/contestation, 14, 149; in *License to Farm*, 158; in *License to Farm* vs *Paper Wheat*, 164–65; narratives as preparation for action, 151–52; and neoliberalism, 149; in *Paper Wheat*, 158
Aid Effectiveness Agenda, 45, 47
Althusser, Louis, 7, 14, 151
Amadae, Sonja M., 97, 98, 105–6
American Revolution: and Constitution, 34; and "country party" ideology, 12; European peasants' rebellion

compared, 22; and fiscal military state, 34; ideological origins, 12, 37; and libertarian old-Whig ideology, 22; and localism, 23; and Lockean liberalism, 36; pamphlet literature, 21; and paranoid-style politics, 22
American Taxpayer Association, 134
Amnesty International Canada, 52
Andrews, Charles, 38n9
Angus, Ian, 13–14, 69, 207, 208, 210
Angus Reid Institute, 70
Aristotle, *Rhetoric*, 117–18
Aumann, Robert, 99
Austen, Jane, 94
auto-ethnography: about, 188, 191–92; ethnography vs, 191–92; and micro level of ideological activity, 10; oral history compared, 191; Vera/Tom story, 193–202; and working class, 15, 193; and working class ideology, 193–94
average people: ideology, 187; knowledge of politics, 190; and populism, 189–90; Vera/Tom story, 193; and working class ideology, 202. *See also* working class

Bailyn, Bernard, 21–22, 23, 26, 30, 36, 38*n*9

Barman, Jean, 201

Barney, Darin, 14, 206

Barthes, Roland, 7

Bartley, George, 172–74, 182

Battiste, Marie, 125

Baudelaire, Charles, 183

Bayer, 166*n*5; LibertyLink, 155

BC Federationist, 172

Begriffsgeschichte school, 8, 10

behaviouralism, 100

Bennett, Bill, 200

Bentham, Jeremy, 102

Bernier, Maxime, 84

Berteig, Alexei, 164

Berteig, Garry, 156–57

Bertelsmann Foundation, 85*n*7

Bhushan, Aniket, 54

Bill C-474, 166*n*6

Bimini's, 178–79

Binmore, Kenneth, 92, 102–3; *Game Theory and the Social Contract*, 102; *Natural Justice*, 102

biotechnology: and canola, 155; dominance of transnational firms, 156; in farming, 156; government regulatory intervention in, 160; information control by firms, 161; in *License to Farm*, 152; public opinion and industry, 163–64. *See also* genetically modified organisms (GMOs)

Bissoondath, Neil, 122

Blaug, Mark, 99

Boessenkool, Ken, 80

Bolingbroke, Henry St. John, Viscount, 22

Borel, Emile, 106*n*2, 107*n*3

Bourdieu, Pierre, 133, 190

Brean, Joseph, 43

Breton, Charles, 70–71

Brick, Howard, 207

Brunner, Otto, 24

Burchell, Graham, 138

Burke, Edmund, 189

Cambridge School, 8, 10

Cameron-Fawkes, Tom, 182

Canada Revenue Agency, 52

Canadian Alliance: ethnic minority voters and, 73; policies, 73; *Policy Declaration*, 85*n*9; visible minority community support for, 79

Canadian Biotechnology Action Network, 166*n*4

Canadian Collieries, 172

Canadian Election Study: 2011, 71; 2015, 63, 78, 81, 82

Canadian International Development Agency (CIDA), 43, 46, 52

Canadian International Development Platform, 53–54

Canadian Northern Railway, 172, 174

Canadian Reform Conservative Alliance Party, 71–72

canola, 155–56, 159

Cantor, Georg, 94

Capital (Marx), 173

capitalism: environmental movement and, 124, 127; taxpayer groups and, 134

Cato's Letters (Trenchard/Gordon), 22

CBC: and multiculturalism, 68; Television, 152; and working class, 200

Charter of Rights and Freedoms: and Aboriginal communities, 85*n*8; and equality, 68–69; and multiculturalism, 68–69, 72, 82; new citizenship guide and, 75; Reform Party and, 72–73

chemical farming: anti-farm movement and, 157; *License to Farm* and, 150; public opinion about, 163–64; and right of choice, 160; and success of farming, 156. *See also* farming/farmers

Chwe, Michael, 94

class: British Columbia and, 192; defined, 170; family history and, 191; identification by workers as, 170; and ideological thinking, 189,

208; laborlore and, 14–15; power
and, 199, 202; shovel-shortening
story and, 173; tensions in laborlore,
171; as uniting workers, 171;
working class sense of politics of,
202. *See also* working class
Clement, Tony, 53–54
Clolow, Zeynep, 11
Cohen, G.A., 209
Cold War: and game theory, 96; and
liberal internationalism, 44
Collis, Stephen, 126
Communist Party, 169, 170, 176,
180–81, 197
Confina, Alon, 212
Conservative Party of Canada (CPC): in
2015 election, 76, 77, 78, 80;
advocacy work under, 52; anti-
statism, 61; and Asian Canadians,
79; Big Break, 43, 48; and "Canada's
principled foreign policy," 43; and
Canadian withdrawal from liberal
democratic compromise, 41–42;
conservative-populist ideological
core, 67; creation of, 61, 66, 67, 72;
and development, 12–13, 42, 47–49,
51, 53–54, 55, 207; and diversity, 68;
efficiency/results orientation, 55;
and equality rights, 63, 75; and
ethnic minorities, 62, 74, 76, 79, 80;
exclusion politics, 62, 78–79; and
foreign affairs, 41–42, 43, 55; and
ICN, 52–53; ideology, 63, 66, 68,
73; and immigrants/immigration,
48, 67, 73, 74, 75–76, 77–78, 80, 84;
inclusion politics, 76, 81;
mobilization of specialized groups
to achieve geostrategic objectives,
52; and multiculturalism, 13, 63, 67,
69–70, 73, 74, 75, 76, 80, 83–84;
122; Muskoka Initiative on
Maternal, Newborn and Child
Health, 47; and Muslims, 62, 77, 78,
79–81; and nativism, 13, 61–62;
neoliberal conservatism, 66; and

niqab, 61, 79–81; and "the people,"
67; perimeter vs core concepts in
ideology, 73, 79; plebiscitarianism,
61, 81–82; populism, 61, 62, 65,
81–82; and private donations for
humanitarian aid, 54–55; and
Reform Party, 13, 66, 74; and
refugees, 78, 80; re-mediation of
information flows, 48–49, 51;
revised citizenship guide, 74, 75;
trade/military emphasis vs
multilateral participation, 43;
unilateral approach, 41–42, 45; and
US ideology, 63, 69; wedge politics,
62, 63, 74, 79–80; and welfare state,
62, 63, 67, 77–78, 79, 83–84;
winning 2006 election, 73; and
women's reproductive rights, 47;
and Zero Tolerance for Barbaric
Cultural Practices Act, 78, 80
Cook, Ian, 141
The Co-op Show, 153
Co-operative Commonwealth
Federation (CCF), 192, 197, 199
cooperative movement/organization:
agricultural political subjects and,
149; cooperative socialism, 149;
Grain Grower's Guide, 152; grain
marketing, 165; mode of
agricultural production, 151–52;
Paper Wheat and, 150, 151–52, 153,
154, 158, 162–63, 164, 165. *See also*
Paper Wheat
Couldry, Nick, 50–51
Coulthard, Glen, 127
Cournot, Antoine-Augustin, 94
cross-disciplinarity. *See*
multidisciplinarity
Cuban missile crisis (1962), 101

Day, R.J.F., 122
Dean, Mitchell, 138; "Rethinking
Neoliberalism," 139
*Deep Ecology: Living as if Nature
Mattered*, 124

definitionalism, 133–34
democracy: conceptual travel of, 4;
    direct, and populism, 4; emergence
    of direct in US, 4; social movements
    and, 116–17
Democracy in America (Tocqueville),
    21, 27
Department of Foreign Affairs, Trade
    and Development (DFATD):
    creation of, 43; name changed to
    Global Affairs Canada, 57
Derrida, Jacques, 7
development assistance: advancement
    of conservative agendas through
    activities, 47; and Canadian
    prosperity/security, 41, 42, 45–46,
    55; conservative agenda and,
    48–49, 57; Conservative
    government and, 12–13;
    conservative values in, 53–54; CPC
    and, 207; under DFATD, 43;
    efficiency in, 55; evidence-based
    analysis, 54; free trade in, 45;
    geopolitics and, 48; geostrategic
    activity, 48; and global citizenship,
    41; Harper's legacy, 57–58; history
    of, 41; humane internationalism in,
    41; humanitarian disaster aid,
    54–55; and independence/self-
    reliance, 56; liberal internationalism
    in, 48, 55; market orientation, 42,
    57; mediation of communications
    and, 42; multilateralism, 41; poverty
    reduction in, 47; public apathy
    toward, 55; public/private
    partnerships in, 47; re-mediation
    of, 51–56; results orientation, 48,
    54; and shaping of international
    futures, 42; and social change, 51;
    unilateralism, 42
development community/organizations:
    changes as mediated geopolitics,
    49; charitable/volunteer
    organizations and, 51–52;
    dissolution of partnership model

for, 51–52; Harper's "Big Break"
    and, 51; information flows and, 42,
    48–49, 51, 57–58; liberal
    internationalist, 51; mediation by,
    56; re-mediation of federal
    government with, 42, 57; results
    orientation, 45; short-term strategic
    partnerships in, 53–54; and social
    media, 53; state relationship with,
    12–13; and transactional
    engagement, 55–56
disciplines. *See* multidisciplinarity
discourse analysis: about, 121; and
    interventions, 127, 129; and truth,
    129
discourse theory: and cultural
    production, 14; and political
    subjects, 14; as secondary resource,
    127–28; and social movements, 207
discourse(s): in agricultural
    biotechnology, 163; centralizing
    power within, 126–27; cultural
    translation between, 125–26, 127;
    discursive space, 127; exclusive,
    120–21; fields of (*see* fields of
    discourse); overlapping, 120, 123;
    theory, 118, 126. *See also* rhetoric
diversity: Bissoondath's slippery-slope
    argument regarding, 122;
    developing respect for, 68;
    multiculturalism and, 68, 123
Dobuzinskis, Laurent, 13
Downs, Anthony, 98

Eagleton, Terry, 15, 188–89
ecology movement(s): deep, 123, 124; as
    ecophilosophical vs ecological, 123.
    See also environmental movement
economics: adaptation of deficit to
    democratic deficit, 4; Austrian
    school, 95, 97; game theory and, 98,
    99–100, 104, 107; and *homo
    economicus*, 102, 105, 140;
    mathematics and, 94, 95, 97, 99;
    multiple equilibria and, 99–100;

neoliberalism and, 101; rationality and, 104; and self-interest, 104; and set theory, 99

Edling, Max, *Revolution in the Name of Government*, 34

Edwards, John, 24

elite(s): CPC and, 66; game theory, and reasoning of, 105–6; and ideological thinking, 189; Reform Party opposition to power of, 72; "the people" vs, 64, 74; taxpayer groups and, 134; and working class parties, 191

Elster, Jon, 92

Engineers Without Borders Canada, 55

environmental movement: axes of significance, 123, 125; and capitalism, 124, 127; cultural translation in, 125–26, 127; as field of discourse, 123; indigenous place-based knowledge and, 124–26; "Mother Earth" vs "ecology" in discourse of, 123–24; productive collaboration in, 126; science vs philosophy in, 125; scientific and traditional knowledge debate, 125; social movement practices, 126; urban, and Prairie farming, 150

Epp, Jan, 158

equality: Charter of Rights and Freedoms and, 68–69; CPC and, 75; exclusion politics and, 79; game theory and, 102–3; inclusion politics and, 76–78; liberal egalitarian concept of, 63, 69; and multiculturalism, 69–70, 80; party-specific meanings, 7; Reform Party and, 72; right-populism and, 69; and welfare state, 78, 79; without special rights for specific groups/interests, 69, 72

Erickson, Paul, 96, 106n1

ethnic minorities: affirmative action for, 75; civic integration of, 77; CPC and, 62, 73, 76, 79, 80; identities, national identity vs, 120, 121; populism and, 76; public attitudes toward, 70–71; Reform Party and, 72, 81; right-populism and, 81

ethnography, 190, 191–92, 195

exclusion: about, 76–77; CPC and, 62, 78; discourse of, 120–21; and equality, 79; and immigration, 64; and multiculturalism, 64, 78, 81; and Muslims, 78; shovel-shortening story and, 173–74; of unskilled workers, 173–74; and welfare state, 81–82. *See also* inclusion

"The Face of Jack Munro" (Wayman), 179–80

Farm and Food Care Saskatchewan, *The Real Dirt on Farming*, 157

farming/farmers: anti-farm movement and, 157, 159–60, 161–62; discursive value of sharing narratives, 163–64; external forces and, 158–60; farmers as complex political subjects, 152; farmers talking to each other vs to public, 164; farmers telling own stories, 154–55; farms as sophisticated, vs family farms, 161–62; freedom of choice, 160; GMOs and meaning of, 156; imperatives facing, 154–55; insecurity of livelihoods, 159; interviews in *License to Farm*, 157–58; in *License to Farm* vs *Paper Wheat*, 164; natural adversaries of, 158; as political subjects, 164–65; public opinion and, 159–60, 161–62, 163–64; self-recognition in narratives of *License to Farm*, 156; transnational corporations and, 159; urban environmentalism and, 150; Vera's story, 195–96. *See also* agribusiness; chemical farming; *License to Farm*

Federalist Papers (Hamilton/Madison/Jay), 36

fields of discourse: axes of significance,
119, 121; defined, 119; environmental
movement as, 123; interventions in,
121, 122; multiculturalism as, 13, 119,
120–23; mutation over time, 122
Filewod, Alan, 153
fiscal military state, 34–35
Fisher, David H., 38*n*9
Flanagan, Tom, 66, 79
foreign affairs/policy: and Canadian
prosperity/security, 44, 45–46;
conservatism in, 44; Conservative
overhaul of, 43; efficiency in, 55;
free trade, 44, 45; Harper's "Big
Break" and, 43; liberal
internationalism in, 44, 57;
"principled," 43, 45; results
orientation, 44; Trudeau
government and, 56–57;
unilateralism in, 45; unilateralism
vs multilateralism in, 44
Foucault, Michel, 7, 14, 103, 137–38,
139, 211
Frankfurt School, 208
Fréchet, Maurice, 106*n*3
Freeden, Michael: and 2013 University
of Virginia workshop, 212; and
adjacent/perimeter concepts, 66;
on analysis of political concepts
through location within patterns,
14, 169–70; analytical toolkit, 6–7;
applicability to CPC anti-
immigrant/nativist themes, 62; on
concepts as relational vs
autonomous, 6; on contestable
meanings, 6; on decontestations, 6;
and decontesting liberty, 22, 37; on
detachment of analysis from
normative position taking through
political engagement, 208; and
essential contestability, 4–5, 7; on
evaluation of empirical/causal
ideological claims, 9–10; laborlore
applied to, 14; on loose, unintended
political thinking, 183; mapping

ideological action, 70; and Marxist
positivist science/ideology binary,
9; on meaning of ideological
concepts, 6; and meso level of
ideological activity, 10;
morphological approach, 5–6, 10,
11, 128, 207; and multidisciplinary
bridge building, 7–8; on normative
obligation accompanying
ideological analysis, 210; and
political thought in social science,
209; rhetorical claims vs ideological
core concepts distinction, 65; on
scope of political dimensions of
human thought, 206; systematic
approach, 5–8; and thin ideologies,
65; Thompson's ideas compared,
169–70, 171; and truth value of
ideological perspectives, 9
Freud, Sigmund, 8, 10, 210

Gallie, W.B., 6, 8, 211
game theory: about, 13, 91; as analytical
method, 104–5; Austrian school of
economics and, 97; Bayesian
statistics and, 100; chess and, 94;
Cold War and, 96; criticisms of,
97–98, 105–6; Cuban missile crisis
and, 101; disciplines and, 91, 98,
104; and economics, 98, 99–100,
104, 107; and end justifying means,
92, 106; evolutionary, 102, 104–5;
and experimental methods, 102,
105; and fairness, 105, 107; gender
and, 97, 98; and justice, 102–3; and
liberal democracies, 91, 92, 103,
107; mathematics and, 95, 96,
107*n*2; and mechanism design, 104;
and minimax theorem, 94–95;
misuses of, 92, 106–7; as
multifaceted, 105; and Nash
equilibrium, 93, 94, 95–96, 99, 104,
107; neoliberalism and, 13, 97, 98,
101, 106; origins, 92–98; and policy
making, 106; and political decision

making, 106; and political economy, 93–94, 105; political science and, 91, 100–1, 102; and politics, 92, 104, 105–7; rationality/rationalism and, 93, 96–97, 101–2, 104; reasoning in terms of players' mutual adjustment, 97–98; and reasoning of political "elites," 105–6; and reciprocity, 97, 103; and refinement program, 99–100; and self-interest, 92, 102, 104; and set theory, 94, 96, 99; social psychology and, 103, 105; and social sciences, 91, 92, 98–99, 104; and strategic thinking, 92, 93, 102, 103–4, 106; and uncertainty in social interactions, 98; uses, 96

Game Theory and the Social Contract (Binmore), 102

Gane, Mike, 138

Gates, Bill/Gates Foundation, 47, 55

gender: and game theory, 97, 98; laborlore and, 15

genetically modified organisms (GMOs): anti-farm movement and, 157; canola, 155–56; in *License to Farm*, 150, 154–55, 159–60, 161–62, 165–66; and meaning of farming, 156; public opinion about, 163–64; and right of choice, 160. *See also* biotechnology

geopolitics: critical, 49; cross-border conceptual travel and, 42; cultural hegemony and, 49, 50; discourse-centred, 49; geostrategic engagements, 50; mediated, 13, 42, 49, 50–51, 56–58, 57; neoliberalism and, 49–50; network-centric, 49

Georgetti, Ken, 181–82, 183

Giocoli, Nicola, 99, 100

Global Affairs Canada, 57. *See also* Department of Foreign Affairs, Trade and Development (DFATD)

Gordon, Thomas, *Cato's Letters*, 22

governmentality: centring of government outside state, 137; and

liberalism, 138–39; policy mobilities studies and, 138; and power, 137, 138; studies, 137–38; taxpayer, 138–39

Grain Growers' Grain Company, 152

Grain Grower's Guide, 152, 166n1

Gramsci, Antonio, 7, 10, 49

Grand Trunk Pacific Railway (GTP), 170–71, 172, 174

Great Britain. *See* United Kingdom

Great Depression, 196–97

Green, Archie, 170, 171, 173, 183

Green, Donald, 101

Growing Forward 2, 155, 166n3

Hamilton, Alexander, 12; *Federalist Papers*, 36

Harper, Stephen: as Alliance leader, 71–72; "Big Break," 51; conservative ideology, 62; and creation of CPC, 66, 67, 71–72; "dog-whistle politics," 80; dominant discourses on development, 50; and ethnic minorities, 76; and Flanagan, 66; and free trade, 44; and Gates, 47; and Hayek's ideas, 80; legacy, 57–58, 84; and liberal internationalism, 44, 56–57; and Manning, 66; and morally driven military interventions, 44; and niqab, 61, 81; and Office of Religious Freedom, 78; and plebiscitarian model of relations, 73–74; and populism, 66, 81; Reform loyalty to, 74; and resource extraction industry, 46; Senegal speeches, 45–46; severance of multiculturalism from welfare state, 83–84; Tom/Vera's attitudes toward, 201; on welfare state, 85n10; and women's reproductive rights, 47. *See also* Conservative Party of Canada (CPC)

Harsanyi, John, 100

Hartz, Louis, 21, 22, 23, 33, 37, 207

Hayek, Friedrich, 10, 62, 66, 67, 72, 73, 80, 95, 97, 106*n*4
Henderson, James (Sa'ke'j) Youngblood, 125
Hepp, Andres, 51
Heron, Craig, 191
Hilbert, David, 94
Hogan, Linda, 125
Hotel, Restaurant, Culinary Workers and Bartenders' Union, Local 40, 178–79
Humanitarian Coalition, 54–55
Hume, David, 94, 97, 103
Humphrey, Mathew, 11, 209, 212

Ibbitson, John, 43, 44, 57
"Ideologies and Conceptual Travel" (2016 workshop), 206, 207, 209
ideology/-ies: about, 6, 188–89; adjacent concepts, 6–7; analysis without advancement of political position/ perspective, 208–9; analytical tools, 6–7, 208–9; behavioural literature on, 189–90; in changing settings, 3; class and, 208; cognitive foundations of adherents, 9; conceptual border crossing, 4–5; contestability, 4–6, 7, 14, 149; core concepts, 6; defined, 170; and elites vs followers, 189; empirical/ interpretive study of, 9; everyday thinking, 15; Freeden's systematic approach to, 5–8; functional explanation of, 210–11; functions, 9; hailing subjects, 151–52, 165, 166; and ideolects, 7; interdisciplinary approaches to, 3; and interpellation, 151, 165; as leading to populism, 189–90; of *License to Farm*, 154–58, 165; linguistic structure of, 7; macro/canonical level, 10, 11, 12, 205–6; Marxist perspectives on, 5; meso/intermediate level, 10–11, 12, 205, 206; micro/everyday level, 10, 11, 12, 15, 205, 206; morphological

analysis of, 5–8, 9, 128; network for analysis, 211–13; normative vs morphological/related analysis, 209–10; in *Paper Wheat*, 153–54, 165; peripheral concepts, 7; and policy, 51; and political attitudes/ behaviour, 9; political science and, 5, 206; and political subjects, 151; political theory vs, 14; power of, 5; as preparation for action, 150–51, 166; psychological dispositions/ orientations of adherents, 9; range of political discourses into research, 206; resistance to structural understandings of, 5; self- consciousness of, 190; and social movements, 207; sociology of knowledge central in studies of, 13; and stories, 151; study of, compared to sociology of knowledge, 128; thin, 65; truth vs, 9; world view and, 190
immigrants/immigration: Conservative government and, 48; CPC and, 73, 74, 75–76, 80; diversity and, 119; economic needs and, 67; funded programs for immigrants, 68; "good" immigrants, 74, 75, 76; as labour, 174; nature of Canadian, 67; as perimeter concept, 61; politics of inclusion/exclusion and, 64; and populism, 61; public attitudes toward, 70–71, 82–83; Reform Party and, 72; "safe" vs "unsafe" sources of, 77; socio-economic status and, 77–78; ties to countries of origin, 48; wedge politics and, 74
inclusion: about, 76–77; discourse of, 120–21; equality in, 76–78; and immigration, 64; and multiculturalism, 64, 81; Trudeau and, 82. *See also* exclusion
Independent (VTLC), 174
Indigenous people: in *License to Farm* vs *Paper Wheat*, 164; and Mother Earth (Pachamama), 123–24; as

"non-taxpayers," 134; *Paper Wheat* and, 154; place-based knowledge, 124–26
Industrial Worker, 171
Industrial Workers of the World (IWW), 169, 171, 172, 174, 198
Innis, Harold, 58n1
Inter-Council Network (ICN), 52–53, 55
interdisciplinarity. *See* multidisciplinarity
international development. *See headings beginning* development
International Development Week, 41, 48
International Woodworkers of America (IWA), 176–81, 182, 183, 200
Ipsos-Reid, 70

Jankovic, Ivan, 12, 207
Jay, John, *Federalist Papers*, 36
Jefferson, Thomas, 12, 35
justice: discovery of truth and restoration of, 118; game theory and, 102–3; political theory and, 115; social contract and, 4, 103

Kairos, 52
Kaltewasser, Cristobal, 63–65, 76–77
Kant, Immanuel, 102
Kaufman, Jason, 38n9
Kenney, Jason, 75, 76
Kerr, Don, 152–53, 154
Kinder Morgan, 126
Kish, Albert, 152
Kymlicka, Will, 70

laborlore: about, 14–15, 170; about Communists in unions, 180–81; camp food story, 176–77; class tensions in, 171; ideology of pragmatism and, 180–82; labour leadership and, 176–83; Munro and, 178–81; organizing of millworkers into union story, 176; shovel-shortening story, 172–74; strike at Bimini's, 178–79; study of, 170;

transgressive, 171; and urban legends, 172–73, 177
labour. *See* workers
labour leadership: as anti-communist/-leftist, 180–81; and being right, 181; and bureaucracy, 175; conservative/anti-democratic ideologies, 183; critical examination of, 182; decision making on behalf of others, 175; directing vs representing union membership, 175; Georgetti, 181–82; ideological radicalism below level of, 193; ideology of pragmatism, 182; ideology shaped by labour movement, 183; and informal ideology, 174–75, 183; as job, 181–82; knowing when to settle/selling deal to members, 181–82; laborlore regarding, 176–83; management of rank/file, 175; Munro as, 178–81; and neoliberalism, 183; split with rank/file, 171; use of ideology, 171–72. *See also* trade unions
Laclau, Ernesto, 8, 10, 126
Lane, Ruth, 103–4
Lasker, Emanual, 106n2
Laycock, David, 13, 207
Layton, Jack, 201
Lee, Arthur, 31
left politics: parties in British Columbia, 192–93; Vera/Tom story, 193; working class and, 191; working class and parties of, 192–93
Leier, Mark, 14–15, 208
Leonard, Robert, 94–95, 106n4
Levy, Daniel, 105
liberal democracy/-ies: and foreign relations, 42; game theory and, 91, 92, 103, 107
liberal internationalism, 44, 48, 51, 55, 56–57
Liberal Party: in 2015 federal election, 56; and Charter, 68–69; Harper's

policy legacy and, 84; and multiculturalism, 82; and niqab ban, 61, 81. *See also* Trudeau, Justin
liberalism(s): breadth of ideological family, 6; definition of, 138; localism and, 23, 36, 37; Lockean, 21, 22, 36, 37; old-Whigs, 22; taxpayer governmentality and, 139–40; in US, 21, 34, 36, 37
libertarianism, 12, 22–23
License to Farm: about, 14, 150; action recommended in, 163–64; agribusiness in, 152, 156–57; agricultural political subjects in, 152, 158–59; agricultural producers in, 151; Berteig and, 156–57; biotechnology in, 152; and competition, 152, 165; content, 157, 161–62; and enlistment of farmers, 156–57; external forces in, 158, 159; and farmers acting in response to challenges, 162; and freedom of choice, 159–60; GMO agriculture in, 154–55, 156; ideological character of, 154–58, 165; insecurity of farmers' livelihood in, 159; as interpellation vector, 164–65; interviews, 157–58; material stakes, 155–56; *Paper Wheat* compared, 158–59, 164–65; problem of information in, 160, 161–62; production/circulation, 155; as script vs film, 164; struggle over GMOs, 165–66; success of, 165; and technologically enabled future, 165; and technology as solution to problems, 158; and threat of regulatory intervention, 160; threat posed by critics of agribusiness, 159–60
The Limits of Economics (Morgenstern), 95
Little Bear, Leroy, 126
localism, 22, 23–33, 34–36, 37; in UK, 25–26
Locke, John, 21–22, 23, 33, 36, 37, 189

Lucas, Louise, 162–63
Lynas, Mark, 157–58

Machiavelli, Niccolò, *The Prince*, 93
Mackenzie, William, 171, 172
Madden, Megan, 160
Madison, James, 35–36; *Federalist Papers*, 36
The Making of the English Working Class (Thompson), 169–70
Manitoba Grain Act, 152
Mann, Donald, 171, 172
Manning, Preston, 66, 72
Marston, Sallie A., 58n5
Martin, Isaac William, 134
Marx, Karl, 5, 9, 10, 127, 130n3, 189, 201, 208, 210; *Capital*, 173
mathematics: axiomatization of, 95; and economics, 94, 95, 97, 99; and game theory, 96, 107n2
Mayer, Hans, 95, 106n4
McCann, Eugene, 133, 134, 136–37
McCormack, A. Ross, 169
McDonald, Bob, 201
McGaa, Ed, 125
McLuhan, Marshall, 119
Meany, George, 181
media: ecology, 119; geostrategic reorganization of, 48; and persuasion, 119; taxpayer groups and, 143; in Tom/Vera story, 200; and working class parties, 191
mediation: of communications/information flows, 42, 48–49; by development organizations, 56; geopolitical (*see under* geopolitics); and social outcomes, 51
Medvetz, Thomas, 133–34
Menger, Karl, 95
Mickleburgh, Rod, 178
Mill, John Stuart, 102, 106
Mills, C. Wright, 175, 180
Mises, Ludwig von, 95
Monsanto, 155, 159, 166n5
Mont Pelerin Society, 139

Morales, Evo, 123–24
Morgenstern, Oskar, 91, 94, 95, 99, 101; *The Limits of Economics*, 95; *The Theory of Games and Economic Behaviour*, 93, 95
Mouffe, Chantal, 126
Mudde, Cas, 63–65, 76–77
multiculturalism: attack on, 122–23; axes of significance, 121; Charter of Rights and Freedoms and, 72, 82; citizenship vs, 122; CPC and, 13, 62, 63, 66, 67, 68, 73, 74, 75, 76, 80, 84, 122; dead ends and creative interventions in, 127; deep diversity and, 120; diversity vs, 123; equality and, 69–70, 80; exclusion politics and, 64, 78; as field of discourse, 13, 119, 120–23; historical periods in discourse of, 122–23; inclusion politics and, 64; institutional closure, 117; multicultural integration approach to, 67–68; Multiculturalism Act (1988), 122; plebiscitarianism and, 74; populist conservatism and, 13; public attitudes toward, 13, 70–71; Reform Party and, 72, 75; rejection of centring of cultural identities, 123; right-wing populism and, 62, 64; separateness and, 122; subordinate inclusion under, 123; Trudeau Liberals and, 82; as universalization of right to belonging, 121; of urban Canada, 67; wedge politics and, 62, 74, 80; and welfare state, 13, 67, 80, 83–84
multidisciplinarity: approaches to political ideology, 3; Freeden's analytical framework and, 7–8; and game theory, 91, 98, 104; macro-level ideology and, 205–6; network use of analytical toolkit, 212; plurality of approaches within, 8; workshops, 207–8, 212
multilateralism, 41, 43, 44, 56

Munro, Jack, 178–81, 182, 200
Muskoka Initiative on Maternal, Newborn and Child Health, 47, 53
Muslims, 77, 78, 79–81, 82–83, 84, 85n7

Naess, Arne, 125; "The Shallow and the Deep, Long-Range Ecology Movement," 123
Nagel, Cherilyn, 157, 158, 160
Narrative Project, 55–56
Nash, John, 93, 94, 95, 96
Nash equilibrium (NE), 93, 94, 95–96, 99, 104, 107
National Farmers Union, 156, 166n2
National Film Board, Challenge for Change (CFC) program, 152
national identity/-ies: deep diversity and, 120; diversity and, 68; ethnic identities vs, 120; multiculturalism and, 119, 120; pertinence to different domains of relevance, 121; "us" vs "them" posing of, 120–21
National Labor Relations Act (Wagner Act), 175, 177
nativism: CPC and, 13, 61–62; and populism, 13; Reform Party and, 72; right-populism and, 84
Natural Justice (Binmore), 102
neoliberalism: about, 106, 139; agricultural political subjects and, 149; CPC and, 66; and game theory, 13, 101; and geopolitics, 49–50; labour leadership and, 183; taxpayer groups and, 139
New Democratic Party (NDP): BC 1972 election of, 176; and BC working class, 192; and ethnic minorities, 76; Tom/Vera and, 199
Next Year Country, 154
No. 1 Hard, 166n2
North-South Institute, 52, 53

Oakeshott, Michael, 97
Oda, Bev, 52

Office of Religious Freedom, 78
Old Regime and the Revolution
(Tocqueville), 27–28
Operation Solidarity, 179, 200
Osborne, George, 143

Paper Wheat: about, 14, 150;
agricultural political subjects in,
158–59; avoidance of issues,
153–54; and collective action, 165;
content, 158–59; cooperative mode
of agricultural production in,
151–52, 165; and cooperative
movement/organization, 154,
162–63, 164; external forces in,
158–59; and farmers acting in
response to challenges, 162;
freedom of choice in, 160; history
of, 152–53; ideological character of,
153–54, 165; and Indigenous
people, 154; insecurity of farmers'
livelihoods in, 159; as interpellation
vector, 164–65; *License to Farm*
compared, 158–59, 164–65; mutual
aid in, 158–59; political orientation
of, 153; price in, 160–61, 162–63;
problem of information in, 160–61;
success of, 165
Paper Wheat: The Book, 152
Paris, Roland, 56–57
Partridge, Edward A., 152, 161, 162
Pearson, Lester B., 41
Peart, Sandra, 105
"People's Agreement of Cochabamba,"
124–25
People's Party of Canada, 84
persuasion: Aristotle and, 118; media
and, 119; rhetoric and, 117
Peters, Samuel, 35
Phaedrus (Plato), 118
Pilon, Dennis, 11, 15
Plato, 121; *Phaedrus,* 118; *Republic,* 115
plebiscitarianism: about, 84*n*1; CPC
and, 73–74, 81; and
multiculturalism, 74, 81; populism

and, 64, 74, 81; and "the people,"
84*n*1
plena potestas, 24–25, 31
policy/-ies: conferences and, 141;
defined, 136; game theory and
making of, 106; and governmentality
studies, 138; ideology and, 51;
knowledge frameworks, 137;
mobilities, 136–37, 138, 141, 145;
transfer, 136; travels/transmission of
knowledge, 145
political economy, 92, 93–94, 105
political knowledge: authored by
taxpayer groups for "taxpayer," 133;
of average people, 190; changes
through movement of, 138;
mobilization, 132, 137; political
reason and, 132; taxpayer
conferences and, 146; taxpayer
groups and, 132
political philosophy: defined, 115; and
interventions, 129; and political
theory, 14, 115; and political
thought, 116, 129
political reason: about, 132; mobilities
of, 136–37; and political subjects,
133; taxpayer groups and, 14;
taxpayer political subjects and, 132
political science: and behaviouralism,
100; and game theory, 91, 100–1,
102; and ideological reproduction,
149–50; and ideology, 5, 206; and
political theory, 129*n*1
political subjects/subjectivity: farmers
as, 164–65; ideology hailing,
151–52, 165, 166; in *License to
Farm,* 152, 158; political reason and,
133; Prairie farmers as, 152; as
prepared to act, 150, 151, 166; and
taxpayer subjectivity, 135
political theory: and interventions, 129;
political philosophy and, 14, 115;
political science and, 129*n*1; and
political thought, 116, 129; and
truth, 128–29

political thought: about, 116, 118; defined, 116; interventions, 127–29; permeability of, 116–17; political philosophy and, 116, 129; political theory and, 116, 129; and politics, 116; and social movements, 116; in social science, 209; temporal/spatial mutation of, 127; and truth, 128–29

politics: average people's knowledge of, 190; farming families and, 196; game theory and, 104, 105–7; interventions in political thought and, 128; interventions vs stasis in, 129; political thought and, 116

populism: conservative core concepts, 65–66; and equality, 69; and ethnic minorities, 81; in Europe, 85n3; migration from US, 62; and multiculturalism, 62, 64; and nativism, 84; and plebiscitarianism, 64; right-, 62, 64, 65–66, 69, 81, 84; Trump and, 84

populism(s): about ideology of, 63–65; and anti-statism, 61; anti–visible minorities and, 61; average people and, 189–90; conservative, 13, 65; of CPC, 61, 65, 81–82; direct democracy and, 4; and elite vs "the people," 64, 74; and ethnic minority citizens, 76; and exclusion politics, 62; of Harper, 81; ideology as leading to, 189–90; immigration and, 61; left-, 64; and multiculturalism, 13; nativism and, 13; niqab ban and, 61; opposition to elite power, 72; and "the people," 64; plebiscitarian, 61, 64, 74, 81; of Reform Party, 13, 71; right-, 62, 64, 79, 81–82, 84, 85n3; strategic dimension of, 64; tax politics and, 134; as thin ideologies, 65; of Trump, 65–66; and welfare state, 79; working class ideology vs, 187

Pouget, Emile, 173

poverty: global, 45; and "non-taxpayers," 134; reduction, 47

power: and class, 199, 202; in communications platforms channelling meaning making, 50; governmentality and, 137, 138; policy mobilities studies and, 138; state as effect of, 137; subject formation outside traditional structures of, 146

Prairie provinces: agribusiness in, 152; agricultural conditions in, 154; agricultural political subjects of, 151; cooperative movement in, 152; expropriation of land for agriculture in, 153–54; ideological ferment in, 149; political movements/parties/institutions, 149

Prime Minister's Office, 43, 74

The Prince (Machiavelli), 93

"Prisoner's Dilemma," 96

Pritchett, Harold, 176

Privy Council Order 1003, 175, 177

Progressive Conservative Party, merger with Alliance to form CPC, 67, 72

Public Choice model of voting behaviour, 98

quod omnes tangit, 25

rationality/rational choice theory: critiques of, 96–97, 210; game theory and, 101–2, 104

Rawls, John, 4, 10, 102, 103

The Real Dirt on Farming, 157

Reder, Deanna, 126

Reece, Florence, "Which Side Are You On?," 183

Reform Party: *Blue Sheet*, 85n9; and Charlottetown constitutional reform, 71; CPC and, 13, 66, 74; creation of, 71; and elites, 72; and equality rights, 72–73, 75; ethnic minority voters and, 73; and Harper, 74; ideology/policies, 73;

and immigration, 81; and multiculturalism, 72, 75; and nativism, 72; and "the people," 73, 74; and populism, 13; rebranding as Canadian Reform Conservative Alliance Party, 71–72; Republican Party and, 75; and US conservatism, 13, 69; and welfare state, 71

refugees, 67, 75–76, 77, 78, 80, 82

Reilly, Katherine, 12–13, 207

Republic (Plato), 115

Republican Party, 62, 66, 75

"Rethinking Neoliberalism" (Dean), 139

Revolution in the Name of Government (Edling), 34

rhetoric: defined, 117; deliberative, 118; and discourse theory, 118; equivalence, and social movements, 13; and expressive genres, 118–19; and interventions, 129; and persuasion, 117–18; as secondary resource, 127–28; and social movements, 207; subservience to philosophy, 121; and truth, 117, 129. *See also* discourse(s)

Rhetoric (Aristotle), 117–18

right-populism. *See under* populism

Riker, William, 101

Rose, Nikolas, 138, 140

Rousseau, Jean-Jacques, 93; *Social Contract*, 93

Rowe, Stan, 125

Sacred Ecology, 125

Saskatchewan Canola Development Commission (SaskCanola), 150, 155, 156, 163–64

Saskatchewan Wheat Pool, 153, 154, 162–63

Schelling, Thomas, 103–4

Schira, Angie, 180–81

Schwarcz, Joe, 158

Schwartz-Shea, Peregrine, 97, 98

Selten, Reinhard, 100

Septennial Act (1716), 28, 34

Service, Office, and Retail Workers Union of Canada (SORWUC), 178–79

Shapiro, Ian, 101

Sheller, Mimi, 136

Simon, Herbert, 102

Sinclair, Jim, 182, 183

Sintaluta (SK), 152, 154, 161

Skinner, Quentin, 10

Smith, Dorothy, 192

Smith, William, 34–35

social class. *See* class

social contract, 4, 103

Social Contract (Rousseau), 93

social movements: and democratic vibrancy, 116–17; discourse theory and, 207; ideology and, 207; political thought and, 116; rhetoric and, 13, 207

social science: political thought in, 209; sedentarist, 136

solidarity: laborlore and, 14; shovel-shortening story and, 173; trade unions and, 182

Solidarity Coalition, 179

"Solidarity Forever," 182, 201

Spargo, John, 173

Speer, Sean, 80

Stevens, Homer, 175

Stolle, Dietlind, 71

Strand, Katherine, 14, 156–57

strategic thinking: about, 93; Austen and, 94; game theory and, 92, 102, 103–4, 106; and policy making, 106

strikes: at Bimini's, 178–79; in British Columbia, 172; collective agreements and, 175; Italian workers, 172–74; in Tom/Vera story, 200; wildcat, 175, 176–77

structural-functionalism, 169, 170, 210

Swyngedouw, Erik, 58*n*5

Syngenta, 159

taxation: consent to, 24–25; government and, 25; without representation, 25

taxpayer, the: and citizenship, 134;
      governmentality, 139–40; "non-
      taxpayers" vs, 134; political
      knowledge authored by taxpayer
      groups for, 133; reason, 14, 133, 140,
      142–45; as symbolic identity, 134;
      taxpayer group advocacy for, 133;
      taxpayer groups aligned with, 134
taxpayer groups: about, 133–36;
      advocacy for "taxpayers," 133; as
      agents of political mobilization/
      ideological production, 14; alignment
      with "the taxpayer," 134; beer tax
      vignette, 143–44; campaigns,
      135–36, 143–45; and capitalism, 134;
      conferences, 140, 141–45, 146; in
      developing world, 142, 144–45;
      directing/shaping of subjectivities,
      144; and elites, 134; and government
      limitation, 139–40, 142–45, 143;
      grassroots involvement, 143;
      international organization/
      mobilization, 142; media and, 143;
      movement of political strategies,
      141–42; and neoliberalism, 139;
      networking, 133, 141; numbers of,
      136; and permanent political
      criticism, 14; and political
      knowledge, 132, 133; practices of,
      135–36; tactics, 141; and taxpayer
      reason, 14; and taxpayer subjects/
      subjectivity, 135, 144, 146
taxpayer subjects/subjectivity: and
      political reason, 132; scholarly work
      on, 132–33; taxpayer groups and,
      135, 144, 146
Taxpayers Alliance (TPA), 143–44
Taylor, Charles, 80, 120
Temenos, Cristina, 141
Territorial Grain Growers Association
      of Sintaluta, 162
Thatcher, Margaret, 75
*The Theory of Games and Economic
      Behaviour* (von Neumann/
      Morgenstern), 93, 95

think tanks, 133–34
Thompson, E.P., 171, 183; *The Making of
      the English Working Class*, 169–70
Tocqueville, Alexis de, 22, 27–28, 30,
      35; *Democracy in America*, 21, 27;
      Old Regime and the Revolution,
      27–28
trade unions: in British Columbia, 192;
      closed vs open shops, 198–99; and
      collective agreements, 175, 177;
      dispute resolution, 177; laborlore in,
      170; negotiation of contracts, 175;
      and Operation Solidarity/Solidarity
      Coalition, 179; for scabs, 178–79;
      and solidarity, 182; working people's
      power and, 199. *See also* labour
      leadership
Tranberg, Janice, 163–64
Treasury Board Secretariat, 53–54
Trenchard, John, *Cato's Letters*, 22
Trudeau, Justin: and aid budget, 57;
      egalitarianism of cabinet, 82; and
      Liberal Party in 2015 election, 56;
      and multiculturalism, 82;
      restoration of constructive
      Canadian leadership in world, 57.
      See also Liberal Party
Trudeau, Pierre, 68–69
Trump, Donald: and Canadian right-
      populism, 84; CPC's politics
      compared, 79; and ethnic
      minorities, 79; ideological success,
      10; makeover of Republican Party
      ideology, 62; "the people" in
      presidential campaign, 64;
      populism of, 65–66, 81
Tucker, Arthur, and "Prisoner's
      Dilemma," 96

Umbach, Maiken, 11, 206, 212
unilateralism, 41–42, 44, 45
United Brotherhood of Railway
      Employees, 174
United Fishermen and Allied Workers
      Union (UFAWU), 175

United Kingdom: attorneyship in representation, 24–25, 29; binding instructions in, 28, 29; electoral terms in, 28; local self-government in, 23–24; localism in, 25–26; *plena potestas* in, 24–25; virtual representation in, 32

United Mine Workers of America (UMWA), 172

United Nations: Canadian support for, 56; Harper government and, 43; Sustainable Development Goals (SDG), 45

United States: attorneyship in representation, 26, 30; binding instructions in, 28, 29–30; bottom-up federalization in, 32–33; conservative movement in, 69; Constitution, 34; decentralization of decision making, 27; *Declaration of Independence*, 33; emergence of direct democracy in, 4; feebleness of colonial governments in, 26–27; fiscal military state, 34–36; and House of Commons as confederation of localities, 26; ideology of political culture, 21; individualism in, 33, 34–35; liberalism(s) in, 21, 33, 34, 36, 37; libertarianism in, 12, 22; localism in, 22, 23–33, 34–36, 37; as medieval society, 12, 22; migration of right-wing populism from, 62; no taxation without representation in, 25; short electoral terms in, 24, 28–29; Tom/Vera's attitudes toward, 200–1; township democracy, 27–28; virtual representation in, 30–32; working people in, 200

Urry, John, 136

Vancouver Trades and Labour Council (VTLC), 174

visible minorities: as perimeter concept, 61; and populism, 61. *See also* ethnic minorities; Indigenous people

von Neumann, John, 91, 94–95, 96, 97–98, 99, 101, 106*n*3; *The Theory of Games and Economic Behaviour*, 93, 95

Wall, Brad, 166*n*6

Walpole, Horace, 12, 38*n*9

Walsh, Camille, 134

Ward, Kevin, 133, 134, 136–37, 141

Wayman, Tom, "The Face of Jack Munro," 179–80

Weber, Max, 37*n*5, 74

Weldon, Steven, 13, 207

welfare state: CPC and, 62, 67, 77–78, 79; equality and, 78, 79; exclusion politics and, 81–82; guaranteed minimum income and, 103; Harper on, 85*n*10; multiculturalism and, 13, 67, 80, 83–84; public attitudes toward, 13, 82–83; Reform Party and, 71; right-populism and, 79; special interest groups and, 81–82

Western Canadian Crop Production Show, 155

The Western Producer, 166*n*1

Western Producer Prairie Books, 152

wheat pools, 165; *Paper Wheat* and, 150. *See also* Saskatchewan Wheat Pool

"Which Side Are You On?" (Reece), 183

Whiggism, 22, 23, 28, 31

Williamson, Vanessa, 134

Willmott, Kyle, 14

Winnipeg Declaration, 192

Winnipeg General Strike, 196

Winnipeg Grain Exchange, 152, 158, 161, 162

Wittgenstein, Ludwig, 103

Wolfe, Tom, 161

Wood, Gordon, 22, 30, 32, 36

workers: class as uniting, 171; flouting industrial relations regime, 177; formal ideologies of, 169;

identification as class, 170;
immigrants as, 174; informal
ideologies of, 169–70; machinery
replacing, 174; marginalized, 173;
reasonableness of demands, 177;
skilled vs unskilled, 173–74; and
union negotiation process, 177;
working class culture binding
together, 170, 171
workers' organizations: formal
ideologies of, 169; split between
leadership and rank/file, 171.
See also trade unions
working class: ambitions of, 201; auto-
ethnography and, 15, 193; culture as
reflection of working class
experience, 170; divisions among,
171; ethnography and, 190; and left,
191, 192–93; as liberals vs socialists,
201, 202; as part of group with
common interests, 202; political
parties, 191; sense of politics of class,
202; trade unions and power for, 199;
as uniting workers, 171; in US, 200
working class ideology: auto-
ethnography and, 188, 193–94;
average people and, 202; cultural
practices and, 190–91;
distinctiveness of, 187; ethnography
and, 190; experience and, 190;

informal expressions of, 14; and
international events, 200–1; lack of
documentary records, 188; left
ideology vs, 187, 191; and left
written canon, 201; populism vs,
187; reconnaissance of, 188, 195;
and socialism, 201; subaltern views
vs, 188; traditional ideological
thinking vs, 189; transcending class
boundaries, 171; of Vera and Tom,
188; Vera/Tom story and, 193–202;
as world view, 187
World Conference on Climate Change
and the Rights of Mother Earth
(2010), 124
World Neighbours Canada (WNC),
51–52
World Taxpayer Associations (WTA),
142, 144, 145
World Taxpayer Conference, 145

Yates, Michael, 191
Young, Iris Marion, 119

Zermelo, Ernst, 94, 106n2
Zero Tolerance for Barbaric Cultural
Practices Act, 70, 78, 80
Žižek, Slavoj, 8, 122–23, 211
Zubly, John Joachim, 32
Zuckert, Michael, 21